Being a teacher in higher education

SRHE and Open University Press Imprint
General Editor: Heather Eggins

Being a teacher in higher education

Peter T. Knight

The Society for Research into Higher Education
& Open University Press

Published by SRHE and
Open University Press
Celtic Court
22 Ballmoor
Buckingham
MK18 1XW

email: enquiries@openup.co.uk
world wide web: www.openup.co.uk

and
325 Chestnut Street
Philadelphia, PA 19106, USA

First Published 2002

A catalogue record of this book is available from the British Library

ISBN 0 335 20930 0 (pb)   0 335 20931 9 (hb)

Library of Congress Cataloging-in-Publication Data
Knight, Peter, 1950–
   Being a teacher in higher education / Peter T. Knight.
      p. cm.
   Includes bibliographical references and index.
   ISBN 0–335–20930–0 (pbk.) — ISBN 0–335–20931–9 (hard)
   1. College teaching. 2. College teachers—Social conditions. I. Title.

LB2331.7 .K65 2002
378.1′25—dc21   2002024620

Typeset by Graphicraft Limited, Hong Kong
Printed by St Edmundsbury Press, Bury St Edmunds, Suffolk

Contents

Preface

Something like this book should have been written by Jo Tait of the Open University. Having co-edited a book on one of her passions, independent learning (Tait and Knight, 1996), she wanted to write about teaching in higher education from a whole-person perspective. The working title was *Inspiring Higher Education*. The book never got written because paid work, in the form of short-term contracts on demanding projects that left no space for this sort of creativity, took precedence. I had often talked with her about what *Inspiring* might say, how and to whom. I became enthusiastic about a book that went beyond hints for practice and tried to take an integrated view of teachers' work. As it became clear that her work on Associate Lecturers in the Open University (for example, Tait, 2002) would stymie the chances of *Inspiring* getting written, I suggested doing a book that would be similar to and different from it. This is it. Plainly my voice is not hers. She wants to say things that I cannot but is not positioned to say some of the things that I do. Yet there is still a sense in which she is an author of this book and I the writer.

John Skelton of Open University Press has been a supporter from Jo's first approach to him through to my detailed proposal. Without him, no book. John Cowan was one of the Open University Press referees. A skilled writer himself (Cowan, 1998), he gave enthusiastic support that ran to pages of suggestions for writing better. More, in fact, than I have been able to accommodate. So too with David Baume, whose generous advice and comments I have valued.

I enjoy writing with my Lancaster colleague Paul Trowler and although he has not directly contributed to this book it has been influenced by the writing we have done together and the work we intend to do. So too with Mantz Yorke of Liverpool John Moores University. He has affected what is in these pages in ways that he may not recognize but which are nevertheless profound.

Time spent working in Dalhousie University's Office of Instructional Development in Halifax, Nova Scotia, and then as a Royal Bank Fellow in

McGill University, Montréal, encouraged my thinking, tested it when I did staff development sessions and deepened my knowledge of North American literature and practice. So too with time spent in Hong Kong universities. In these ways Alenoush Saroyan, Ron Smith, Cynthia Weston, Helen Wong and Alan Wright have challenged me and helped me to think better.

This appreciation previews some themes I develop in this book: the value of friends to learn from, talk to and be at ease with; the importance of collegiality and collaboration, regardless of distance; and, perhaps most significantly, its tone says that feelings matter in writing. In teaching too.

Part I

People, times and places

It is easy to assume that being a good teacher is a personal responsibility, dependent on whether you prepare thoroughly, speak well, read books on teaching, use the right technology, smile a lot, give sensitive feedback to students and so on.

There is something in that. Teaching well does depend upon the individual and these first six chapters contain plenty of suggestions about things that you can do to enhance your teaching. But not upon the individual alone: rather, upon the individual in the community. Part, but only part, of the explanation is that teaching is not just performance in the presence of students. I use 'teaching' to refer to all the planning, preparation and other activities that teachers do to help student learning. Most teaching, in my sense of the word, happens out of contact with students. This backstage work is shared work in a way that classroom performance is not because course and programme design, assessment plans, module evaluation arrangements, resource decisions, admissions and teaching policies, for example, are teaching activities that implicate teams. (I am using 'course' and 'module' interchangeably and using 'programme' to refer to the whole curriculum that leads to an award.)

Besides, while our doings, thinkings and feelings are individual, we do, think and feel with scripts that are shared with others. What we understand about being a teacher in higher education is very much a personal understanding *and* it draws upon shared ideas of what teaching and higher education are, ideas that will vary from department to department and between now and then. Our expectations as teachers, the practices we take for granted and our beliefs about what is good are influenced by the contexts in which we are. In one setting it is easy to be a good teacher because normal practices sheepdog everyone into teaching well. In those departments it would take a perverse talent not to teach well. In others, it takes grit to teach well, although it is easy to get by with information-peddling and plenty of testing. Being a good teacher is about personal skill deployed in an environment rich in appropriate affordances.

The thinking associated with complexity theories exposes some implications of this connectionist perspective. If teaching is an outcome of the interaction between individuals and (social) environments, and if individuals are themselves interactions between, among other things, history, biology, culture, thinking and shifting emotions, then (a) outcomes will be somewhat unpredictable and (b) interventions will also have uncertain effects. This book contains lots of suggestions for teaching well but the impact of any suggestion on any person in any setting is not determinate because what happens emerges from complex interactions whose outcomes are not precisely predictable at the individual level. In other words, becoming a better teacher, like educational and social change in general, is not a certain business but a matter of trying to act well in the light of what we understand experience and research to be saying about what is generally likely to turn out to be stimulating. And, to repeat a point, being a teacher is not just an individual achievement, so becoming a better teacher is a social and a personal process.

These six chapters review research about the settings in which academic staff work and try to teach better, about what encourages them to enjoy it and what discourages them. They introduce ideas about how academic staff (faculty) learn to teach and how they might learn to teach better. This is followed by consideration of what it is to be a new faculty member; of how more established faculty's enthusiasm for teaching may be sustained; and of the implications of the marginal position of part-time teachers.

Chapters 1 to 9 follow a common format. I begin by sketching my stance and the key points I want to emphasize. A longer section follows, containing a more formal review of research which prepares the way for an exploration of implications for alert practice. The penultimate section contains a few ideas for taking things further and I end each chapter by recommending a couple of readings to those who want to know more. Although I am writing for teachers in higher education, some of the things I suggest cannot be done without support from programme leaders, heads of department or deans, which means that some sections are written more for these mid-level leaders than for teachers alone. Just as my audience varies, so too does my voice. The summaries of research, experience and implications are written quite transactionally but the other sections are freer and more personal. When I review research I do use technical terms. Some, such as 'formative' and 'summative' assessment, are useful and unavoidable. Some, such as 'declarative' and 'procedural' knowledge, come from disciplines, notably philosophy and psychology, that help to ground research on good thinking. Others, such as 'affordances' and 'feedout', are there because they allow me to make a point distinctively. This technical language is less in evidence when it comes to implications of research for practice.

I

Being at work in higher education

A stance

Being a teacher in higher education is about you, and your work environments, and your non-work environments. The stance is that each influences
the other. For example, your non-work environments affect the way that
work feels. Reviewing research into stress in the workplace, Briner (1997:
63) noted that as far as people referred for occupational stress counselling
were concerned, 'the limited evidence available suggests that the sources
of client difficulties are more usually connected with life outside work'.
Life counselling is outside the scope of this book but that omission is not
intended to signal that what happens outside work is a closed system with
no connection to it. The interplay is acknowledged but only explored
insofar as it helps us to understand better the experience of being a
teacher in higher education.

Academic work is the main concern of this book. It is seen as a complex
net of expectations, tasks and communications. Being a teacher is a part
of this net, although the act of selecting this one role for deliberation is as
artificial as selecting your work while keeping issues of identity, personhood
and non-work systems in the background. Regardless of whether teaching
invigorates research, whether research sustains teaching or whether they
compete like ferrets in a sack, teaching and research are networked to
each other as well as to administration, pastoral work, self-advancement
and other academic functions.

So, teaching is a web of communications, activities, beliefs and such like.
If this were represented in a simple sketch it might look like Figure 1.1.
The stars stand for elements of the work of teaching, which will include
beliefs, understandings, activities and procedures. The lines invite you to
imagine some of the many, many connections between the elements, with
the heavier lines showing connections that have become 'hot-wired' through
frequent use so that they are almost automatic patterns of reaction to a
particular task that is to hand. In this scheme of things, connections are

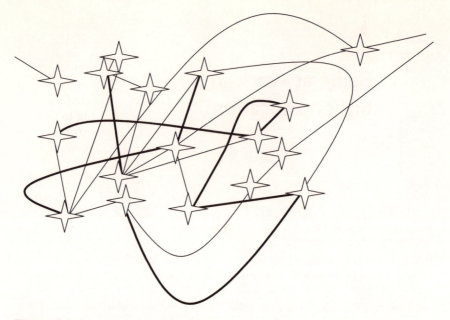

Figure 1.1 A system of connections

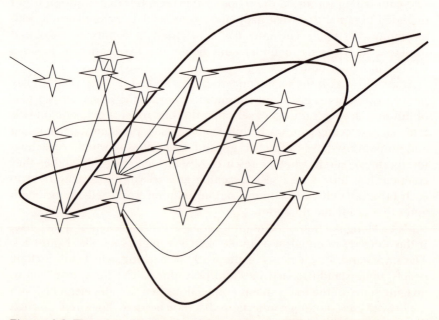

Figure 1.2 The same elements but connected with different weights for a different purpose

bidirectional, although unidirectional patterns get learned. Figure 1.2 shows the same elements but in this case a different set of strong connections is fired up as the task changes. This complex of elements that are variously involved in teaching is connected to other work systems, such as administration, as suggested by Figure 1.3, and then to others still, as Figure 1.4 suggests. Such systems are dynamic in the senses that: (a) the number of elements involved changes over time and according to the task and context; (b) elements decay or drop out of the system; (c) new elements enter it as new connections are formed. In other words, a sketch does not capture the dynamism that makes connectionist systems learning systems. That only reinforces the general point that although it may be analytically convenient to explore some aspects of teaching as if they were free-standing entities, connectionism (Boden, 1991; Dennett, 1991) and human systems thinking (Luhmann, 1995) point us in the direction of complexity, towards understanding teaching as more, say, than a set of tips that work.

This chapter connects teaching to the experience of work in general but this is not to imply that our experience of being teachers is determined by work environments. They do relate to the ways in which we have experience of being teachers and people but they do not determine those experiences (Halford and Leonard, 1999; Webb, 1999).

Key points

1 Around the world, professional work, including academic work, is changing.
2 The impact of structural changes is by no means uniform.
3 Changes may imperil the psychic rewards that motivate many faculty.
4 However, individuals can have some choice about the ways in which changes impact upon them.
5 Local actions, particularly at departmental level, can also preserve psychic rewards in the face of unwelcome structural changes.

Research

Experiences of intensification

Work was changing at the end of the last century, especially middle-class work. Leadbeater (2000) provides a readable account of the changes that come with the development of knowledge economies. Sennett (1998) wrote

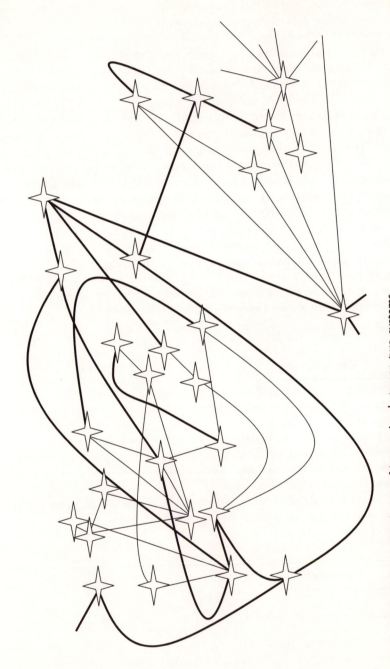

Figure 1.3 A simplified view of interaction between two systems

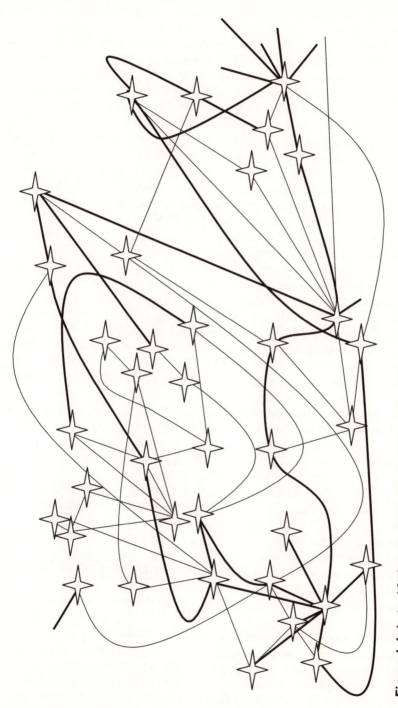

Figure 1.4 A simplified view of interaction between three systems

of a consequent corrosion of character which he attributed to new work environments of fixed-term, often part-time, jobs making greater, faster and more intense demands. He, like others, saw that many middle-class jobs went to people who had the necessary knowledge and skills and presented the right sort of personality as well. By the end of the century, success in the job market needed this emotional labour of self-marketing, and concomitant 'soft skills' such as interpersonal fluency, empathy, self-awareness, enthusiasm, flexibility and self-monitoring. Gee and Lankshear (1997) have sketched a similar picture of the demands that 'fast capitalism' makes on workers and the discourses they use.

Webb (1999) wrote that in the UK 5.8 million people worked in education, medical, welfare and government jobs. He argued that their work had changed and that they were increasingly directed and controlled, trusted less and monitored more. Where their work had once been reliant on reciprocity and cooperation, they were being displaced by market relationships, insularity and competition. A growing cadre of (mainly male) managers now tries to coordinate the (mainly female) workforce, using the old 'hard' management command and control discourses of tight job specification, codes of practice, inspection and numerical performance indicators. Alongside this were shameless expectations of conscientiousness and over-work and the assumption that shortfalls from best practice should be attributed to a lack of staff competence or commitment. There have been similar British analyses of management (Glynn and Holbeche, 2000), schoolteaching (Bottery, 1998; Helsby, 1999), social work (Balloch *et al.*, 1999) and public sector work in general (Exworthy and Halford, 1999). Newspapers have predictably reported that stress levels were rising in all sorts of middle-class occupations. Academic life, once considered a low-stress area, has increasingly been understood to be stressful for a growing number of faculty (Fisher, 1994; Currie, 1996; Soliman and Soliman, 1997; Doyle and Hinde, 1998). Faculty (academic staff) widely report longer hours of work, more marking to be done, raised expectations of publication and service to the community (for example, Blackburn and Lawrence, 1995; Thorsen, 1996; McInnis, 2000). These changes can be especially threatening for faculty who were appointed primarily to teach and who may be clustered in newer universities. Ramsden's Australian evidence is that many academic staff publish little, which suggests low levels of research activity: in the early 1990s, 'three quarters of respondents in the older universities published no books, 60% no book chapters, and 20% no articles' (Ramsden, 1998b: 357). The HERI Faculty Survey said that in 1998–9, 25.3 per cent of faculty in the USA reported 'spending 0 hours doing research and/or scholarly writing per week', compared to a figure of 20 per cent in 1989–90 (Sorcinelli, 2000: 17). Less active researchers may see demands to do research as a threat to teaching excellence and as an assault on their identities (Lucas, 1994; Bailey, 1999). More active ones get locked into the intensifying world of sustaining perfomativity and reputation, which often means subcontracting their teaching to academic wage labourers who, let it be clearly understood, often teach very well.

Academic staff also say that they now work with a more diverse (Upcraft, 1996) and/or less capable (McInnis, 2000) student community on curricula fragmented by modularization and the proliferation of electives (Gaff and Ratcliff, 1996; Blackwell and Williamson, 1999). Resource complaints are endemic. They make work more demanding when conscientiousness leads faculty to try to maintain best practice without the resources that make best practice easy. Instead, they have to struggle to do the job as they wish it to be done. McInnis (2000) reports that 30 per cent of his 1,554 Australian respondents in 1999 said that the lack of up-to-date equipment and technology hindered their work. The 1993 figure was 22 per cent. Forty-six per cent of the 1999 respondents and 36 per cent of the 1993 respondents said that their work was hindered by teaching too many students, which is another face of resource limitations. And, as universities are becoming more managed, faculty can see themselves as less 'professional', less trusted, more called to account and spending more time on record-keeping and documentation. 'Hard' managerialism gives these 'backstage' tasks an importance that many faculty feel is unwarranted. This not only steals time from activities they like (research and teaching) but also adds to the proliferation of tasks, meetings and roles (Altbach and Lewis, 1996; Currie, 1996). Experiences of intensification – of having more, more complex work to do and more roles to juggle – are exacerbated by having to do work that is a distraction from the 'frontstage' business of teaching and researching. Claims that teaching and research are really improved by this 'backstage' work are seldom appreciated by academic staff.

There is a view that institutions have become 'greedy', asking for more without caring sufficiently for the humans who work in them. In Martin's (1999) survey of 160 staff in Britain and Australia 88 per cent of faculty said that they did not feel valued. Interestingly, 77 per cent of leaders felt the same. The full-time workforce is also 'greying' (Karpiak, 1997). There are certainly mid career professors with a vitality for teaching (Walker and Quinn, 1996; André and Frost, 1997), but others face stagnation or cynicism (Karpiak, 2000). When faculty are surveyed, it appears that alienation (Everett and Entrekin, 1994) and stress are growing. In addition to the reports of stress that were mentioned earlier, alienation, or at least suspicion of management, is regularly reported (Fourie and Alt, 2000; Newton, 2000), as a predictable response both to attempts to introduce change and to the belief that administrators are trying to run higher education institutions (HEIs) on their terms and for their unacademic purposes. Lastly, greedy demands can particularly affect women academics (Caplan, 1994; Chilly Editorial Collective, 1995) and staff from minority groups. Not only do they tend to be disproportionately represented in the lower levels of pay and status (Doyle and Hind, 1998) and have less secure employment contracts (Leslie, 1998; Chitnis and Williams, 1999), they also get called upon to do a disproportionate amount of service work (Tierney and Bensimon, 1996).

As the discourses of the market place are applied to HE, so academic staff increasingly have to attend to competition and image management, as well as to the substance of research and teaching. One face of the market economy applied to HE is increasing casualization, with it being said that 60 per cent of undergraduate teaching in the USA and 40 per cent of that in the UK is not done by full-time, tenured faculty. I mistrust the figures but believe the general message. This means that many teachers, often women, have to juggle short-term and part-time jobs while trying to land a full-time tenure-track position. There are more of these casual staff than there are full-time vacancies, so there are disappointments. At the same time there are reports of a loss of collegiality throughout HE (Tompkins, 1992). There is less time to socialize and people spend less time in the university because they are on a fees-per-hour-of-teaching contract or because they get interrupted there, which disturbs their pressured writing schedule. 'Hard' managerialism threatens collegiality: at best it uses 'contrived collegiality' (Hargreaves, 1994), when people are corralled into groups to produce plans that advance priorities decided by senior managers. The opportunity to share and discuss good practice and problems in teaching and learning is increasingly lost and the emotional support networks are disorganized.

It is important to modify this glum picture in two ways. First, these changes have uneven impacts. For example, 77 per cent of the 312 male and 74 per cent of the 251 female psychology faculty in Doyle and Hind's (1998) survey reported that their administrative loads had increased, which means that 23 and 26 per cent, respectively, reported no change. Second, any objective changes to conditions of work take on meaning in conjunction with other elements in people's systems of connections. A person's job expectations, goals, self-theories, gender, health, care responsibilities, race, job status and age are some of the elements that will mediate the ways in which objective changes in the work environment are understood and experienced. A dynamic systems approach recognizes that changes in the workplace will tend to have somewhat predictable general effects *and* that these effects will be unpredictable at the individual level because their specific meanings emerge through the interplay of the changes with other elements in the net. Large-scale changes in the workplace have effects which have some indeterminacy about them. This cuts two ways. On the one hand it means that changes can be more or less troubling depending on the moderating effects of other elements in the systems. This means that the experience of intensification should be affected by a faculty member's academic department, their self-theories, expectations and suchlike.

On the other hand it suggests that the impact of any intervention, such as an attempt to make a department a more collegial community of practice, is likely to be dampened by the unchanged elements in the systems of meaning-making.

Work motivation

McInnis (2000) found that between 1993 and 1999 the level of Australian faculty's overall satisfaction with the job fell from 67 to 51 per cent. Fifty-six per cent added that their work was a source of considerable stress. This picture seems to be recognizable in other English-speaking countries. Many of us have no choice but to stay in academic professions but others have choice. Yet Altbach and Lewis (1996: 48) reported that although 'the vicissitudes experienced by the profession have been considerable, the professoriate is by no means demoralized. In all but three [out of 14] countries 60 percent or more agree that this is an especially creative and productive time in their fields.' I suggest four ways of resolving this apparent contradiction. First, Altbach and Lewis (1996: 13) write that 'Many report finding intellectual pleasure in their work', a pleasure that is frequently identified with research activity. Second, Blackburn and Lawrence's (1995) finding that most faculty in the USA wished to do a little less teaching was accompanied by an insistence that they did want to teach. Surveys consistently report that face-to-face teaching work is a source of reward, although its attractions are besmirched by large classes, poorly prepared students, lack of resources, recording, planning and accountability requirements, etc. (Doyle and Hind, 1998). Third, many academic staff do find 'spaces' for their own interests. For example, an ethnographic study of an English university found that underlying what was in many respects a worsening situation was a significant residue of autonomy, work enrichment and development (Trowler, 1998). Fourth, academic work can have emotional rewards. Karpiak (2000) writes of mid-life faculty's call to care, community, creativity and consciousness, accepting, though, that some get drawn into crisis and stagnation.

This is a picture of intrinsic motivation, of people getting psychic rewards from their work. They may want to be satisfied *with* salary levels, promotion prospects and the ways in which they are managed (hygiene factors) but they are mainly satisfied or fulfilled *by* the intellectual challenge of research, the joys of teaching and the emotional quality of the communities of practice in which they work (motivating factors). Psychic rewards and opportunities for fulfilment and self-actualization in the workplace are major sources of faculty motivation: Doyle and Hind (1998) report that their 582 psychology teachers in HE showed high levels of intrinsic motivation on standard measurement scales. Although faculty can be demotivated by lack of resources, poor pay, 'hard' managerialism and low status, they are not, in the main, satisfied by improving these hygiene factors (Evans, 1998). Hargreaves (1998) extends these ideas by pointing out that attempts to enhance the quality of education by specifying school-teachers' work in ever greater detail, requiring more documentation of policies and practices, and using the accountability methods of 'hard' managerialism to try to ensure compliance run a serious risk of damaging education because teachers then find it hard to get the psychic rewards that make the work worthwhile. The concern is that this will lead to re-cruitment and retention problems and muffle the creativity, flexibility and care that are so important in people-working professions.

As long as schoolteachers and academic staff can find spaces for the work that thrills them and as long as they can get some fulfilment from face-to-face teaching, from interaction with colleagues and, in HE, from scholarship, then changes that make the workplace more challenging stand a good chance of being accommodated because staff can still feel some sense of control and reward. But, following Hargreaves, there is a danger that reforms steer people towards backstage activities that they mislike and make it harder for them to get the psychic rewards they seek from the frontstage ones that they enjoy. Referring to schools, McCulloch and col-leagues (2000: 83) wrote:

> In the face of such constant, mandated change and of threatening accountability procedures . . . teachers may learn helplessness . . . believing themselves to be victims who are scarcely able to shape the patterns of their work and find rewards in it. The ensuing passivity, disillusion and defensiveness, sometimes manifesting themselves as cynicism, obstructionism or anger, are hardly conducive to good schooling . . . stress and 'burn out' are more likely.

Of course, disillusioned people continue to do academic work and some are mainly motivated by extrinsic rewards, but because professional work requires the non-routine exercise of expert judgement, it thrives on creat-ivity, intuition, dynamism, insight and the other qualities that come from pleasured commitment, not from extrinsic motivation.

These ideas about motivation are extended in Chapter 4. Enough has been said here to establish that faculty's motivation is at risk from changes in the world of work generally and in HEIs in particular. Their profes-sional identity as teachers may be especially vulnerable because teaching is often, but not invariably, ranked second to research and because many of the changes described in the previous section bear most heavily on teaching-related activities. To put it another way, one way of strategically redefining academic work is to avoid many of the changes by concentrating on re-search, erasing teaching from one's professional identity. Yet, although structural changes may not favour a commitment to teaching, I want to suggest that it is still possible for individuals, especially when they work in well led subject departments, to teach well and enjoy it. A short account of research on faculty's mental well-being sets out some of the bases of my claim.

The mental well-being of academic staff

Edworthy (2000) reported that stress in further education colleges could be fuelled by: a lack of resources; over-full timetables; problematic students; a breakdown in communication between 'management' and others; apparently discriminatory practices, with some people not being rewarded for their achievements; meetings; shared workrooms; car parking; and the erosion of the psychic rewards that come from working well with students. Much the same is likely to be true of higher education. Yet while such conditions affect the incidence of mental dysfunction at the group or population level, they do not *determine* the well-being or dysfunction of any individual. Structures and environments have influence but people draw on the same repertoires of scripts and schemata yet experience the same environment in different ways thanks to their biographies, expectations, self image and dispositions. So, 'the effects of stressful conditions are not uniform but depend on individual differences in personality – for example, the pattern of motivation and beliefs of those exposed to a stressor – as well as other external conditions that make a difference in the way situations like this are experienced' (Lazarus, 1991: 414).

To give another example, it is widely held that people with Type A personalities (a strong need to control and achieve, competitiveness, showing chronic haste and impatience, tending to be confrontational) are more liable to stress than are the more laid-back Type B people, which means that the same changes in work conditions can stimulate very different effects on Type A and Type B people. Again, the workplace is only one of the environments in which an individual acts and the impact of the work environment is related to the 'personal capital' that the individual invests in it (Halford and Leonard, 1999). So a work environment that is not conducive to mental well-being is likely to have greater impact on people for whom work looms large in their lives than for those who treat it otherwise.

That is not to deny that structural factors are significant: for example, women workers often have to manage 'double careers' as employees and as home-makers, so it is not surprising that women may be especially vulnerable to stress (Thorsen, 1996). Yet HEIs and communities of practice, such as departments within them, differ in the emotional ranges that may be expressed, with some expecting emotions to be hidden (Hochschild, 1983), while others permit greater authenticity (Putnam and Mumby, 1993). In such ways workgroups moderate structural variables. At the individual level, well-being is associated with a sense of control: those who feel that they have a suitable degree of control in their environment tend to feel less stressed and threatened than those who feel less empowered (Fisher, 1994). Rahim and Psenicka (1996) suggested that feelings of having control related to the extent to which stress was reported in situations of role overload. Perry and colleagues (1996) found that new faculty with a low sense of control were less successful than colleagues who were rated highly on the locus of personal control. Thorsen's definition of stress implies that control is central: 'Stress [is defined] as that which occurs when one perceives that the demands of the environment clearly exceed the resources to handle them' (Thorsen, 1996: 472). As noted above, there is also a dynamic element to this. Some research on workplace stress has suggested that the fact of change is as significant as the nature of the change itself (Murphy, 1988; Fisher, 1994). New entrants into a workplace may not have problems with some of the things that vex established workers who have known different conditions and who may view the present through an interpretative filter of nostalgia. It can be argued that changes affect established workers' perceived levels of control in their environment, and possibly have an impact upon their self esteem. 'Evidently', concluded Murphy (1988: 324), 'it is less stressful never to have had control than to have had it and lost it.'

Furthermore, where some will attribute things to stable forces that are outside their control, casting themselves as victims (of their own lack of intelligence or innate character, for example), others explain the same situation in terms of changeable factors (not working hard enough or thinking carefully enough, bad luck etc.) that will change or that they can affect (by working harder or working smarter). Self-theories (Dweck, 1999) matter, connecting to the meanings we make about work and life in general. Some people's self-theories, consolidated by repeatedly seeing themselves as lacking control or as failing, amount to learned helplessness, which has been seen as a contributor to stress and dis-ease. Seligman (1998) argues that optimism can be learned, or, to use Dweck's language, self-theories can be encouraged that support perseverance, strategic thinking and a tendency to see oneself as having potential in situations that will generally afford some spaces for manoeuvre. Environments of certain quality – ones that are person-centred, empathic and empowering, ones in which people are encouraged to make attributions to factors that they can influence – are conducive to learned optimism and positive self-theories and make fulfilment and self-actualization in the workplace more likely.

There is a lot of evidence that being a teacher in higher education is compromised by intensification, the unwanted importance being placed on backstage work and inflationary expectations of research output. However, teaching can still offer valued psychic rewards, especially if we can find ways of retaining control where it matters and teach ourselves ways of experiencing that are affirmative, not defeatist. This view of teaching is about technique and commitment, but also about integrity, self-knowing and persistent attempts to turn others' expectations to our advantage. It is to such ways of being a teacher in higher education that I now turn.

Informed practices

This section follows connectionist metaphors in exploring ideas about practices that help to make the workplace congenial to our work as academic staff. The metaphors imply that action could be taken at many levels – national, state or provincial, professional association, HEI, department or team, and individual. It could also take many forms, addressing beliefs, structural inequalities, emotions, practices or sources of dissonance, for example. Notice, though, that connectionism implies that the outcomes of any action are often uncertain because there is no one-to-one correspondence between change in one element and change in any other. Recognizing that interventions at one place in a system may not connect to other elements in ways that lead to the intended outcome, Fullan (1999) argues for *systemic* action to encourage change. This implies that attempts to improve faculty's experiences as teachers would involve action at several levels and in several forms. Even then, complexity theories tell us that the unchanged elements in the system may be connected in ways that dampen the effects of the interventions and attract the system back into more or less the same cycles of behaviour (Knight, 2002d: Chapter 6). Here and throughout this book I am criticizing widespread, individualized approaches to teaching quality that say that we can all be good teachers if we get the right messages and act seriously upon them. If that were the case, it would follow that tepid teaching would be an individual, moral failing whose remedy would lie in making people go to more workshops and take their own teaching more seriously. I argue the opposite, saying that if guilt is in order then those who connive in systems that make it so hard for excellence to emerge should be feeling guilt, not honest teachers. Better teaching does, of course, take well informed people with goodwill and individuals can become excellent, but widespread good teaching needs systemic expectations, processes and leadership to favour it. I have suggested, though, that there is a case for saying that higher education environments are progressively becoming more inimical to good teaching. Ironically, much more attention is simultaneously being paid to educating individuals to teach better. One interpretation is that this steady normalization of the discourses of personal professional development is a ploy to make the victims responsible for their own rescue. An implication would be that teachers could often be kinder to themselves by recognizing the limits to what they, alone, can achieve. There are other sites for intervention to improve teaching quality, as a glance at Figure 10.1 will indicate.

I think the academic department is the prime site for educational improvement. Ramsden (1998a: 63) identified it as the key organizational unit in universities: 'There is evidence that the environment of academic departments – including their leadership – influences the quality of teaching and learning in universities.' Departments can be considered as 'activity systems' (Blackler, 1993), as the organizational sites in which workloads are determined and done. They are also communities in which the meanings of change are explored and constructed. The emotional quality of work is partly created in subject departments, and stress and joy are experienced (or not) through the mediation of their structures, routines and cultures.

Obviously, departments are connected to the HEI and are subject to its budgets, policies and accountability procedures. Yet departments in the same institution differ considerably as work environments. In secondary schools and HE it has been found that attitudes, self-theories and workplace cultures vary from department to department within the same institution and between departments teaching the same subject in different institutions (Knight and Trowler, 2001). In other words, departmental-level action may be the most promising way to try to affect the ways in which institution-wide structures are perceived in faculty's working lives. Informed teaching practices, then, would largely be local practices, although 'local' does not mean 'disconnected'.

Underlying the practical suggestions that follow is a distinction drawn by Dr Rob Buckman, a Toronto oncologist, television presenter and comedy performer. Talking about alternative medicine to an audience of physicians and medical students he argued that there was slim research evidence that it made patients medically better, although he acknowledged that four alternative treatments did seem to do some good. But, regardless of medical effectiveness, it often made them feel better and for this reason cancer doctors such as himself should take it seriously. Some of the practices I mention below can reduce the objective workload but others are justified because they can touch the way we feel about what we do. Box 1.1 contains ten suggestions for things departments can do to ease the experience of work.

It is somewhat misleading to single out leaders and identify things that they might do because there is a case for saying that leadership is not so much what a head of department does as practices that are distributed throughout systems – the dynamic outcomes of webs of connections (Knight and Trowler, 2001). Yet, there are people who are recognized as leaders. Leithwood and colleagues' (1999) account of what good leaders do establishes some benchmarks for leadership practices that are sensitive to the quality of working life. Good leaders:

Box 1.1   Department-level actions to ease the experience of work

1 Taking time to think about 'the ways we do things around here' and why it is thus. Most organizations do pointless things and resist doing things better. For example, an enormous amount of time is spent on grading student work but there is a case for marking less (Knight, 2000; and Chapter 9 of this book).

2 Seeking appropriate efficiencies. That does not mean reducing the staff time needed to teach a course, only then to fill it with fresh busy-work.

3 Using known and simple systems for keeping records. One way to get such systems is to assume that no records are needed *unless* a compelling case can be established to the contrary.

4 By extension, trying to substitute professional interactions for bureaucracies and paperwork, and trusting that colleagues will do good things in their own ways *unless* there is good reason to operate on low-trust assumptions.

5 Helping support staff to be as effective as possible. This may mean, for example, encouraging them to close their doors sometimes so that they can work without interruption.

6 Managing meetings well. This advice is so often repeated that there must be some doubt whether it really is practicable.

7 Working on the assumption that long hours of work on compliance activities (marking, teaching preparation, record-keeping, course planning, writing specifications, doing self-evaluations) is a sign that there is something wrong in the department, not a failing in the individual.

8 Having a workload distribution system that is fair and based on known criteria. Resentment makes a workload seem heavier than it might otherwise feel.

9 Fostering collegiality. A great deal of learning can happen through collegial interchanges and, at the same time, great security can come from mulling over problems or discussing problems with others. Collegiality may reduce workloads by stimulating new ideas and the support and sense of belonging may help to make them feel less intense. Writers on modern organizations (for example, Hesselbein *et al.*, 1996; Allee, 1997; Goleman, 1998) commend teamwork, equality and collaboration.

10 Routinely approaching new demands and problems as things that can be accommodated in ways that should not cause great upsets to the department. This is learned optimism at a departmental level.

---

1 Ensure that strategies for problem-solving are available and shared.
2 Periodically clarify, summarize and synthesize perspectives on progress.
3 Stimulate commitment to task completion.
4 Promote innovation and collaboration.

5 Draw out all team members' knowledge.
6 Surface their assumptions.
7 Encourage the expression of diverse opinions and open enquiry.
8 Foster the development of shared interpretations.

For me the first four often mean that leaders listen to what colleagues say and then put together 'mock ups' as objects for further consideration. An example of this is the case of a team required to respond to a demand that all coursework be second-marked. The leader introduced discussion by saying that this need not mean second-guessing a first marker's grades, but could be a way of inspiring professional conversations about students' achievements on a particular task and about appropriate ways of producing marks and advice for improvement. Framed like this, the task became more manageable and worthwhile. The leader then presented draft guidelines and second marking protocols for discussion and revision. In this way a problem that tied some departments in knots was quickly brought to a collegial conclusion without a feeling that a new burden was being imposed. This leader, who brought similar creativity to the university's demand that the department introduce a staff appraisal system, helped to make innovation, collaboration, task completion and problem-working a matter of practice. Leithwood's next four points are more directly about evoking collegiality and incorporate the common advice on the development of interpersonal relations based on mutual respect, trust and tolerance of well intentioned failure. A remark that applies to all eight points is that improvement is a slow and incremental process, not a matter of root-and-branch change. So, in addition, leaders do well when they:

9 Recognize that colleagues have different biographies, bring different things to deliberations, learn faster or slower and have different needs.
10 Know that learning comes from errors, which means that well intentioned errors are acceptable, even desirable.
11 Accept that people learn best when their sense of self is not under threat, which means that confrontational methods have their limits and that respect is important.

A holist view of people and their work lies behind these ideas about leading. It is quite neatly captured in a summary of a professional development course that McLeod and Jennings (1990: 69) ran for IBM (UK). It included '*gestalt* work, personal construct theory, guided affective imagery, Chinese philosophy, psychosynthesis, and using the right-hand side of the brain'. While leaders will seldom dare to act publicly on the basis of 360° views of people as systems of feelings and thinkings, being and doings, we may benefit from doing it for ourselves. Box 1.2 contains 14 ideas.

Box 1.2   Things individuals can do to ease the experience of work

1 Take the view that working long hours is a sign of incompetence, not a mark of distinction. Campbell and Neill (1994) write that the hours British schoolteachers work would be evidence of poor professional practice in some other countries.
2 Having taken a view of how much time to spend on work you are required to do (and remember that backstage teaching work is usually less satisfying than interactive teaching), roughly allocate time to individual tasks. For example, it might be that a book review is worth the time it takes to read the book plus reflecting time plus two hours writing time; written comments on essays might be fitted into five minutes apiece by restricting yourself to headline points; skim all e-mails except those that matter, except when you are very busy when it makes sense to delete them unread. Etc.
3 Think frequently, write often. Many of us can easily find ourselves straining to write and wasting a lot of time in the process. One novelist remarked that she had written her next book and all that remained was to put the words on the page. Writing is easiest when we know what we want to say. I find travelling time, especially walking to work, excellent for drafting. Following Boice's (1992) findings that the new academics who succeeded were those most likely to do some writing almost daily, I then aim to write what I have walked when I get into the office.
4 Get comments on first drafts of teaching materials, not on near-finished products. It saves a lot of time if others identify things that need changing before you have committed a lot of effort to making them look good. In general, the less the 'be perfect' driver operates and the more we naturally and easily seek advice from trusted colleagues, who do the same, the better.
5 A lot of academic practice fetishes data collection, although it is not clear that much is achieved by it. Why do we *really* create and keep assessment data, minutes of meetings, etc.?
6 Try to learn 'one touch' techniques. That means dealing, on receipt, with any emails, memos or letters that will take only minutes to handle. An alternative, of which I do not approve, is to heap these papers up and ignore them until the seventh reminder arrives. I expect we all have colleagues who are adept at this dark side of the work-reduction force.
7 Decide how long a meeting is worth and leave once that time is up. Many meetings are worth none of your time: keep face by contributing electronically and pithily in advance.
8 Say 'No'.
9 If students can learn from each other, advise each other and give feedback to each other, your time can be saved. Chapter 9 argues that these practices, well used, are good for student learning.
10 Read widely. It sounds counter-intuitive to recommend a ruthless approach to marking lab reports only now to suggest reading 'off piste'. The

idea is that it can be more invigorating to read things that can help you to re-see your research, teaching and job than to add another dreary empirical study to a stilted bibliography. Read to vivify.

11 Physical fitness is frequently associated with mental well-being. The endorphins that come from exercise can make work feel different and even make teaching performance more lively. Body work, in the shape of the Alexander technique, mindful breathing exercises, meditation, yoga and t'ai chi, to name a few, makes a difference to a lot of people who find that bodily well-being makes work easier – that swimming at lunchtime makes for a better afternoon's work.

12 Confessional practices, self-help work, emotional cleansing, neurolinguistic programming are some of the courses that people use to try to allow mental energies to work for them, not against them. Work demands can become lessened as a result.

13 Recommending that you develop 'personal mastery' may only be rephrasing things already said, inviting you to appraise your self-theories, to look for opportunities to do things that you value and to appreciate how to maintain and enhance personal and professional vitality. Peter Senge's work contains popular and well established advice on this. I prefer his *Fifth Discipline Fieldbook* (1994) to his other books.

14 Colleagues seldom seem to recognize one's successes and institutions often see that one's worth is defined by failings, not achievements. Nor am I good at praising myself for things achieved. I have felt better and worked better, though, when friends have nudged me to be kind to myself and celebrate things I do well. We all gain, as people and as faculty members, when we have friends, colleagues and leaders like them.

Action points

The last section contained a selection of things that could be done to try to sustain a good work–life balance and to contain sources of dis-ease at work. You may have found things there upon which you would like to act. I recommend three other ways of engaging with these ideas.

1 Get together with a friend or two and roam over questions such as: 'How could *we* make it better round here?'; 'What do *we* do to make things difficult for ourselves?'; and, if these are good friends, 'How do you see me giving myself a hard time?'

2 Again, gather together good people and spend social time looking on what you, as a group, do well. No griping allowed. From there, move on to looking for opportunities to create successes in the future. What could we have done well in two years' time? How could we enjoy getting there?

3 Read *Working with Emotional Intelligence*.

Further reading

Daniel Goleman's (1998) *Working with Emotional Intelligence* is a strong and readable book on the importance of self-knowledge and self-regulation in the workplace. I associate it with the humanistic psychology of self-actualization that has developed from the work of Maslow and Rogers. This 'third way' in psychology has insightful critics who say that it is more about individual autonomy than benevolence, which is the social face of self-actualization. This implies that it inclines to sociological naivety: for example, by marginalizing issues of formal and informal power relationships. That said, the tradition has much to say about what individuals can do for their own fulfilment in the workplace and in life generally. Goleman also has a complete section on 'The emotionally intelligent organization'.

Richard Sennett (1998) gives a lively analysis of what is happening in the world of white-collar work in his book, *The Corrosion of Character*. A theme of this chapter, though, is that the structural changes that he describes can be mitigated through one's own self-theories and through sensitive communities of practice. Paul Trowler and I elaborate that in chapters 5 to 10 of *Departmental Leadership in Higher Education* (Knight and Trowler, 2001).

2

Learning teachers, learning students

A stance

In Chapter 1 faculty work was considered in something of an undifferentiated fashion but now the work of teaching is increasingly to the fore. Where Chapter 1 considered ways of being in work environments, this chapter is more about ways of learning in them. I develop this position with reference to activity theory, 'actor . . . network' thinking and ideas about the interplay between the explicit and tacit. These theories lead to the simple proposition that learning is something that happens in normal social practices, as well as more formally when learning is intentional (Eraut, 2000). Once established, those ideas about situated learning are used in Chapters 3 to 6, where motivation and the different experiences of being a teacher are explored. A stance that unites these four chapters is that the quality of our work settings affects, by infusion, what we learn, do and feel. Some work environments are good learning environments and provide a superb place from which to manage a career (see also Chapter 13). In some the daily practices exude enthusiasm whereas others leach it away; some make it easy to succeed as a novice while others make it easy to hope for retirement. Being a good teacher is indeed affected by policy statements, staff development workshops and command of new teaching techniques but the ways in which they all work out, motivate and influence us is enormously dependent on the way a workgroup, department or institution routinely rolls along. Good environments – teams, departments and universities – make for abundant good learning

Key points

1 Learning is more complex than might be assumed. (So good teaching is as well.)

2 Good teaching is a personal and a social triumph. (Good learning too.)
3 Despite obvious differences, there is symmetry between teachers' and students' learning. Understandings of how people learn can inform our learning as teachers and what we do to promote student learning.

Research

Knowledge, knowing and teaching

Ohlsson (1996) identifies two sorts of knowledge. His first is procedural or practical knowledge, comprising sensori-motor skills (driving a car, throwing a ball) and cognitive skills (chess). His second is declarative, propositional or higher-order knowledge. It includes concrete facts (the mass of super-massive black holes is about 0.5 per cent of the mass of their galaxies), abstract knowledge of principles (Newton's laws of motion) and abstract knowledge of ideas (the Enlightenment). Practical knowledge is about learning to do and higher-order knowledge is about understanding. Crucially, he suggests that 'successful performance', which is what practical knowledge is about, 'is neither a sufficient criterion for, nor a necessary consequence of, understanding' (Ohlsson, 1996: 50; see also Wertsch, 1998: 132). If this is so, then tests of understanding need not be good predictors of performance, nor need polished performance betoken good propositional knowledge. There are profound implications here for the design and implementation of learning–teaching sequences which have as their goal the development of complex procedural–propositional achievements.

Shulman (1987) rejected the view that teaching is no more than procedural knowledge in action and insisted that its propositional, intellectual basis mattered too. His model of pedagogical reasoning and action comprised: comprehending the setting and what is to be taught; transforming it by preparing, representing, selecting and adapting; instructing; evaluating; reflecting; and forming new comprehensions. He argued that these processes called for seven sorts of knowledge. He had schoolteaching in mind but I know of no better account for higher education, where attempts to improve teaching are also so often obstructed by 'incomplete and trivial definitions [of professional knowledge] held by the policy community' (Shulman, 1987: 20). The seven types are:

1 Content knowledge: science, art, geography etc.
2 General pedagogical knowledge: knowledge of principles and strategies for curriculum and class management in general.
3 Curriculum knowledge: knowledge of the materials and programmes that are the tools of the trade.

4 Pedagogical content knowledge: a 'special amalgam of content and pedagogy . . . [teachers'] own special form of professional understanding' (Shulman, 1987: 8).
5 Knowledge of learners and their characteristics.
6 Knowledge of educational contexts: of the characteristics and effects of groups, classrooms, school district administration, communities and cultures.
7 Knowledge of 'educational ends, purposes, and values and their philosophical and historical grounds' (Shulman, 1987: 8).

It is usually easy to fault lists like this one. I do not want to haggle over what seems to me to be a serviceable sketch of the pedagogic terrain but I do think that there is an eighth type of knowledge to be added:

8 Knowledge of self, including awareness of our self-theories (how we tend to explain success and lack of it), our preferred identities (who we wish to be seen as), the values we tend to act out, and our emotional drives and needs (Dweck, 1999; Moshman, 1999)

The eighth is prominent in descriptions of the expert practitioner in people-working professions (Schön, 1983; Palmer, 1998), where the self is an important means by which work is done and so personal integrity, in the sense of an integration between what we do, what we want to do and the values that we want to live, is important. Learning to be a teacher therefore means learning about one's own values, self-theories, thoughts and identities as well as gaining the other forms of knowledge needed to encourage that valued, complex learning which can involve the student as a whole person. If Chapter 1 had much to say about the importance of having a sense of personal influence over the work environment, this chapter complements it by recommending appreciative self-enquiry as a way of giving it directions. 'Appreciative' is an apt word because it says that the enquiries should be judgemental (appreciation as weighing or judging), but it reminds us to be kind to ourselves and avoid the self-laceration that can be implied by commonplace recommendations that we engage in 'critical reflection' or 'critical enquiry'. Ludema *et al.* (2001) have more to say about the business of appreciative enquiry.

These eight forms, which blend propositional and procedural forms of knowledge, come from different sources, notably: (a) scholarship in subject areas such as history, German and music; (b) pedagogical settings and their affordances, such as texts, materials, finances, curriculum, organizational arrangements; (c) 'research on schooling, social organizations, human learning, teaching and development and the other social and cultural phenomena that affect what teachers do'; and (d) 'the wisdom of practice itself' (Shulman, 1987: 11). The list implies that some – perhaps much – learning comes with the experience of being a teacher. While recognizing

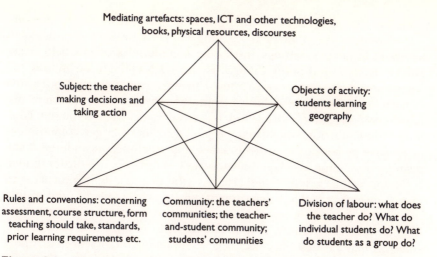

Figure 2.1   Elements of a teaching and learning system (after Engeström 2001)

that the knowledge that teachers in higher education need is different from the knowledge students need, I want to suggest that both roles involve learning; that there are similarities between learning as a teacher and as a student; and that, following Shulman's point that knowledge comes from different sources, they both learn from the environment and communities of practice, as well as from more intentional and formal activities.

Teaching as one face of learning

Figure 2.1 shows teaching as an activity system, although it would be less misleading were the line connecting subject and object to be broken, which would make it clear that teaching is not sufficient to produce the planned learning outcomes. I want to comment on just two of the figure's triangles. The first, connecting subject, object and community, makes it clear that action (and the thinking that suffuses it) is not individual action but an individual-and-social matter. The second shows that action is influenced by three sets of affordances (opportunities and possibilities): mediating artefacts, which individuals appropriate to their activities; rules, codes, expectations and the like; and the division of labour between actors. Notice that affordances bring limits. Rules for course design help teachers by reducing the number of decisions they have to make, tools help them do it and the division of labour which gives the programme director a say on whether a course design is acceptable also gives the designer a source of advice or guidance. Yet each of these affordances actually or potentially limits what the designer does. There is more about affordances in Chapter 10.

Figure 10.2 extends the thinking behind this activity system diagram and elaborates the point that learning happens through the mediated interplay of people, settings (including communities of practice), rules and artefacts. At this point, though, Figure 2.1 is enough to continue the connectionist perspective of Chapter 1 by suggesting that what is learned or taught is the outcome of shifting connections between different elements. Activity systems interconnect and are often bunched together in communities of practice, which may be joined to make larger communities of practice or constellations of practice. For example, an undergraduate degree programme may be understood as a complex activity system which is located within a subject department (the community of practice). In many universities, subject departments are loosely coupled to the institution, which is more a constellation of activity systems and communities than an integrated entity. A minority of HEIs, notably small liberal arts colleges, may be described as large communities of practice, in which departments (which are communities of practice in their own right) are tightly coupled elements of the larger community.

Power relations of differing and shifting kinds suffuse these networks, which can be as turbulent as a bag of cats, the word 'community' notwithstanding. Such internally created dissonances are one source of change, while changes in the relation of networks with their environments also create dissonances that can alter the activity system itself. Some systems try to protect themselves by putting a lot of effort into boundary maintenance, fighting off change with the 'not invented here' routine. Others, especially vibrant learning systems, treat boundaries as places to learn, and they sponsor boundary-crossing, boundary-pushing activities as ways of strengthening themselves through continuous adaptation (Wenger, 2000). Analyses such as these are compatible with sociological 'actor . . . network' thinking, which is concerned with networks,

> which configure ontologies. The agents, their dimensions, and what they are and do, all depend on the morphology of the relationships in which they are involved. For example, a very simple variable such as the length of the network, or the number of connections that an actor has with different networks, determines what the actor is, wants and can do.
>
> (Callon, 1999: 186)

I return to the theme of change in Chapter 12. Here I simply say that naive views about the impact of teaching on learning – and, by extension, of how we learn to be better as teachers – are not easily reconciled with the simplified complexity of Figure 2.1; nor is it helpful to imagine the teacher as a lone, heroic figure whose achievements are hers, or his, alone.

Figure 2.2 presents learning in a different way. 'Teaching' is not mentioned: indeed, there is an implication that we should begin by asking, 'How is learning possible?' and accept that a legitimate answer will be 'It happens', which has radical implications for the ways in which we try to promote student learning *and* for our own learning as teachers. Engeström (1999), currently the best-known proponent of activity theory, is critical of the work of Nonaka and Takauchi (1995), which, modified by ideas taken from Kolb (1984) and Spender (1998), underpins this figure. I agree that Nonaka and Takauchi's analysis is not as good as Engeström's when it comes to exploring the dynamics of what he calls 'expansive learning' episodes. That said, I stand by Figure 2.2 as a pointer to the significance in the long-term operations of workgroups, communities and systems of: tacit knowings; the dialectics between tacit and explicit; the interplays between individuals and groups.

I will begin by looking at the four major areas, emboldened and numbered 1 to 4. The double-headed arrows connecting them indicate two-way flows between these four cells but they fail to show that there are leaks in the system and that what ends up in one cell has an uncertain resemblance to anything in either of the cells with which there is communication. Although Figure 2.2 looks like a hydraulic system, the reality is more like a plasma.

The left-hand side of Figure 2.2 distinguishes between a person's tacit knowing and explicit knowledge. Much knowing is tacit and the more expert we become as teachers the more intuitive and automatic our practices will tend to be. Although it may lie somewhat outside the reach of consciousness, tacit knowledge is the bedrock of experts' fast, intuitive judgements and actions. They find it hard to put this expertise into words and are likely to find that their skill crumbles if they try to bring to bear the calculative rationality that the textbooks teach novices (Dreyfus and Dreyfus, 1986). This implicit knowing comes from many, often informal, sometimes subliminal sources (Eraut, 2000) and is liable to elude consciousness (Donnelly, 1999). Some of these sources are shown by the arrow that points diagonally from the top right corner to the practices of the community or system and also by the one coming from the top left which alerts us to the contribution of things as diverse as our own experiences of being taught and of learning, parenting, films, television, faiths, beliefs and travel. In the words of Anderson and Skinner (1999: 252), 'learning occurs "through the job" rather than "on the job" and is supplemented by technical books and attendance at short seminar/presentations on specified topics'. Again, 'Good office designs can produce powerful learning environments. But much of that power comes from incidental learning. For example, people often find out what they need to know by virtue of where they sit and who they see rather than by direct communication' (Brown and Duguid, 2000: 72). Rosenholtz's (1991) research into Tennessee elementary school teachers, Becher's (1999) interview study of professionals and Chivers and Cheetham's (2001) survey of 452 people in 20 professions all say much the same.

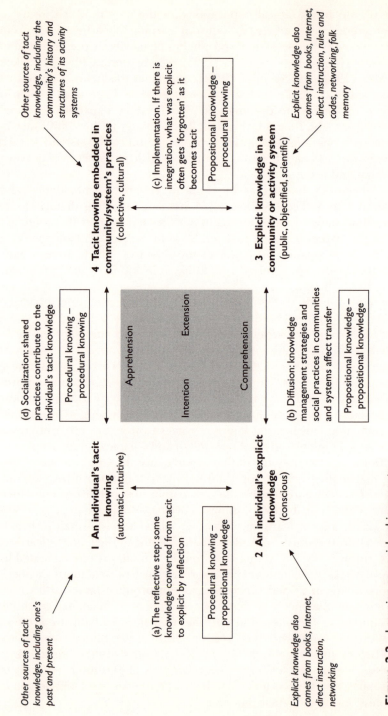

Figure 2.2 Learning as social achievements

Explicit knowledge of how to teach, perhaps related to McKeachie's world-famous *Teaching Tips* (1994), is linked to implicit knowing. It is stabilized and commodified, coming partly from direct instruction, books and the like, and partly from trying to capture tacit knowledge through reflection or metacognition. In the past 20 years a great deal of faith has been put in the notion of 'the reflective practitioner' and the idea that reflection *in, on* and *for* practice is a promising way of improving the quality of espoused theories (propositional or explicit knowledge) and of practice (procedural knowledge and tacit knowing). As with many enduring educational ideas, its rhetorical appeal has outstripped the evidence. Schön's (1983) account of reflection-in-action has been criticized for inconsistency (Eraut, 1995). Meanings (and confusion) have proliferated as the term has attracted more advocates. Some objections, well captured by Donnelly (1999), are that reason has only limited access to that which drives our actions, which rather limits the promise of reflection for improving practice. Others note that reflection easily gets confused with any old thinking, which devalues it (Parker, 1997). A related problem is that reflection can become 'closed-circle' thinking where the essential rightness of existing thought and action is confirmed or is only mildly troubled. A further objection is that researchers with psychological expertise in learning theory are inclined to talk of metacognition (Hacker *et al.*, 1998; Moshman, 1999). They see reflection only as a *means* to metacognitive awareness, which includes knowing what one knows, having strategies for getting and using knowledge, and knowing one has those strategies. Where reflection is a means to an end, the concept of metacognition carries with it an idea of what the ends of reflection might be. This returns us to the idea that it is unwise to praise reflection indiscriminately, and that it is not unchallenged as a way of conceptualizing the conversion of some tacit knowing into explicit knowledge. These themes are revisited in Part 2. This summary has been enough to caution against putting overmuch faith in reflection (or metacognition) as a means to improve teaching or any other practice. That is not to dismiss it completely, since I argue in Chapter 11 that it is necessary *as a part of* good self-evaluation.

The right-hand side of Figure 2.2 is about the social nature of expertise, referring to the interplay of tacit and explicit knowings in a workgroup, community or system. The main difference is that there is usually a greater emphasis on getting explicit knowledge into practice: that is to say, on turning the propositional knowledge that has been identified as useful into improved procedures. These change management processes are outlined in Chapter 12 and in many books and papers (Fullan, 1991, 1999), so it is enough to notice here that there are very good reasons why these processes no more lead to practices that mirror faithfully the plans than do attempts to bring individual tacit knowing, as expressed in action, under the control of explicit knowledge.

The connection between explicit and tacit is bidirectional, which means that explicit knowledge can, in some measure, be constructed by interrogating the tacit knowledge embedded in practices. This is no easier a task at the workgroup level than it is at the individual level, not least because there is a long history of treating the contingencies of tacit workgroup knowledge as defects that account for practice falling short of theory. Although the rationalist ontologies and epistemologies that are behind these assumptions are not strong in modern philosophy, they still fascinate some who downplay specifics and seek generalized, context-free, easily transferred and commodifiable knowledge.

The direct horizontal links between the individual and the community suggest that people learn, as individuals, from groups and that groups also learn, sometimes slightly, from individuals. So, a new faculty member entering a community brings her tacit knowledge, expressed in the way she teaches, and her explicit knowledge, which might be seen in her contributions in teaching committee, to the community and thereby affects it. In this case there is a likelihood that the community's practices and policies will make a greater impact on her, socializing her into established ways, as modified by *her* influence on the community's knowing and knowledge. This 'apprenticeship learning' (Guile and Young, 1998) is a theme of the next chapter.

Following the remark that Hewlett-Packard would be invincible if Hewlett-Packard only knew what Hewlett-Packard knew (Dreyfus and Dreyfus, 1986), there has been a great interest in how these horizontal links can be improved so that socialization is better (top row, right to left and, to a lesser degree, bottom row, right to left) and the community has access to the sum of individual knowledge (bottom row, left to right). Of course, this implies that there are serious concurrent attempts to turn as much tacit knowledge as possible into codifiable, transmissable explicit knowledge (Nonaka and Takauchi, 1995; Davenport and Prusak, 1998). The strategies used to move and change knowledge need not delay us here. It is sufficient to note that there is a lot of emphasis on 'knowledge management' by means of encouraging informal interactions, collegiality and non-formal learning opportunities, whence unexpected, unplanned and fruitful learnings will happen.

At the shaded centre of Figure 2.2 is Kolb's (1984) sketch of the mental activities associated with learning. Unfortunately, his complex account of experiential learning is usually trivialized as a learning cycle and the psychological and philosophical depths get missed. In fact, experiential learning means much more than just learning from physical activity; Kolb represented his ideas with a cone (the 'learning cycle' was its base); and cognition was kept in place as one part of human experience. For Kolb, learning involved a dialectic between apprehension, which he described as something that could go beyond the reach of cognition, and comprehension, an active process of selecting and sense-making directed at that which is apprehended. His account had a second dialectical interaction, that between intention (which is rather metacognitive with its call to look inwards and reflect) and extension (which is outward looking, concerned with action and engagement). This picture of learning as something emerging from interacting processes complements the overall theme of Figure 2.2, that it is varied and dynamic. If Figure 2.1 alerts us to the range of influences on what we do, think and feel in workgroups, networks and communities, Figure 2.2 suggests that we learn in many ways simply by being so connected. 'Actor . . . network' thinking points in the same direction, to the complex plasma in which we are, act and learn.

This has considerable implications for thinking about how best to foster continuing professional development or to help students to learn. For example, it has been suggested that 'Teaching and education, from this perspective, are not simply matters of putting students in touch with information . . . they are matters of putting students in touch with particular communities' (Brown and Duguid, 2000: 220). It also puts the business of learning as a teacher in a different light because it suggests that the quality of the department, team or other workgroup contributes considerably – perhaps more than anything else – to pedagogical learning, and that one's worth as a developing teacher is not reducible to workshops attended or certificates earned.

Informed practices

Let me turn from teachers to students. Much of what we expect students to learn may be propositional but not only are there many professional disciplines in which procedural knowledge is valued, there is also an increasingly strong conviction that higher education should also develop generic attributes and contribute to students' employability. Whatever precise meanings are given to 'employability', there is a tendency to identify it with the possession of core, or key, skills at the very least. 'Employability', like many aspects of professional competence, is essentially a procedural, 'knowing how' concept and so wherever higher education claims to be enhancing student employability, it follows that the curriculum should be designed to sustain the creation of procedural as well as propositional knowledge. If Figure 2.2 is a fair model of how some learning happens, then it has enormous implications for such complex learning goals. If employability includes skills, then the curriculum needs to be skilling, which means designing it to be a medium in which tacit knowledge grows and which contains plenty of opportunities for the tacit to seep into explicit forms and disperse through the connections that constitute learning communities.

This is all the more so with teachers' professional development, partly because teaching is a complex set of learning achievements and partly because it is about stimulating equally complex propositional and procedural learning in others.

What would count as good learning about promoting learning? Shulman's analysis suggests that this professional learning should be wide, covering all but the first of his seven forms of pedagogical knowledge. Ideally it would involve diverse practical teaching experiences on the principle that tacit knowledge arises from what we do and that what we do is influenced by the activity systems and communities in which we are. There is something here of an idea that has sometimes been practicable in school-teacher training, namely that learner-teachers should work in several different settings, each of which is suffused with an effective commitment to children's learning. Teachers in higher education who by choice or necessity have worked in several departments come closest to those student teachers. There is, though, a good chance that what they shared will have been average or indifferent practices, especially in communities dedicated to research, where teaching may have been enjoyed as a sideline without there being any great appreciation of the importance of fostering complex and diverse student learning. It is not enough to hope that we can learn to be teachers largely through being in several activity systems committed to effective student learning. Table 2.1 identifies other means of learning to teach better.

Action points

Being a good teacher has been clearly associated with the affordances – the opportunities or possibilities – that a department contains, so that teaching quality is closely related to the ways in which a department routinely operates and the opportunities for learning that it creates. This puts heads of department in a position to have a considerable impact on their colleagues' teaching. One way of capitalizing upon this is to consider what people might learn about teaching from the ways in which a department routinely operates. It might be useful to get an outsider to help with this task because insiders can find it hard to see the learnings that are inexorably promoted by subliminal practices. This review should lead to some incremental actions to enrich the messages embedded in 'what we do around here'.

Perhaps a qualified *in*action point is appropriate for individual faculty members. Learning to teach better may involve being mindful about that as an aim and then trying to do it easily, in small ways, with what is ready to hand. *Bricolage* – tinkering – has a lot going for it as an approach to

Table 2.1 Some opportunities for learning for teaching

Learning opportunity	Comment
Seeing: observation of teaching	The quality of teaching observed does relate to the quality of learning that can come from observing others but the quality of conversation between observer(s) and observed (perhaps students too) may be more important. A *good* observation schedule (many are awful) can make observation a better learning experience.
Seeing oneself teaching (video)	Nothing shows us more clearly the quality of our body language as teachers, especially when the video is speeded up. Diction and audience reactions are also mercilessly exposed. Although self-observation is a powerful tutor, most of us still find it hard to change what we see because what we do has become so natural – a part of who we are.
Seeing: team teaching	The need to teach means that this participant observation is not ideal *as observation*. However, there is a power that comes from working with others, planning and reflecting with them. This joint engagement in *doing* gives the participant observer a distinctive understanding of what is seen, revealing things that might be lost on non-participants.
Seeing through students' eyes	A lot can be learned about teaching by observing classes in a subject with which you are unfamiliar, perhaps by enrolling in adult education classes.
Seeing as a way of learning. These forms of learning by seeing are prone to three problems: (a) it is hard to be alert to and see most of what happens; (b) it is hard to become estranged, to see as if through an outsider's eyes; (c) it is hard to use the seeing to make a regular difference to doing.	
Reading books and journals	There are now quite a lot of thoughtful publications on the first four of Shulman's types of teaching knowledge. They tend not to deal with the other four forms and, although there are general publications on these themes, it can be a major intellectual effort to try to bring the discourses together.
Reading groups	Tend to be short-lived. Advantages include the incentive to read about teaching, the learning that comes from talking in groups of equals about teaching and the new community that is formed, perhaps briefly.

Table 2.1 (Cont'd)

Learning opportunity	Comment
Reading on the web	Clearly, the quality of sites and lists varies. The reason I value reading from the web is that it is always possible to join or start a conversation.
	As a solitary activity reading can be convenient and appealing to people skilled at text-processing. As with seeing, there is the problem of applying general ideas to specific times and places. Reading may be most powerful when it is part of conversations among people who treat each other as near-equals.
Doing: changing the stationery	A lot of learning can come from simply changing the stationery that faculty use in their normal teaching work: for example, changing the coursework cover/feedback sheets is a powerful way of spreading new ideas about assessment.
Doing: changing student evaluations	Traditional student evaluations of teaching produce numerical data which can be valuable but which are often abused and unhelpful for teaching improvement purposes. Asking students what they would improve, why and how is a better way for teachers to learn, especially if students do it in groups.
Doing: asking alumni	This extends to alumni the idea of doing better student evaluations. Graduates of a few years' standing can see their undergraduate learning and the teaching experiences rather differently from how they did as students. Asking alumni can help teachers to appreciate the learning that lasts.
Doing: curriculum development/ innovation	Earlier suggestions have foreshadowed the comment that the more that others can be involved the better. 'Others' might be students (giving qualitative feedback and suggestions for improvement), colleagues in the department (an expert audience commenting on what they hear), colleagues in other departments working on similar developments (sources of hints and warnings, collaborators in planning).

Doing: action research	I define action research as systematic enquiry that is geared to making a difference to a situation or practices in identified sites. It can be similar to curriculum development but it need not be confined to curriculum matters and it should be better grounded in research literatures and enquiry practices than some development projects are.
Doing is a powerful way of learning, particularly given research suggesting that small-scale and incremental changes have particular staying power (Huberman, 1993; Fullan, 1999). *Bricolage*, or tinkering, is a practicable approach to change and learning that is on a human scale. Lack of ambition can be the flip side.	
Disrupting assumptions about what we do	Scholars working within critical theory and associated stances regularly invite us to look behind things we take for granted, ask whose interests are served and consider whose are injured. Acts of deconstructing why things are as they are and why it seems normal for them to be so may initiate new learning (because we may see things afresh) or may lead us to consider practices that had hitherto seemed inappropriate.
Disrupting your practices	A lot can be learned by almost haphazardly disrupting your established practice and watching what happens (revert to it if the disruption looks harmful). For example, where you use small groups, sometimes lecture instead; don't centre seminars on you but make them occasions for small group talk leading to reports back to the whole seminar groups; restrict written feedback to three main comments; etc.
Disrupting you	This is an invitation to work on the eighth form of teaching knowledge, which is about self-theories and personal influence, and ask why you think, feel and do as you do; what you know about alternatives; and whether they will remain 'alternatives' for you.
Imagining	What if . . . ? How could 'if' become 'is'?

These four prompts to learning are intended to try to shift it from the well grooved paths of common sense and habit and to counterbalance a tilt towards doing in these suggestions.

teaching improvement, although there are times when rapid and radical learning is necessary, as when one is becoming established as a teacher, facing review by powerful people with different ideas about good practice or working in a project that compels experimentation. Nor in praising mindfulness in small things do I mean to offer a principled justification for being an educational ostrich and not considering anything new. Yet small changes can be big changes in the sense that theories of complex systems say that a run of small changes can amount to something noticeable and that enough of them may trigger a substantial or phase change (van Geert, 1994). Networks can sometimes change radically when sufficient new connections are formed and enough old ones forgotten.

Finally, the more we feel that the ways in which we learn are similar to the ways in which students learn the better, especially if we can frighten ourselves by trying to learn tough, new material.

Further reading

The Social Life of Information (2000) is a readable summary of Brown and Duguid's work. They explore the idea that learning is a social phenomenon ('where one person's knowledge ends and another's begins is not always clear': p. 106) and argue that it happens in ways that are easily overlooked (because we are so accustomed to see learning in terms of planned events) and that 'knowledge doesn't market very easily . . . it's hard to detach and circulate' (p. 215).

Although Lee Shulman's 1987 article 'Knowledge and teaching foundations of the new reform' comes from his concern with schoolteacher education in the USA, his analysis of what we need to know in order to teach well is a good one. Re-reading it, I am struck by the gap between the professional development practices it implies and what pass as 'teaching in higher education' programmes in several states, provinces and nations. Start reading it on page 5.

3

Being a new teacher

A stance

The first years in academic work are a time when tensions between different calls on our energies and on our range of identities resolve into a pattern that can suffuse a career. These years, then, are important for new academics and it is important that they are well guided in their early years. For example, Boice argues that 'the first years for new faculty are formative and lasting . . . early experiences in the classroom . . . and in other academic activities, such as publishing . . . , predict more about career habits than any other formative period . . . Once under way, career paths may be hard to change' (Boice, 1992: 40). Again, 'you will discover in some future year that your career as an academic . . . [has] been affected by your decisions now – at the start' (Gibson, 1992: 129). If early socialization is deficient, then the longer-term prospect for higher education is a worrying one, especially when higher education is increasingly mandated to extend and improve its performance – by teaching more students better, and by enhancing students' key or transferable skills, for example (Harvey and Knight, 1996; Jones, 1996). New academics' postgraduate work will have prepared them as researchers but not for these new and extended teaching roles. If their early experiences in their first academic appointment do not provide a good grounding in these new orientations, they are likely to use their own experiences of being taught as the template for their own work. Personal frustrations and institutional disappointment may ensue because our learning experiences, as clever people who have become good at the academic game, are not trustworthy guides to helping students – an increasingly diverse group of people – with the complex business of understanding subject matter, developing subject-specific and other skills, appraising their self-theories and refining their metacognitive processes.

This chapter contains advice for new entrants into academic life and ideas about approaching a balance between the scholarship of teaching and the rival charms of the scholarship of discovery.

Key points

1 Emotional unease and stress are to be expected: role conflict, overload and feeling like an impostor are usual among new academics.
2 Induction and mentoring practices are variable in quality and new teachers should be prepared to take a responsibility for their own learning and passage into the community of practice.
3 As was said in the previous chapter, much learning comes from the natural, normal business of being in a community of practice. Once this is understood, new teachers are better able to capitalize upon it.
4 Developing the scholarship of teaching means taking risks, although specializing in the scholarship of discovery means taking other risks.

Research

The increased risk of being a new academic

Teaching and academic life generally have changed in the past quarter of a century and will continue to become different. Henkel records that the experience of becoming an academic in Britain in the 1960s and 1970s was that of 'another era . . . a golden age in which individuals were free to pursue their own goals at their own pace' (Henkel, 2000: 167), which could be a very leisurely pace. Posts were easier to get, a first was a great help but a PhD was not vital, especially in polytechnics where research was not something that staff were generally expected to do (although people did research out of interest or to undergird their teaching). Young staff 'were assumed to be functioning, independent practitioners, within the dominant norm of self regulation' (Henkel, 2000: 169).

The 1980s and 1990s were different. Senior academics saw their younger colleagues having 'a more sophisticated understanding of the demands of an academic career and the skills and knowledge to be successful. They were also perceived to be more focused and efficient in the allocation of their time' (Henkel, 2000: 265). Young faculty members had paid a price for these gains. Scientists often had to do up to ten years of post-doctoral work before getting a permanent academic post, if, indeed, they ever got one. To survive in this risky environment they had to be ready to change directions to accommodate work and opportunities on offer. Degrees of academic independence on appointment were found to vary, especially between pre- and post-1992 universities. In the humanities and social sciences Henkel found wide differences 'in the extent to which individuals . . . had had to struggle to achieve their ends' (Henkel, 2000: 174). The experience of short-term contract work was common and was combined with a constant pressure to compete, particularly by publishing. The importance of networking and becoming recognized as a member of the community of practice was emphasized. These newer academics expressed strong commitment for their subjects and had 'incorporated theory and practices from pedagogy in their approaches to teaching' (Henkel, 2000: 265), not least because appointing committees looked for evidence of teaching competence. Consequently, tensions were commonly reported between the imperative to perform as a researcher and the market need to be seen as a good teacher, tensions that many faculty continue to feel throughout their careers. Regardless of discipline, the 1980s and 1990s appointments game was more complex and riskier than it had been in the 'golden age' of the late 1960s and early 1970s. The risk to individuals is obvious but the risk to HEIs that feel themselves to be competing on every front for funds, students and reputation is hardly less.

Paul Trowler and I (Knight and Trowler, 1999, 2000; Trowler and Knight, 2000) have studied the experiences of people entering their first full-time post and what follows draws heavily on that work. Their words help us to appreciate the personal risks in steering a passage for tenure. The next section builds on their insights in offering advice to academic leaders and new faculty members on how new staff can embrace a scholarship of teaching.

New teachers talking

Course-based induction arrangements were available everywhere but they were not a good fit with actual learning needs. One informant said, 'I didn't go [to that induction session] but that's . . . because I'll ask next door', and another, 'In actual fact the most effective way of helping me to get into things is just informal.' The quality of this learning through the job was variable. We heard horror stories of people arriving to empty or blasé departments. For example, '[I needed to know] where do I get a desk from? Who do we contact to get the computer plugged in?' Some had virtually to induct themselves: 'It wasn't really induction. They said it was but I had to find things out I wanted to know and different people were telling me different things. So I just learned it by asking and looking at the handbook. Even then I wasn't sure what the handbook means' (Trowler and Knight, 2000: 32). Mentors should have been provided (CVCP, 1992) but often weren't.

> We have this mentor – I think I've met her once and that's it. I mean, we got this great big handbook about the role of the mentor and all about how you should behave with your mentor. [But] she was in [a different section of the school] so I didn't see her in the normal course of [things] and she obviously didn't really understand how I

worked . . . So I only saw her once and she never got in contact with me and I thought 'well I haven't got time to contact her.' And yet at university [level] they put such a lot of time and effort into this, training them and . . .

[Mentoring] was probably successful because we were committed to having regular meetings. The bottom line was that the mentor was prepared to put times in their diary, and we kept to it . . . we were very rigorous.

(Knight and Trowler, 1999: 27, 28)

It was very clear that becoming an academic was largely a departmental business and that departments, even those teaching the same subject but in different HEIs, differ sharply from each other. 'There are strange experiences here that when I talk to people in other departments say wouldn't happen to them. Things that other people would be encouraged to do in other departments you are sometimes discouraged from doing because it means you wouldn't be a faithful psychologist' (Trowler and Knight, 2000: 29).

What we heard from our informants and from other research studies is that for new academics, like older ones, 'learning occurs "through the job" rather than "on the job" and is supplemented by technical books and attendance at short seminar/presentations on specified topics' (Anderson and Skinner, 1999: 252). Again, 'on the job learning, working alongside more experienced colleagues and team-working are related forms of learning which are of the greatest importance to the [452] professionals we researched' (Chivers and Cheetham, 2001: 71). This emphasis on the significance of learning in activity systems which often cohere in communities of practice runs the risk of inadvertently evoking rosy visions of happy workers laughing as they harmoniously strive for the greater good. Activity systems and communities of practice may be sites of learning, good and bad, but that does not mean that we should ignore the realities of power, dysfunction and discontentment. Some of our new faculty informants talked about differences to be navigated within departments, not least around competing accounts of the nature of the subject area itself:

there are divisions . . . It's very difficult to talk of [this subject area] as . . . It's quite strange . . . to define what [this subject area] actually is. I'm sure that if you asked anybody in [this subject area] they would come up with something completely different because it does cover such a wide range of areas, basically anything that . . . challenges traditional mainstream knowledge.

(Knight and Trowler, 2000: 76)

[My colleagues] don't liase with each other so you have to create the coherence and piece all of this together . . . There's lots of little micro-politics happening here because of people's own agendas. One person will encourage you to do one thing and another will get you to do something else because of theirs . . . and it's also part of the induction process of learning what the micro-politics are . . . That's something no one really tells you about but it's part of the assimilation process, the way the academic world is; the forward agenda and the hidden agendas.

(Knight and Trowler, 1999: 29)

In such settings a fluid approach to creating a work profile is an advantage, which implies that professional identities may be created afresh:

You have to present yourself as . . . being good in all these three areas [teaching, research, service] and then it's actually hard to take yourself back out of that and say 'well what originally was I interested in', or 'what did I think I was good at?' . . . You have to have this very fluid identity.

(Trowler and Knight, 2000: 34).

I could see that [my priorities] might shift . . . if I moved into an area and the Department or Dean said to me, 'You're here to write books' . . . Obviously, then I would have different views of [my priorities].

(Knight and Trowler, 2000: 77)

In some cases the need for such identity work caused stress. The informant whose words follow left academic life shortly after this interview. A close personal relationship had been lost to the job and she saw no chance of another while doing this work in this place. Elder members of her racial community criticized her apparent collusion with the white men [*sic*]. She felt overworked and, in my view, with her sense of self on the edge of tatters.

I didn't come to this university as a blank slate [but] . . . when I say something . . . what I have to say isn't considered . . . I went to the Dean and I said 'I don't want to be socialized into this system. I don't know how long I'm going to last here because there are so many things that are against who I am, in conflict with who I am as an individual' . . . [There are areas in which I] can't say the kind of things I really want to.

[Trowler and Knight, 2000: 34]

This woman, like the previous informant, found that there were extra role expectations for women.

I do feel from talking to colleagues and students that women do get a disproportionate number [of pastoral visits from students] . . . it is women who get caught for a lot of that . . . I frequently get students coming to see me and I'm not their academic counsellor at all but they may have an academic counsellor . . . whom they don't know or don't get on with and so they tend to seek out women, I think, who they see as sympathetic . . . [it] takes up a huge proportion of my time and is emotionally often draining . . . but you're always left with a sense of 'I didn't do enough, I should have done more.'

(Trowler and Knight, 2000: 35).

The problem is not simply that faculty work long hours, for this is true of many professions. Multiple roles and multiple, usually tacit, expectations, allied to a lack of feedback from departmental managers, were great sources of uncertainty and unease:

I get more stressed out about things than I used to [when working in industry]. I think that the reason for that is partly because I don't feel completely confident about knowing how to do things that I do know . . . In other jobs I've had there were mainly three threads and now there's probably five threads.

From the point of view of a new member of staff there are insecurities. On top of that you have 'Am I doing it to a good enough quality?' None of [these] things are easy to pin down. In the early days, I went through a crisis of confidence.

(Knight and Trowler, 2000: 73–4)

The quotations that follow give a flavour of the demands of the three main areas, research, service and teaching. This tripartite distinction is crude and will be replaced later in the chapter. It will do for now, though.

The pressure to do research, in the sense of original enquiry, is considerable and too well known to need much attention here. New academics were acutely aware that in the social sciences and humanities research could easily cease because other people daily demanded service and teaching whereas research tended in these areas to be a much more self propelled activity with few, if any, short-term deadlines. Deferring research activity was easier than not preparing a seminar, although the consequences of sidelining research could, in the long term, be far greater than those of 'winging it' in teaching. The rational mind might try to insist on this worldview but practices differed. Furthermore, new academics were not always as fluent in all aspects of the researcher's art as they needed to be. For example, 'I do need to get down to the writing, but it's not easy and I'm not finding, it's not flowing when I sit down with paper: I've still got a desk covered with heaps and heaps of paper and I still don't know how to file them yet, other than in the bin' (Knight and Trowler, 2000: 75).

A Canadian informant said that he felt cold when he tried to write, irrespective of how high the central heating was running. He could sit in Arctic weather gear and feel frozen, in more than one sense. It is not only that tenure, security and career hinge upon this scholarship of discovery; so too do professional identity and, correspondingly, elements of self-identity and self-esteem as well. Since all informants enjoyed enquiry in their subject/areas, it was debilitating to feel that they were not doing enough good, for-publication research. The significance of this in the context of this book's theme of being a teacher is to remind us that there are strong competitors for any investment we make in teaching.

Administrative and service work also compete for time. By administration I mean taking responsibility for the running of programmes or activities (being in charge of admissions, publicity, examinations, master's programmes, ICT matters etc.). 'Service' I use to mean contributing to the community outside the HEI (by giving public talks, representing the institution in local associations, serving national professional associations) and to the HEI as a whole (for example, by being an academic adviser for a group of students, sitting on faculty, school or institutional committees, participating in student societies). What people are expected to do and its 'exchange value' – the value it has when it comes to trying to get tenure or promotion – vary nationally and according to the status of the HEI. Like research it can voraciously consume time but unlike research it is seldom such a good investment in terms of career advancement. Yet service and administration are hard to resist and conscientiousness leads many people to serve so well that their own career interests suffer from the consequent lack of investment in research and teaching.

> [There's] just me [as personal tutor for the first year]. So I've inducted them all and now I'm just waiting for the knocks to start on the door. I'm allowed a hundred hours now but I've used that up already typing up registers and organizing induction.
>
> The admin thing has consumed me since I got here . . . I've just found it's taken up every minute so both teaching and research have suffered . . . Admin seems to be something which grows into as much space as you can give it.
>
> (Knight and Trowler, 2000: 74–5)

The dangers of service and administration are more acute for some than others. Tierney and Bensimon (1996) observed that women and people from minority groups face particularly high demands for service on committees because HEIs feel that these are people who should be widely visible even though they are often few in number.

It would be quite understandable if new academics faced with demands such as these chose to satisfice by doing a good, basic job of teaching. Our informants aimed higher. We gave them a list of four goals for teaching in higher education: to develop content mastery; to promote an understanding of subject principles and concepts; to foster 'transferable skills'; and to promote personal qualities. Most of the new academics we spoke with chose just one or two of these four aims, but 'content mastery' was not normally one of them. They were choosing the more difficult teaching aims, ones that could be associated with attempts to encourage student understandings and/or that have an impact on the student that goes beyond the subject alone. These are praiseworthy, complex and demanding ambitions to have because it is hard enough to teach advanced subjects for understanding and it is harder still to care for the development of skills and qualities at the same time.

Perhaps surprisingly, all but two of the new faculty members we interviewed had teaching experience. Their past accomplishments did not necessarily transfer smoothly to the new job, as might be predicted from the emphasis in Chapters 1 and 2 on the significance of context and contingency. For example,

> teaching at the moment is much more of a strain in this job than has been previously. The demands are higher, and the student dissatisfaction greater. There's much more of a sense that they are 'paying' for their education and they want it delivered as a consumable item in a very neat package . . . I'm becoming less committed to [teaching] in a sense that it doesn't pay the dividends that it should. It's getting away from my research.
>
> (Knight and Trowler, 2000: 74)

Help was wanted but 'you were just given the course title and that was it!' (Knight and Trowler, 2000: 74). Again, a Canadian said, 'I don't think that in terms of teaching I got any help – no that's not right, I got some notes from someone who taught the course before, I got some assignments' (Knight and Trowler, 2000: 74).

So, uncertainty and tension come from a drive to do well in these three main areas of activity (teaching, service and research). The three have not been well reconciled in HEIs. In practice they tend to compete, having different champions, attractions and accountability systems. The problems of creating identities in places criss-crossed by the demands of these three areas are exacerbated by the choices that also have to be made within each area. Uncertainty and tension come from juggling the demands of different courses, formal and informal commitments, writing and reading, senior and junior students, email notes and joined-up prose, administration and delegation. Heavy workloads made choice necessary for well-being, not an option to maximize pleasure. Yet, despite having to put in a lot of hours, all except one of our informants were, in some sense, coping and most said that in many ways they were enjoying it. But it is not clear how long the juggling act could be sustained, especially as one ball, research, often seemed to be getting dropped by all except those working in the natural sciences. One said, 'I'm already 101 hours over my normal timetable since September. That's on top of my 37 hours a week', while another gestured wearily as she said, 'I've learned how to juggle 15 balls, and the thing is that on the table over there is still another 20 balls' (both quotations from Knight and Trowler, 2000: 75). A problem is that

It's not a job that you can go home, switch off, sit in front of the telly or go down the pub or whatever. You're always thinking 'I should be doing some work.' Even things like reading a novel is a dreadful thing to do because I could be reading something for my work . . . in terms of personal life it's a very time consuming job both in physical time and emotional time which is maybe one thing that I hadn't fully recognized when I came here. I think it's been hard trying to juggle home and family and work responsibilities.

(Knight and Trowler, 2000: 76)

There were a few cases when personal identity had been defined in a way that put professional identity in *this* job in its place and where social support helped to maintain boundaries between life and work as one of its subsets. For example,

it's not a culture she [my wife] is unfamiliar with, so she understands where I am coming from, and she is also very adamant about in some cases keeping the job side [in perspective] . . . She'll say 'enough is enough' and that's good because I tune in and play with my kids. I refuse to let anything associated with this job deter my life with my children and my wife. And I simply won't allow it to happen, I'll leave the job if I find that it [is] the case where I cannot do this without my family suffering because I'm totally confident of being able to do well elsewhere.

(Knight and Trowler, 2000: 76)

But, despite the risks described by that teacher and the costs paid by others, informants did celebrate the freedom and opportunities of academic life and liked the experience of being in enquiring, learning environments. As one said, 'You can be your own manager, you have more freedom. You can work at your own pace' (Knight and Trowler, 2000: 73). Yet even there the pluses could have their minuses. Freedom evoked isolation. The very architecture of their working spaces, with cell-like rooms and lack of space where people come together and organic collegiality might be, symbolized both freedom and isolation. The opportunities were liked but some felt isolation keenly: 'Well, you could turn up here and sit in this office and nobody would know whether you're alive or dead. You could be dead actually . . . the cleaner would come and move you out . . . For an awful lot of the rest of the time I actually haven't known whether or not I'm doing the right thing' (Knight and Trowler, 2000: 73).

Most of our new faculty informants liked or loved their work, which is consistent with Altbach and Lewis's conclusion that 'the vicissitudes experienced by the profession have been considerable, the professoriate is by no means demoralized. In all but three [of fourteen] countries 60 per cent or more agree that this is an especially creative and productive time in their fields' (Altbach and Lewis, 1996: 48). Nevertheless, new academics' work took a great deal of time, usually involved living out role conflicts, often produced stress and was prone to leave them feeling isolated and bereft of a supportive departmental community. Few were able to defend out-of-work space. Some didn't care. This account converges with the stories in other studies with larger samples and different enquiry methods, especially those done by Boice (1992) and Menges and associates (1999). If this is a fair sketch of what it is often like to be a new entrant into the academic professions, how are new academics to engrain good teaching practices, to become disposed to care about teaching well and to commit to renewing their integrity and vitality as teachers?

Informed practices

Many of those concerned to improve teaching practices argue that this depends on improving the rewards for teaching well (see, for example, Wright and associates, 1995) and on then engaging with 'the scholarship of teaching'. The term is attributed to Boyer (1990), who said that academic work comprises the scholarships of discovery (commonly known as 'research'), teaching, integration (a boundary-spanning activity of synthesis) and service (which includes the application of scholarly knowledge). There should be parity of esteem between the four forms, with faculty well disposed to all of them, although not doing them all in equal measure at any one time. These ideas have caught the imagination of those with interests in curriculum, learning, teaching and assessment (because it makes the object of their research seem more significant) and of the larger community of staff, instructional and educational developers (because it assumes theirs is important work). There are ambiguities here, though. For example, in what sense is it appropriate to talk of a scholarship of teaching in higher education but not in elementary education, when elementary school teaching is arguably the more complex activity? How might scholarship enhance practice – is it necessary for good practice? What might be the relationship between the scholarships of teaching and integration? Is the scholarship of teaching really just a part of a scholarship of practice? Papers edited by Kreber (2001) suggest that scholarly teaching entails an intention to keep improving teaching by reflecting on practice and looking further afield for inspiration. That inspiration may be found in research papers, be mediated by works like this, be stimulated by real or virtual communities or be 'home grown' through small-scale research, such as action research that engages with relevant literatures.

Kreber's contributors agree that these developing personal knowledges should be shared and open to peer appraisal.

For new academics to commit to the scholarly inclinations described in Kreber's collection means finding a story they can use to justify the risks of (a) an activity, teaching, whose outcomes are somewhat indeterminate and vulnerable to student evaluations and (b) not investing so heavily in the growth stocks of research or in the social capital of service. The second of these risks is reduced when there is parity of esteem between Boyer's four forms of scholarship, but since that is rare, it is common to look for a story that brings teaching and research together. Although 'Most academics argue that good research is necessary for good teaching' (HEFCE, 2000: para. 23), the research evidence about the relationship does little to support the idea that good researchers are good teachers (Knight and Trowler, 2001). The alternative is to depict the scholarship of teaching as some mix of research and teaching, but many blends are possible and their proponents seem to agree only that teaching is important and that it should be associated with 'research'. Stories may be constructed to order from these opinions, although local departmental practices will give a clue about scripts that are most likely to be applauded in a given context. But it is not necessary to buy into claims that there is a special scholarship of teaching in order to justify teaching well. A pragmatic story is that teaching is a significant part of contracted work and should be done well as a moral matter, for self-esteem and out of prudence in times when governmental mandates and quality assurance regimes make teaching quality a public concern, not a private foible. If this also leads to systematic enquiry (research) and publication, so much the better. So, if teaching has to be done and done well, its risks cannot be avoided. Sidestepping tussles about the scholarship of teaching, I can now turn to things departments and new academics can do to embrace good teaching.

The claim that we all learn from departments' taken-for-granted practices can be illustrated by thinking about what an imaginary but plausible department does. In this department some established and senior members get away with:

1 Cancelling classes so that they can attend meetings and conferences.
2 Taking weeks to return coursework (six months is not unknown).
3 Using illegible and overcrowded overhead transparencies, complemented by queasy photocopies.
4 Basing their teaching on their research which is specialized to the point of tedium and too advanced for most students.
5 Saying 'I don't think that this technology stuff is worth it.'
6 Claiming to foster fashionable skills without it being clear how they are doing so.
7 Acting as if learning only took place when they spoke.

8 Treating seminars as an opportunity to criticize students' interpretations.
9 Giving feedback on course work that is too tied to the specifics of the task to be of much value for improving future work.
10 Being heard to say, 'It's only undergraduate level'.
11 Fearlessly criticizing (constructively and in the interests of quality, they say) course proposals and novel practices.
12 Using the claim that they are promoting student autonomy to reduce their workloads by expecting students to teach themselves.
13 Acting as if they were by definition reliable and accurate markers.
14 Setting tough tests [of information, usually] 'to really sort the students out'.
15 Etc.

This incomplete list identifies questionable practices that it is easy to fall into. Unchallenged, this blend of bad teaching practices that are tolerated because a professor has got so much on with important committees, important research and being important (for example, 1, 2, 3), and practices that are mistakenly valued (for example, 4, 9, 11), makes a dreadful learning environment for new academics and a corrosive one for established ones committed to good teaching. Traces of some of these practices can be seen in my work, although I keep tinkering in pursuit of the ever-receding horizon of teaching excellence. My shortfalls do need attention but what matters more is that these practices should be publicly identified as matters of concern, things to be tolerated only on condition that people are trying to give them up.

Having made a predictable point for this book, namely that much learning to be a teacher in higher education comes from how our departments are, I turn to the more familiar topic of mentoring and planned induction. The literature on mentoring, and not just mentoring in higher education, contains long, holier-than-though lists of what mentors should know and be like (for example, Fay, 1975). More helpful is Cox's (1997) account of his 18 years' experience of running a mentoring programme for new academic staff. He advises that departmental mentoring practices should be set within a carefully designed, campus-wide programme of mentoring and professional support, which implies having someone in the HEI with responsibility for the programme. This approach is more costly than the haphazard arrangements that are commonly found, but Cox's enquiries indicate that it improves the quality of induction practices and is appreciated by new academics. They choose mentors from a university-wide list of those willing to do the job, trained to do it and then rewarded for doing it. Cox suggests a menu of activities that could be used to organize regular meetings between mentee and mentor and he adds that the programme coordinator should prompt both of them to make sure that meetings do take place regularly.

The new academics Paul Trowler and I talked with were not mentored within such a purposeful programme structure and, although they seem to have coped, our work was not designed to see what the costs of this lackadaisical approach are. There are indications that they may be unacceptable. Boyle and Boice (1998) conclude from their research, mainly in New York, that 'spontaneous mentoring' reaches only about a third of new teachers. When induction is essentially tacit, they say that 'the single biggest advantage of natural mentoring goes almost exclusively to white males already in the old-boy network' (p. 159). Worse, since there are few systematic mentoring programmes, the implication is that most new staff get by on their own. They agree with Cox that 'the systematic mentoring that we have depicted here works better than spontaneous, natural mentoring' (p. 173). Drawing also on Boice's important book, *The New Faculty Member* (1992), they suggest that some key features of effective mentoring in higher education are that:

1 'Mentoring programs, if they are to be successful, appear to require the services of a program coordinator' (p. 160).
2 '[M]entoring for new teachers works as well (if not better) between strangers and members of different departments as with traditional pairings' (p. 160). Mentors from the same department can be suffused with taken-for-granteds whereas outsiders can help new faculty to see better what is going on and the possibilities it could afford. This distance can also make it easier for mentees to disclose difficult thoughts and feelings, especially when it is understood that the mentor will not have a say in whether the probationary period is completed successfully.
3 The earlier mentoring starts, the better.
4 The programme coordinator should ensure that meetings go on for at least several months. By then the pairs often feel bonded in a self-sustaining relationship.
5 Although mentees value mentors who show interest, give support, have empathy, exhibit knowledge and competence, it may not be advisable to have a friend as a mentor. There are two different ways of explaining this. One is that mentoring should expand perspectives where friends are likely to share them and may be less good as conduits to new networks. Second, in some systems mentors do contribute to summative judgements on mentees' performance. In these circumstances friends may not be the best mentors.
6 Mentors often say they benefit. This echoes a common finding that teaching is a way of understanding something better.

Recommendations for induction and mentoring arrangements have more to say about the arrangements than the content, which is understandable given that what is said and done depends upon the new academic's past, the job, the department and the HEI. However, it is worth repeating a theme of Chapters 1 and 2 which is extended in Chapter 4 by referring to a study by Perry and colleagues (1996, 1999). They found that those new faculty who were the most positive about their early careers had a high locus of internal control – that is to say, they believed themselves to have some control over the ways in which they responded to external demands and pressures. Those who were least likely to be happy with their work tended to see themselves as victims, as having little power in the face of malign circumstances – they had a low locus of internal control. Fortunately, these attributions can be changed (Perry *et al.*, 1996; Seligman, 1998; Dweck, 1999). Accordingly, good professional socialization might help new academic staff to see the possibilities they have for fulfilment in work: mentoring and induction might be empowering. For example, mentor and mentee might look at the pressure caused by role conflict and identify priorities, efficient work habits and coping strategies, all the time working on the assumption that we contribute to the ways in which we experience our situations. This would not be a case of the mentor saying 'be like me to succeed' but of helping the mentee to capitalize on what they do well, what they *realistically* could do better without great cost, and to identify and then use the affordances in their work environment. This implies telling the new staff member to clarify with the departmental chair or head what is really expected and going to count in terms of getting through probation, getting tenure and getting ahead. Yet another way of coming to see how priorities can be set and of identifying places where coping, not excellence, is the thing to do is to ask for suggestions about ways of reconciling the contradictions that will usually be tangled up in the head of department's response to those questions.

Sometimes these affordances are not obvious, which is why it helps if mentors have had some training. For example, Boice (1992) found that the new academics who made the grade tended to have a different attitude to writing to those who fell. Torment came from trying to get big, clear stretches of time to write. For sure, academic life can provide them but it tends to provide them most to those people with a strong locus of internal control who are likely to be active in finding ways to carve them out of schedules that too easily get clogged up with busywork. More success comes from finding space to write something almost daily. It doesn't have to be polished, it doesn't have to be a lot and editing is as valid as creating fresh prose. Academic life can afford an average of an hour a day for people who want to claim it. The mentors who have the most to offer are those who know that this is generally good advice about writing to give junior colleagues.

To give another example: researchers consistently find that new teachers are prone to worry that they will be found out as frauds, caught out by smart students. They, the new teachers, are not always confident enough to reply: (a) 'I don't know'; (b) 'Can anyone else suggest what the answer could be?'; (c) 'How could we find a good answer?' These are not the evasive responses that insecure new teachers might imagine but ones that carry powerful messages about the way that scholarship really is. New academics also tend to try to forestall 'being found out' by giving information-dense lectures (Boice, 1992; Gibson, 1992). This is a bad idea for several reasons. The most obvious are that it makes preparation too hard, leads to break-neck lecturing that still doesn't get through everything, overwhelms students and has the nasty effect of suggesting that higher education is about amassing lots of recondite information. (Amassing information is very important in some subjects, especially in the early years of a programme. However, that ought not to be the default option. Besides, medicine and dentistry are two information-rich subjects that increasingly use other ways of helping students to get the information they need.) Skilled mentors recommend a different approach to lecturing, with far less content and more emphasis on understanding key principles (Knight *et al.*, 2000: Chapter 5). Better teaching, less preparation, less stress and less vulnerability should follow.

Trained mentors should be able to challenge content fixations and recommend ways of teaching more efficiently by giving advice on the lines of the suggestions in Box 3.1.

Box 3.1   Advice that mentors might give to new teachers in higher education

1 Save time assessing student work. It is not likely to be feasible to start with radical approaches (Knight, 2000) but there are piecemeal possibilities, including giving better feedback more efficiently (see Box 9.3).
2 Teach to strength. Begin by relying on teaching techniques with which you are comfortable. Aim to supplement them and enhance them over time. As was noted above, research with schoolteachers gives good reason for valuing tinkering, incremental but unremitting change (Huberman, 1993). There are times for wholesale change efforts but these first years may not be them.
3 Time spent on thinking and planning to teach is well spent, especially when this reflection involves exploring more efficient ways of doing things. I believe that I save a lot of time through the synergies of planning the year's teaching in advance. I think it also makes for a more cohesive course. Face-to-face teaching then becomes a matter of recreating the summer's brainstorming, which makes term time less fractured than it would be otherwise.
4 Aspire to a course planned in student learning hours, not contact hours. Traditional thinking defines a course in terms of face-to-face contact hours

but what matters is student engagement with worthwhile learning activities, of which lectures and seminars are but a part. Replacing some of these face-to-face activities with student-managed tasks can give you more time and commit students to better learning tasks. Those tasks must be worthwhile and well designed (see also Chapter 8).

5 There are good educational grounds for valuing group work as a learning method (Slavin, 1996), and expert teachers find many ways to incorporate it in the suite of tasks that engages students (Thorley and Gregory, 1994). Well managed it can save your time, especially when group assessment replaces individual assignments, or when students know that the group is the first place to go with questions or uncertainties.

6 Look for ways of becoming committed to reading about teaching (in your subject). Some staff development centres sponsor reading groups and it is not unknown for subject departments or programme teams to do the same. Professional and subject associations often publish pedagogic newsletters or journals. In Britain the Institute for Learning and Teaching produces *Active Learning in Higher Education*. It, like equivalents in some other countries, is not subject specific and although it is based on educational expertise and some research it is intended to be accessible to a nonspecialist audience. There is now quite a slew of books written for people anxious to teach better.

7 Network. There are few dilemmas that are not eased by asking for advice on the internet. In the UK there is a Learning and Teaching Support Network (www.ltsn.ac.uk) which may be able to help through one of its 24 subject centres and/or through its generic centre. There is also the Deliberations site (www.lgu.ac.uk/deliberations), the SEDA list (www.seda.demon.co.uk) and the ILT (http://www.ilt.ac.uk). Australasia has HERDSA (http://www.herdsa.org.au/), Canada has the STLHE (http://www.tss.uoguelph.ca/STLHE) and the USA has POD (http://lamar.colostate.edu/~ckfgill/aboutPOD.html).

8 Get good student feedback. Good feedback can quickly and precisely show us how to do better and, by implication, what to leave alone. By this I mean ask students what they would like to change and how they would change it. Push them to be specific. My students usually rate my course handbooks less highly than I think they should but they are stumped when I ask how I should improve them. It usually emerges that there isn't really a handbook problem but that what their ratings seem to be saying is that they find it hard to get an overview of the complex, steadily emerging structure of my non-standard course designs. The point is that the standard tick-box approach to evaluation is remarkably unhelpful.

9 Get a sense of how your teaching might develop over the next two or three years and lay plans accordingly. For instance, most people find it better to change a face-to-face course into a largely on-line one over two or three years, first getting teaching and learning materials on-line and then tackling the trickier task of setting up good on-line learning and teaching routines.

Action points

1 Do whatever it takes to hold fast to a sense of your own agency and power to make a difference to what you experience, whether that is through becoming more assertive, better at time management, more aware of self-limiting attributional styles or more ready to set and stick to priorities.
2 Complement that sort of self-work by searching out ideas for working efficiently and sustainably, a sample of which is given in Box 3.1. If no obvious sources present themselves, ask for suggestions through electronic lists.
3 If you haven't been given a good mentor, imagine ways of finding one or two people to act as guides. Given what Boice and Cox have to say, it is worth agitating for good mentoring support.
4 Departmental heads and chairs should recognize the importance of mentoring but they should be much more concerned about what daily practices say. They determine which of the messages that come from mentors, research, policy statements and the like get taken seriously by new academics.
5 Some institutions do not require new staff to get formal teaching qualifications or accreditation. Since there is a strong international trend to expect new (and, in some cases, established) academic staff to be warranted as teachers, it would be unwise not to look for ways of getting nationally recognized accreditation. In the UK, the Institute for Teaching and Learning is the national body to approach (http://www.ilt.ac.uk).

Further reading

Robert Boice's *The New Faculty Member: Supporting and Fostering Professional Development* (1992) is about becoming established in North American higher education. It combines years of research, done with a psychologist's care, and a staff developer's commitment to using research to improve practices. It is a thorough and thoughtful book of value to those in full-time and part-time positions alike.

More recent North American research is set out by Robert Menges and associates in *Faculty in New Jobs* (1999). Although they write more as researchers than as staff developers, I think that the chapter on 'feeling in control' by Ray Perry and colleagues, which argues that new academics who think that they can, by and large, have some control over what happens to them in most situations tend to be happier and more successful than others, contains a significant message for educational and staff developers working with new faculty.

4

Feeling motivated

A stance

Motivation for teaching is not separable from motivation to do the whole academic job, although it is possible to consider what tends to be enjoyable and what tends to be distressing just with reference to the work of teaching. Nor is it possible to say confidently that some things are 'motivators' and others are 'stressors'. One reason is that liking and dreading teaching are feelings created by real individuals experiencing complex situations. It can be convenient to think about those situations with the help of abstractions such as 'stressors' and 'motivators' but the terms are not the emotions, nor the causes of the emotions – they are convenient labels to help, not to displace, understanding of what is happening. Another reason is that a stressor for one person is not for another, and may even motivate a third by providing a welcome challenge. Indeed, a challenge to one can be understood by another as a subtle manoeuvre by management to get workers to exploit themselves and, as such, as something to be subverted. Echoing Chapter 1, like much of this chapter, my claim is that motivation and discomfort are created by individuals in networks of others, all of whom are engaging with multiple tasks in shifting settings. This means that suggestions about sustaining motivation to teach well and limiting the stressful possibilities of teaching (and academic work in general) must be about what the individual and the community of practice can do. They will be suggestions to be artfully adapted, not prescriptions for sure-fire success.

Implicit in this is the idea that much of what passes as research into motivation might better be seen as research into control. Agreed, incentives and accountability procedures help to make teaching something to take seriously but extrinsic motivation that compels or cajoles is reckoned to be dysfunctional. Extrinsic motivation

> refers to any instance in which the reasons for one's actions are some
> separable consequences, whether they be interpersonally administered

(e.g., praise, monetary payments, or the opportunity to do other, more interesting tasks) or self administered (e.g., praising self statements or presents to oneself). Extrinsic rewards are frequently used and widely advocated as a means of motivating individuals – for example, as a way of motivating professors to teach.

(Deci *et al.*, 1997: 61)

My emphasis is upon intrinsic motivation. Csikszentmihalyi (1997: 73, 76) writes that:

the intrinsic reward from learning is the enjoyment one gets here and now, from the act of learning itself, and not from what follows later from having acquired the knowledge ... An activity is intrinsically rewarding when the actor experiences it as worth doing for itself, not just as a means to future, external goals.

Key points

1 Intrinsic motivation is generally preferable to extrinsic motivation, where rewards or punishments are the drivers. However, people can become comfortable with external prompts, especially when they understand the rationale and can integrate it with their own priorities.
2 Motivation is not a bolt-on quality. Communities of practice, such as departments, work in ways that encourage or deter. With individuals, motivation and distress are expressions of who we have come to be.
3 People can help themselves to be more motivated or less stressed. This is not, though, an endorsement of heroic self-help manuals, such as those of Hay (1999), which imply that you can change anything and that if you fail, then it's your fault.
4 Sometimes the thing to do is quit or mentally shrink-wrap the work and invest your life in better things.

Research

Extrinsic and intrinsic motivation

Enthusiasm for teaching may not be what mainly motivates academic staff in the workplace: 'It is likely', writes Bess (1997: 432), 'that most faculty have chosen their careers in anticipation of the opportunity to conduct research and write about it.' Research has intrinsic appeal to the mind, may excite the emotions and has choice associated with it, particularly in the humanities and social sciences. Although researchers can also be confident teachers who enjoy teaching, academic staff commonly say that they would like to teach a little less (Blackburn and Lawrence, 1995). Some, though, are not as secure and try to avoid teaching or, if they cannot, invest as little of themselves in it as possible, which enables them to hold some belief that they could be much better if only they really had the time and really tried. So, as I said in Chapter 2, teaching is frequently a secondary priority. Being a teacher is a part of being a faculty member that competes or coexists with other identities. There need not be a serious conflict between being a teacher and being attracted to the scholarship of discovery, as Kenny (1998) argues in a review of ways in which departments in US research-led universities can encourage greater research/teaching synergy.

Nevertheless, it is widely accepted that there is a problem with teaching quality. There are governments and legislatures who, true to their principles of distrusting professionals, especially public-sector professionals, have addressed it by sponsoring 'discourses of derision' (Ball, 1994), which question academic staff's commitment to teaching and/or their competence to teach. Increased control and regulation follow, sometimes in the form of expensive inspection systems, often in the form of paying cash-strapped institutions for compliance with state mandates. Other extrinsic motivational devices include appraisals, student evaluations, classroom observation and tenure hearings to get staff to take teaching seriously, and prizes, promotion prospects and limited teaching development grants to make them keen to teach well.

The problem is that if extrinsic motivational tactics involve too many sticks and too much control, they can be damaging. Writing of schools, Ryan and La Guardia (1999: 78–9) said that, 'top-down, controlling reforms to raise standards are not only unlikely to produce higher quality education, they are instead likely to *lower* the effectiveness of schools' (emphasis added). Deci and colleagues add that

> several studies have shown . . . that making extrinsic rewards salient as a means of motivating people to do some activity undermines their intrinsic motivation for the task . . . Threats of punishment, the imposition of deadlines, competition and evaluations . . . have also been found to have the same deleterious effects . . . the more they are used in an attempt to motivate or control, the more likely their consequences will be negative.
>
> (Deci *et al.*, 1997: 63–4)

This may seem counter-intuitive. Deci and colleagues acknowledge that extrinsic rewards are necessary and often greatly appreciated. 'The problem', they write (p. 64), 'is that rewards and other such motivators are all too often used in an attempt to control – or at least people experience them that way, which has the same negative effect.' Furthermore, when good practice relies on rewards and punishments, practice needs to be specified in enough detail for finely graded measurements to be made of performance so that

rewards and punishments can be appropriately applied. As far as professional work goes, this is hard, if not impossible, and the system for discip-
lining and rewarding can become contentious, producing rancour that
harms teams, departments and institutions. And extrinsic motivation may
not work; if it gets compliance it may not get commitment. These low-trust
work environments are expensive, largely inappropriate for the knowledge
economy (Leadbeater, 2000) and unsuited to complex professional work.

In contrast, educational environments 'characterized by trust, openness,
sharing, supporting, understanding and realism' (Troman and Woods,
2001: 119) are associated with a commitment to quality and with happiness and well-being. This thinking can be traced back to the work of
Maslow, who believed that people need to satisfy basic needs, such as food,
shelter and security, before searching for affiliation, love, esteem and,
ultimately, self-actualization. This motivational pyramid is suggestive but
by no means complete or uncontested. Two ideas, though, are important
here: first, that basic, essentially extrinsic motivations fade into the background as those needs are slaked; second, that self-actualization – for
example, as a parent, teacher, lover or soul – is the intrinsic good which
people strive to get. An implication is that extrinsic motivators need to be
satisfied but that when that is more or less done, then they are not, *by and
large*, sources of satisfaction and fulfilment. This is reflected in Herzberg's
two-factor theory of motivation, which proposed that some aspects of working life, such as work conditions, supervision, company policy and administration, be treated as hygiene factors, matters that needed to be satisfactory
but which contribute little to fulfilment in the workplace. Where hygiene
is bad, dissatisfaction is evident. It does not follow, though, that good
hygiene brings satisfaction. Motivators, not hygiene factors, make for satisfaction. Motivators include opportunities for achievement, recognition, the
work itself, responsibility, advancement and growth. Some factors, including salary, security and peer relations, have an ambiguous position, which
means that they may not contribute greatly to satisfaction and fulfilment.
Commenting upon Herzberg's ideas, Elton (1996) added that motivators
could become 'negative satisfiers' when the workplace stifled people's
natural attempts to get the satisfaction of achievement, recognition and
enjoyment. He endorsed work that associated Herzberg's motivators with
intrinsic motivation and hygiene factors with extrinsic motivation, but
emphasized that the distinctions between intrinsic and extrinsic are subjective and contingent. This is an important warning against reifying
motivators and hygiene factors, against implying that motivational factors
have similar meanings regardless of time, person and setting. Something,
such as salary, may be a hygiene factor, a motivator or a negative motivator,
depending on the person, their goals and their experience of the workplace.
So, hygiene factors, which would be at the bottom of Maslow's motivational pyramid, need attention as well as motivators, which is something

that can be overlooked in the veneration of intrinsic motivation. They often need to be dealt with before intrinsic motivation can be groomed. This analysis suggests that well judged management and teaching incentives are necessary but not sufficient for encouraging commitment to teaching as an activity that calls upon initiative and inspiration. Equally, bad management and lack of incentives might be expected to provoke motivational crises in the form of apathy or stress. Higher education staff (Fisher, 1994; Doyle and Hind, 1998), along with schoolteachers (Campbell and Neill, 1994) and social workers (Balloch *et al.*, 1999), tend to experience stress levels greater than population means.

That said, some mandates or other extrinsic influences may become, over time, integrated into other values and perhaps taken up as one's own. Integration and identification can be seen as staging posts on the way to intrinsic motivation, which is where the goals come from within, rather than from those external mandates. This analysis of extrinsic motivation challenges a common belief that goals must be freely chosen, although it does not mean that unwelcome goals have the same motivational potential as ones that get integrated. Latham and colleagues (1997: 132) suggest that,

> If assigned goals from a dean or department chairperson are given in a supportive manner, if they are given with a rationale, and if the goals are within the perceived legitimacy of the authority figure's role, they can be as effective in energizing the performance of a faculty member as are goals that are set participatorily.

Even so, the common-sense strategies mentioned above for encouraging people to take teaching seriously and to adopt teaching well as a goal are not quite enough. In addition to general problems with relying on extrinsic motivation to shape people's goals, there are specific problems with using them to make teaching valued. For example, there is the problem of parity of esteem, so a chair awarded for teaching excellence can be seen as the stigma of a mediocre researcher. Besides, it is hard for academics to believe that promotions really are based on teaching skill when there is urgency about getting research grants and publishing, particularly as the lack of valid and reliable ways of distinguishing degrees of teaching competence (Luntley, 1999) means that promotion panels are well advised to look for evidence of reasonable commitment to teaching and then differentiate between applicants on the basis of grants and publications. Resource restrictions further limit these attempts to make teaching an important professional goal, which do not, in any case, have much penetrative power when it comes to faculty who are in positions where they can be indifferent to new pedagogical initiatives.

To understand the appeal of intrinsic motivational strategies for improving teaching quality it is useful to appreciate that teaching is an emotional activity in which psychic rewards are important:

[School] teaching cannot be reduced to technical competence. It involves significant emotional understanding and emotional labor as well. It is an emotional practice . . . without attention to the emotions, educational reform efforts may ignore and even damage some of the most fundamental aspects of what teachers do.

(Hargreaves, 1998: 850)

Nias (1996: 306) argues that unless there is personal commitment, school-teaching 'becomes unbalanced, meagre, lacking fire – and in the end, therefore, unsuccessful', adding that 'To place the development of teachers' affect in the forefront of our concerns is ultimately to safeguard children's education.' ('Affect' is psycho-speak for feelings and the emotions.) Brookfield (1999) and Palmer (1998) have made similar claims about the importance of these psychic rewards to teachers of higher education. They are not teaching for the money. Nor can they be compelled to teach well, not least because teaching is not something that can be reduced to a set of unproblematic procedures to be diligently implemented. Teaching well demands insight, intuition and initiative, and teachers are vitalized by an intrinsic commitment to the work, which, in turn, is abetted by the psychic rewards of doing the work well, of feeling good because learners learned, enjoyed and perhaps laughed as well. Teachers' motivation, as understood here, is more about positive affect than stick-and-carrot control and this is doubly so when the aim is to encourage creativity, flexibility and freshness. Good teaching flourishes when motivation to teach is part of the fabric of the job, when the work and its social settings make it relatively easy and quite natural to teach well. This is a view of motivation for teaching as something that is social as well as personal, which is a restatement of the connectionist thinking pervading these opening chapters. Where there is a lack of commitment to teaching, the problem is personal-and-social, an interplay of an individual with a history and a community of practice. This means that the ideas for enhancing teaching motivation that close this chapter are more about what departments and teams can do than about how individuals can pep themselves up. Sometimes communities of practice have little effect on calloused teachers and sometimes stressed individuals get no relief from their workgroup but, in general, feelings about teaching and work are coloured by the individual *and* the community.

What helps people to take teaching seriously and try to do it well? A selection of the key personal themes André and Frost explore in *Researchers Hooked on Teaching* is:

(e) love for the profession and the people, *agape* – the overflowing love that seeks nothing in return; (f) dialogue and co-learning with students; (g) enthusiasm and even drama in the theater/classroom; (h) the essence of professional accomplishment; (i) the finding of one's voice; . . . (k) sensitivity to learning styles; (l) commitment to helping students develop deep, personal insights; . . . (n) integration of individual research interests into the classroom; (o) love of one's subject; . . . (r) intellectual and emotional refreshment.

(André and Frost, 1997: xiii)

The social side of motivation is confirmed by this commentary on the importance of fun as a motivating force:

An additional facet of post 1970s psychological research has been greater attention to positive emotions . . . fun at work . . . the mechanisms of pride. [Psychologists] make a strong plea for organizations to engineer a sense of job enjoyment and happiness (which they distinguish from job satisfaction) by improving physical working conditions, remodelling organizational culture and enhancing communication. Mild shifts in positive mood or affect can, they contend, improve task perception and decision-making, face-to-face bargaining . . . conflict resolution . . . performance appraisal . . . absenteeism and labour turnover . . . The benefits of the 'feel good' factor are echoed by [writers] who say that love, empathy, zest and enthusiasm are the *sine qua non* of managerial success and organizational 'excellence'.

(Fineman, 1996: 544–5)

This social-and-personal theme is repeated when thinking about the significance of goals as motivators. In line with the position taken above, that motivation, valuing and affect are interwoven, expectancy theories say that people commit most strongly to goals that are worthwhile and achievable with a reasonable amount of effort. Although these theories may imply that people are more clear, consistent and mindful about goals than is really the case, they usefully indicate that motivation is related to goals. Goals, of course, can be changed and, where something such as teaching is concerned, that is a social and an individual matter. As is stress.

Stress

In everyday use, stress is a 'diffuse, non-specific negative state' (Fineman, 1996: 546) and the experience of stress is characterized by emotions 'such as anger, anxiety, sadness, despair, depression and disappointment. Stressed people undoubtedly *feel* their distress or illness' (Fineman, 1996: 546). It is well known that high levels of stress lead to the arousal of a cortisol flood in the body and that when it is sustained it is associated with increased susceptibility to several forms of physiological harm (Marmot, 1999). The likelihood of mental harm in the form of depression, substance abuse and burnout is also increased and courts are increasingly ready to award damages when employees can trace such harm to toxic workplaces. However, as Briner (1997) points out, it is not clear when negative feelings, which are part of the human condition, should be understood as stress, nor what it means to name them as 'stress'. Stress is subjectively experienced and hard – perhaps impossible – to measure with any degree of reliability (raised cortisol levels are not good guides to affect, to how a person *feels*). It is also difficult to alleviate precisely because something that causes stress for one person may mildly irritate another and not affect a third. A further complication is that we need some stress – 'eustress' – to function. But what one person feels as stimulating eustress, another feels as distress.

Definitional difficulties notwithstanding, negative stress is a matter of concern. Forty-three per cent of Americans are thought to suffer adverse health effects due to stress and the proportion of US workers feeling highly stressed doubled between 1985 and 1990, leading to a US$11.31 billion market for stress management programmes, products and services in 1999 (American Institute of Stress, 2001). A newspaper article (*Guardian*, 12 October 2000: 16) highlighted the following points from the International Labour Organisation's report on mental health in the workplace: 'Depression in the workplace is the second most disabling illness for workers after heart disease'; 'The self reported occurrence of anxiety and depression in the UK ranges from 15 to 30% of the working population'; 'anxiety levels are set to dramatically increase in the coming years.' Troman and Woods (2001: 62) report that bullying, 'the misuse of power and the humiliation of individuals', is endemic in schools (and in workplaces generally). Headteachers are the main perpetrators. Quite apart from the ethics of bullying, it is 'likely to be educationally counter-productive . . . more suited to the schools of the nineteenth rather than to those of the twenty-first century' (Troman and Woods, 2001: 76). An implication is that heads of department and other leaders in higher education may see themselves acting decisively as managers with the interests of the community at heart, but where some see this as efficient management, others feel bullied and infer constructive dismissal.

Stress, in the negative sense of the word, is common when things that should motivate are misfunctioning so that, for example, instead of having a feeling of reasonable autonomy workers feel threatened by a lack of control. Marmot *et al.* (1999) bring together two models to account for work stress. The effort–reward imbalance model says that, for example, 'having a demanding, but unstable job, and achieving at a high level without being offered any promotion prospects, are examples of high cost-low gain conditions at work' (p. 120), and predicts greater stress as a result. The demand–control model focuses on jobs that make high demands over which the worker has little control. People who report lower amounts of control, less varied work, less use of skills and less satisfaction have the most sickness absence and risk of heart disease Marmot and colleagues (1999: 126) put the two models together and say:

Whereas the emphasis of the demand-control model is on change of task structure (such as job enlargement, job enrichment, and increasing the amount of support within the job, etc.) the reduction of high cost–low gain conditions includes actions at all three levels – the individual level (e.g. reduction of excessive need for control), interpersonal level (e.g. improvement of esteem reward), and the structural level (e.g. adequate compensation for stressful work conditions by improved pay and related incentives, opportunities for job training, learning new skills, and job security).

Stressors are mediated by individuals' perceptions of the amount of social support they have, in this case social support in the workplace, particularly support for teaching. Griffiths and colleagues (1999: 526) concluded that 'The perception of teacher stress itself was affected by social support.' They argued that social support is not an objective phenomenon, backing it up with evidence that some teachers reckoned there was good social support, while others in the same school said there was little. This implies that a team or department may have a lot of meetings with people often working together on teaching tasks, yet, paradoxically, faculty could still feel short of social support. It is quite easy to appreciate that this could happen where faculty members row over fundamental values. For example, some faculty might see learning as students mastering bodies of information transmitted by lecturers and texts, while others might believe learning involves students making defensible meanings with support from the teacher. These paradigm wars can be stressful and leach motivation. However, the absence of values conflict does not mean that social support will be sufficient even if a department has adopted collegial practices in research, teaching and administration. Hargreaves (1994), who is generally well disposed to collegiality, has pointed out that it can be 'contrived', where people are told to work in teams on tasks that are not of their choosing. This can be more destructive when some people think it important that their voices are fully heard on most issues, act accordingly and make others into listeners, although listeners would have been contributors had they managed to force their way into the microseconds of space the loud-mouths left. These listeners, who are often women, can feel demeaned. Sennett (1998), arguing that modern work practices cause a corrosion of character, claims that people have to learn to mask themselves in order to comply with contrived collegiality. Such ideas point to the need to find out what practices mean to people in the workplace and warn against trusting that a department in which things are done in teams is one to which people feel affiliation and in which they feel supported. Meetings, it should be remembered, are one of the most hated features of professional work.

As with so much about being a teacher, workplace stress is an environmental matter (in that some features of workplace life regularly evoke stress reactions) and an individual one (in that you might hardly notice something that makes me feel bad). It is to the individual that I now turn.

Motivation and the constructed self

Understanding what encourages people and what distresses them is easier when groups, especially large groups of somewhat similar people, are concerned. Individuals are not predictable like that, which is partly a result of neuro-physiological differences and partly a resonance of the specific timbres of the concepts, feelings, values, beliefs and information that each has learned. While individuals in the same culture learn in more or less the same physical environments, using a common stock of scripts and schemata (Strauss and Quinn, 1997), subcultural variations combine with individual differences and small group interactions to produce distinctive shades of meaning and affect. Yet, in so far as differences are learned, often unconsciously, it is possible to believe that they can be unlearned or modified if people learn to scan their environments so as to see more opportunities for fulfilment or less cause for distress. Briner (1997), Cooper and Cartwright (1997) and Hogarth *et al.* (2000) observe that primary interventions (changing the workplace) are less popular with employers than secondary or tertiary interventions (running stress management programmes and offering treatment to highly stressed people, respectively). A consequence, which may or may not be intentional, is that it can then appear that stress or motivational torpor gets attributed to individuals who should therefore *buck themselves up*. Enough has already been said to show the limitations of that view, but the underlying idea that people are active constructors of motivation and stress is an important one. If some people thrive in a setting while others fret, might there be something the fretful could learn from the flourishing?

Dweck's ideas align with other work on self-efficacy (for example, Bandura, 1997) and on practical intelligence (Sternberg, 1997). Put together, they suggest that some forms of success in life and in the workplace are related to the theories that people hold about themselves and their explanations of success and failure. Figure 4.1 schematizes these ideas.

People who persist in the face of difficulty, which means the people who are the most likely to succeed (all other things being equal) on novel tasks and with fresh problems, are most likely to fit into cell A. Sometimes they will justifiably attribute success or failure to things outside their control (cell B) but if they keep explaining things like that they may be moving into cell D, perhaps to cell C. Entity theorists (cells C and D) are vulnerable to learned helplessness, which can paralyse effort (Peterson *et al.*, 1993). Alternatively, if they are intelligent people who have always found things easy until now, they are likely to crumble when they do face difficulties because their beliefs tell them that there is nothing to do but stop trying or

	Attributions	
	Internalist (high internal locus of control)	**Externalist** (low internal locus of control)
Incrementalist: things are malleable, people make a difference	**A** Effort is important: the more effort you make, the more you are likely to succeed. People here see intelligence, for example, as a social and practical achievement, not as God-given	**B** Luck, fate and chance play a great part in life. Some people have all the luck, others don't. That said, luck might change, especially if our efforts make us well placed to seize the chance
Entity theorist: things are fixed and people have little chance of making a difference	**C** Fixed traits, such as intelligence, essentially determine what we can and cannot do. People here believe that they will do well because they are naturally clever or fail because they were born stupid	**D** Specific circumstances keep holding you back or usually explain your success: the boss, for example, likes you or hates you. This victim thinking can foster inertia: 'What's the point of trying?'

(Self-theories)

Figure 4.1 Self-theories and attributions

give up. Dweck is clear that even highly intelligent entity theorists can learn helplessness and that cell C and D people are more likely to be quitters. I want to draw two points from this. The first is that certain self-theories and attributional tendencies make for greater persistence and success. Second, we learn to prefer cell A, B, C or D patterns of thinking and we can learn to change our preferences. Box 10.1 suggests six ways in which programmes can encourage students away from cells C and D and towards cell A.

The upshot is the assertion that the experience of being a teacher is something that people construct for themselves, with the workplace as the source of raw materials. If the materials are rotten only an exceptional artist will be able to make anything very pleasurable out of them. Even there, though, it depends. For example, teaching in a degree factory could feel good after schoolteaching, with its long hours, multitasking, compressed time, shoddy surroundings, demanding children, lack of intellectual stimulus, limited autonomy, derisory rewards and scant recognition. Lazarus (1991) suggests that it might be worse to have had a lot of control in the workplace and then lost it than never to have had it in the first place. The point is that whatever HEIs and communities of practice might do to feed motivation, actions are individually interpreted. There are no motivational panaceas. Some people are disgruntled, while others in the same circumstances are gruntled.

To conclude, five themes that recur in this literature on goals, extrinsic and intrinsic motivation, hygiene factors and motivators are:

1 People seek affirmation and affective rewards.
2 Positive feedback is valued, partly because it can be a reward in its own right and partly because of its helpfulness.
3 Feelings of appropriate control and autonomy are important.
4 Goals are best when they are valued and likely to be achievable with appropriate effort.
5 Self-theories matter. When people believe that they are not talented or smart enough to succeed, then learned helplessness is likely to stop them trying.

Informed practices

Table 4.1 lists some popular suggestions for things individuals can do to enhance their motivation or lessen stress, although 'evidence as to the success of stress management training is confusing and imprecise' (Cooper and Cartwright, 1997: 10). Attempts to help individuals may improve short-term coping but are liable to fail with extremely distressed people and where the stress comes from outside the workplace. Helpful suggestions, such as not taking work home, may be good for some people but not for others. Griffiths and colleagues (1999) found that this could lead to a lower sense of efficacy and self-esteem (because the work wasn't getting done), yet cutting down on non-work activities to concentrate more on work was associated with higher blood pressure and heart rate in the evening. Furthermore, the self-help and therapy books are coy about something that is well put by one of Herskowitz's patients, who said, 'I could write several volumes about what I learned about myself in analysis, but I've got the same damned symptoms I started with' (Herskowitz, 1997: 13). Knowing that you know how you tend to see the world, understand yourself, explain success or judge the likelihood of effort paying off is not the same as being able to be different. Reflecting on who you are and developing the metacognition that goes with it is a necessary but not a sufficient step to being different, whether as a person, faculty member or teacher. That takes commitment, persistence, help and, in many cases, some change in the workplace as well.

Informed motivational practices are sensitive to the whole working environment. For example, a major study of social work staff in the UK highlighted organizational issues as prime sources of dissatisfaction: 'I like the job but I hate the organization', said one respondent (Balloch *et al.*, 1998: 335). '[M]ost stress was caused by aspects of the work attributable to something or somebody else, factors outside the individual's control' (Balloch *et al.*, 1999: 69). Major problems included threats to job security, promotion prospects and the emphasis put on managerial paperwork at the expense of client-centred professional activities. The more these social

Table 4.1 Things people do to reduce their experience of stress or to improve their motivation

Action	Comment
1 Reappraising assumptions, 'frames' and attributions	If it is accepted that we can have choice in the ways we feel and understand what is, then we can learn alternatives and, in so doing, break from the frames that limit our perceptions of our selves and our potentials.
2 Taking salutogenic actions	There is a lot of research on the all-round benefits of bodily well-being (principally to do with exercise and dietary care); mind–body work (aikido, yoga, various breathing arts); mind/spirit care (neuro-linguistic programming, voice dialogue, meditation); and medication (herbal or prescription treatments, aromatherapy).
3 Appraising non-work support systems	People with active social lives tend to be healthier and live longer (Marmot *et al.*, 1999). Workplace stress can be dissipated with others, who may also show different ways in which experiences can be felt and understood.
4 Rewarding ourselves differently or better	We often don't reward ourselves for achievement – writing a programme specification, preparing properly for all classes, getting work marked on time. That is a pity because celebrating something we hoped to do anyway affirms the goals and grooms our general sense of self-efficacy.
5 Reviewing goals and priorities	It can be inspiring to imagine what we would like to have achieved in, say, six months and to think through what we would need to do to achieve it. Making it a priority to pursue attractive and just-within-reach goals is a good motivational strategy. Meretricious and over-ambitious goals tend to cause problems.
6 Improving time management	There are lots of books and websites giving near-similar advice on ways of compressing backstage work to make enough room for teaching and other forms of scholarship. It often means unlearning habits and beliefs about how you ought to behave, which is one reason why these excellent ideas are so widely ignored.
7 Managing demands better	'35% of men and 45% of women report that imposing excessively high self expectations is a major source of pressure' (Doyle and Hind, 1998: 74). Many people have a 'be perfect' driver that is fuelled by a belief that other people are smarter, work harder, write better,

Table 4.1 (*Cont'd*)

Action	Comment
	have more fun. They make life hard for themselves because their ideas of normal are absurd. One route to being less stressed and more motivated is to be kinder to oneself and to enjoy ipsatively, not normatively.
8 Creating appreciative spaces	This means doing things that are likely to go well and spending time with people who appreciate what you say and do *and* whose appreciation stimulates ideas about doing different and better.
9 Experimenting with job redesign	Academic work tends to be rich with opportunities to change a job, rather in the manner of rebuilding a boat at sea. Sometimes this is impossible. If so, consider personalizing your workspace – there are those who say that certain colours induce tension or gloom, which can be compounded by poor lighting. Others say that thriving pot plants can make a difference.
10 Seeking training, looking to learn	Feelings of incompetence feed stress. Competence brings psychic rewards and sometimes the 'flow' experience of being pleasurably immersed in the work as well (Csikszentmihalyi, 1997).
11 Riding the boundaries	Identifying and defending boundaries is necessary for demand management work. Boundary-crossing, whether by extending networks, trying new things or reading in fresh fields, can bring the exhilaration of learning.
12 Resisting bullies	Unions and professional associations are necessary sources of advice when the workplace feels toxic because of senior colleagues' management practices.
13 Challenging structural inequalities and unfairness	*Shared* resistance to unfair, and hence demotivating, practices is important, a point well made by a number of feminist writers: the Chilly Editorial Collective (1995), for example.

work staff were doing things that they did not see as important parts of the job, the more cause for concern there was about their scores on the General Health Questionnaire, which was used to assess the relationship between their perceptions of their work and their estimates of their own well-being. Findings such as these, set alongside research perspectives on motivation and stress, help to show how organizations and workgroups might be reformed to help motivation and minimize dis-ease. Table 4.2

Table 4.2 Departmental actions that can help people to commit to teaching

Suggestions	Motivational theme				
	Competence and self-theories	Worthwhile and achievable goals	Sufficient autonomy	Positive feedback	Affirmation and rewards
Be concerned that people can get the psychic rewards that make teaching something to choose to do, a source of pleasure (usually) and a contributor to self-esteem	✓	✓	✓	✓	✓
Reduce surveillance, paperwork and bureaucratic accountability			✓		
Although it is rarely possible to do anything substantial about the quality and affordances in the physical environment, it is worth remembering how primary school teachers vitalize bleak teaching spaces by means of plants, posters and colour		✓			
Examine departmental calls on time: is there scope for simplifying or reducing what is done?		✓			
Talk of good teaching as an outcome of commitment, concern, persistence and learning. 'Persistence, enthusiasm, and liveliness are traits that consistently distinguish effective teachers from average teachers' (Walker and Quinn, 1996: 328). This discourse challenges the belief that teaching is a gift, so that those who are not 'born teachers' are wasting their time trying to become good teachers	✓				

Reward *commitment* to and *enthusiasm* for teaching (traditional teaching awards demand po-faced evidence of achievement). Make these rewards public and significant ✓ ✓

Encourage new teaching practices; for example, lecturing less about content coverage and more about meaning-making ✓ ✓

Encourage teachers to tinker with their teaching practices, enjoying things that work, looking to learn from those that do not ✓ ✓

Stimulate team discussions of the expectations that should be foremost in teaching practices. These will change as some expectations become embedded and new concerns arise ✓ ✓

Hold teaching improvement seminars asking, 'What is new in the discipline and how can we teach it?' or 'How can we encourage students to value their work and to enjoy their achievements?' ✓

Make more use of 'giving an account': face-to-face, professional conversations about successes and how 'we' could make incremental improvements to practice ✓ ✓ ✓

Negotiate module learning goals within the agreed programme framework or specification but only have a few (three to five) good achievable goals per module; having more invites failure, 'cooking the books' and self-deception ✓ ✓

Use these goals to inform faculty evaluations and appraisals ✓ ✓

Table 4.2   (Cont'd)

Suggestions	Motivational theme				
	Competence and self-theories	Worthwhile and achievable goals	Sufficient autonomy	Positive feedback	Affirmation and rewards
Model these evaluations/appraisals on giving student feedback: stress the role of effort and good thinking in achievement, encourage incremental self-theories and 'learned optimism'	✓			✓	✓
Discourage norm-referenced ways of judging teaching; be cautious about criteria-referenced ways; encourage ipsative (self-referenced) thinking because it is sensitive to individuals in context (which means it is more genuine as a way of looking at achievement and thinking about development)	✓		✓	✓	✓
Redesign student course evaluations to identify what they like and what goes well. Ask for advice on what might be improved and suggestions for things to add	✓			✓	✓
Programme leaders and heads of department might use staff appraisals or course and programme review to negotiate attainable but challenging teaching intentions for the coming year	✓	✓	✓		✓

suggests actions that can be taken in communities of practice to enhance motivation, relating them to the five main motivational themes summarized above. Any combinations of actions that are fit for the purpose may be used, often in association with ones taken from Table 4.1.

However, things are not so simple because 'changing any part of the work environment will have mixed effects, some of which may be detrimental to some employees' well-being' (Briner, 1997: 64). For social work staff, 'Work was not the only source of stress. Staff with caring responsibilities for dependent adults and other children have to deal with these and other home pressures on top of work' (Balloch *et al.*, 1999: 69), which is consistent with Briner's (1997) observation that stress in the workplace does not necessarily originate in the workplace. He adds that 'only 20% of the variance in subjective ratings [of job conditions] can be explained by objective conditions' (p. 68). There are, then, no quick fixes and one-size-fits-all solutions but there are pointers to help individuals and managers to ease the strain of academic work in general and teaching in particular. The aim is, of course, that teaching should be enjoyable, not a source of stress.

Action points

Heads of department, deans and other leaders ought to wonder about the contribution that communities of practice make to the commitment faculty have to teaching and the job in general. There is a strong case for reflecting upon the extrinsic/intrinsic, hygiene factors/motivators balance and using prompts, such as those in Table 4.2, to consider whether departments and teams could be nicer places to be. A starting point would be to consider when it would be beneficial to displace hard managerialism (directive and controlling) with soft managerialism (incorporative and encouraging). Individuals can reflect on Table 4.2 or consult books such as *Working with Emotional Intelligence* (Goleman, 1998).

Further reading

Working with Emotional Intelligence combines advice about what individuals can contribute to their own motivation and success with a view of effective workplaces. Carol Dweck's *Self-theories* (1999) and Martin Seligman's *Learned Optimism* (1998) are accessible books by psychologists with strong records of research into motivation and attributions.

5

Maintaining teaching vitality

A stance

Attempts to improve teaching quality have often concentrated on beginning teachers, but there are many reasons, summarized below, why older faculty may lose teaching vitality (and some, of course, never had it). Most of them teach but they can choose not to engage in instructional, educational or professional development activities, despite professional obsolescence creeping up on them as higher education faces new teaching mandates, works with a more diverse student body, embraces new technologies and continues to confront financial difficulties. Furthermore, these are the people who set policy and approve programmes and courses. My position is that they *should* be committed to student learning and abrim with knowledge of good teaching, learning, assessment and curriculum practices.

Once, as Bland and Schmitz (1990: 52) observed, 'definitions saw vitality as being basically a faculty issue . . . vitality was usually considered a faculty "problem".' Later analyses attribute vitality to the interaction of the institution, communities of practice and individuals, which is an extension of Chapter 4's account of motivation to a large and important group of academics who are at risk of losing any taste for teaching that they once had. Beginning with an explanation of why older faculty may become silted up as teachers, this chapter suggests ways of sustaining teaching vigour. It assumes that anything these established teachers do will be most effective when departmental and institutional practices are favourable to it.

Key points

1 Established academic staff are harder to reach than those who *have* to look good as teachers.

2 Chapter 4 described the limits to extrinsic motivation. It is generally less effective when used on late-career staff, so it is all the more important that efforts to enhance their commitment to teaching do not rely upon it.
3 Teaching vitality is most likely to be sustained in communities of practice where good teaching scripts or 'memes' have become established.

Research

There are two main stories about careers. One is about the growth of expertise and skill, a story of progress to infinity and beyond. It is implicit in taxonomies that identify the performances characteristic of assistant, associate and full professors. For example, at Alverno College,

> [Experienced assistant professors should] . . . develop a more comprehensive view of the curriculum which they are able to incorporate into their teaching. They expand their awareness of students and their learning needs. They integrate feedback from peers and students into their teaching and assessment practices . . . Full professors . . . extend the range of perspectives they integrate. They take leadership in exploring the teaching enterprise within and across disciplines. The results of their scholarship are seen in teaching practices within and outside the institution. They provide direction in identifying and addressing significant teaching concerns.
>
> (Mentkowski *et al.*, 2000: 262)

Whatever the appeal of this way of seeing a career, it was always assumed that the top of the career pyramid would be reserved for a minority. In the mid-1980s, 38 per cent of tenure track professors in the USA were full professors (Schuster, 1990), and being aged 50 and one of the 32 per cent who were still associate professors would be a mark of failure. With slim chances of promotion in the past ten plus working years (there is no compulsory retirement age in the USA), there are few incentives for these 'also-rans' to commit to anything at work, unless they have their own intrinsic reasons. An alternative way of seeing careers is sensitive to evidence that the traditional 'company man' career is nonsense. Careers are not like this for people with care responsibilities, for those who work part-time, for those who are confined to one geographical area, for those who have no great interest in moving upwards and for those who are reinventing themselves. Besides, jobs are not for life, work is ever-changing and the star companies of today are likely to be the dogs of ten years time. A good understanding of what careers really are is a precondition for thinking about how best to help established academics to commit to teaching.

Drawing together her empirical work on the 'graying professoriate', Karpiak (2000) pointed out that mid life (which for most of us nowadays is late career) could be a period of stagnation and crises, especially as we begin to estimate the years left to us. Yet, for many of her informants it was the time of a 'second call' to care about and for others, to value the quality of community and social relationships, to be creative and to deepen self-awareness. This second call and its emphasis on generativity, or giving to the next generation, can be channelled through teaching and be, as Karpiak reports, a source of teaching vigour. One of her informants said, 'I wish and I hope the university recognizes that there is maybe 10 years left in me, that I could do something really special' (Karpiak, 2000: 133).

The seven fictitious sketches in Box 5.1 illustrate the diversity of established academics' commitments to teaching, which can be related, albeit somewhat loosely, to research into career phases. The following commentary on them draws upon Huberman's (1993) research into schoolteaching careers. Although it is insensitive to academic staff's need to choose among several forms of scholarship, I think that it provides a useful way of understanding the interplay between people getting older and their commitment to work.

He describes an initial or socialization phase (see Chapter 3) which leads to a sense of belonging and liberation from strict supervision as a basic repertoire of skills is consolidated. It is a time of greater ease, relaxation and psychological comfort. Stabilization generally follows, a time of 'consolidation, affirmation, relaxation, integration, effectiveness . . . [it] is the phase described most positively by teachers in our sample' (Huberman, 1993: 245). While teachers in this phase may be relatively open to outside influences, their sense of rightful autonomy, associated with an awareness of their own competence, can put them, like Cheryl and Jed, beyond the reach of suggestions that there are new things to do.

The following phase is usually one of experimentation or diversification, but that need not signify a willingness to invest in teaching improvement. Promotion is a matter of importance and it is well known that in higher education this may mean concentrating on the scholarship of discovery and, as in Carl's case, playing safe. Likewise, Huberman found that some schoolteachers commit themselves to making a better job of running the system and concentrate on management and leadership. The attractions of administration and research can take attention from teaching so that practices established as a teaching assistant run automatically, probably with some degradation caused by trying to teach more efficiently so as to free the time for promotion-enhancing work. Bessie is a good example of the way in which diversification can contribute to indifferent teaching practices. In her case it almost seems that diversification and the attendant images of busyness and importance are ends in themselves.

Box 5.1 Seven established teachers and their commitment to teaching

Mitzi is about 50, has been an effective head of department for a dozen years, writes one or two books a year for the sixth form/undergraduate market, enjoys sport, is passionate about her subject and teaches it with gusto, intelligence and humour. Once she was a successful teacher of urban adolescents. It shows.

After seven years in post, Cheryl is brash and self-opinionated, has served her apprenticeship and knows all the answers. She doesn't want to spend time on learning about learning and teaching any more; she has done that and is putting it all into practice – effectively, she reckons. Students don't much care for it though.

Carl is ten years established and reluctant to take risks because he has more to lose now, when he is on the edge of promotion in a fairly turgid teaching environment. He doesn't want negative feedback from students, who are happy with a system in which they get the marks if they do the work, although he is quite interested in developing his teaching. He has started wearing a tie to work.

Shirley is in her last ten years as a professional academic and one of the hardest working people in her college. She has a sharp, critical mind, a great way with people and enthusiasm for her subject and for talking. Written feedback on students' essays is lengthy, detailed and caring. It is also late, bogged down in specifics and hard to read. Her teaching is good on its own terms and stirs students up. Whether it contributes much to programme goals is another matter. As a teacher of the old school, she is great.

Bessie is a full professor, active in the national affairs of the subject community and internationally well connected. Scarcely a pie exists that does without her finger. Being good at interpersonal communication, she can talk well with students and easily improvises in student-prompted lecture/seminars. However, she doesn't teach much, and her lack of preparation can infuriate colleagues and inconveniences students who cannot get readings, miss handouts and want better guidelines on assignments. Marking can take months to do. She will endorse most innovations as long as they do not trouble her licence to 'wing it'.

Jed had tried a number of new ideas in his early years, inspired by Bill McKeachie and Trudy Banta. A lot hadn't worked for him, often because he was still learning so much, and was inexperienced, and didn't follow advice any too well. Now, freshly tenured at age 33, he responds to all suggestions for change with the mantra that he has been there, tried it, found it doesn't work and is against it.

Etienne has 28 years in the same place, isn't a full professor and is a teaching enthusiast. He is wondering how to get his courses fully problem-based and totally reliant on authentic assessment. He is working in a project to enhance the contribution higher education makes to students' generic attributes and thinking about ways to teach that help students to develop their professional identities. He is always tinkering with what he does and how – he is continuous quality improvement personified.

The stabilization and diversification phases are not as well defined as this taxonomy makes them seem – they can span decades or collapse into a dozen years if a ceiling is reached early (as when life circumstances lead to the choice to stay in an institution where promotion and stimulation are unlikely). There may be pulses of diversification, followed by stabilization. Elements of self-doubt or reassessment may intrude or grow into an unhappy stage of their own – 40 per cent of Huberman's teachers experienced a distinct phase of self-doubt. Interestingly, women employed on a part-time basis or who maintained an external interest in order to counterbalance their scholastic investments were the least vulnerable to it.

Regardless of whether teachers experience a phase of doubt or not, Huberman (1993: 246) wrote that 'We did notice a general displacement of energy in the second half of the career: a tendency towards less activism and less commitment in the pursuit of greater serenity.' This period, corresponding to the onset of what Jung described as 'internalization', may be associated with a more relaxed, laid-back attitude. This last phase, of relative disinvestment, is sometimes spiced with

> scenarios of negative focusing: attachments to the past; severe criticisms of the evolution of schooling; difficulties with students; social isolation at the school. There were also scenarios of disenchantment, often associated with dashed hopes, with unsuccessful or 'betrayed' reforms. With the feeling of being devalued or not taken seriously by younger colleagues . . . [Nevertheless] secondary teachers have as many chances to finish their careers 'well' though positive focusing, as they have to finish their careers 'poorly' through negative focusing.
>
> (Huberman, 1993: 247)

Yet he also found that 'a large "family" of teachers with 30–40 years' experience . . . remain surprisingly energetic, open, committed and optimistic. By contrast, the younger teachers . . . are clearly more conservative and dissatisfied' (Huberman, 1993: 246). Etienne may be one, Mitzi another and Shirley a third, although her impact is curbed by a lack of self-awareness or the power to do anything to change ingrained practices.

Without denying that many settled faculty have a zest for teaching, anecdotes and a limited body of research indicate that there are plenty of reasons why others can become accustomed to practices that might not have been particularly good in the first place and which look shabby now. A stuck career and the allure of research have already been mentioned as factors connected with withdrawal from work and resistance to change. Box 5.2 describes nine other things that militate against a commitment to teaching well. Although older people are the most open to such anti-teaching forces, settled faculty in their thirties may also be affected by them. People like Etienne and Mitzi have been tinkering and learning throughout their careers but, as educational developers around the world

Box 5.2   Nine factors militating against a commitment to teaching

1 Loss of rewards: 'Many [especially mid-career academics] felt that the world in which their academic identities had been shaped had fundamentally changed in a way that affected key sources of satisfaction and self esteem in their professional lives. The conditions under which they felt themselves to have made a distinctive contribution to higher education were being undermined ... For those who were not researchers and whose sources of reward and fulfilment were being displaced, it was difficult to see what might be substituted' (Henkel, 2000: 217). This echoes research into stress that concluded that 'it is less stressful never to have had control than to have had it and lost it' (Murphy, 1988: 324).

2 Disillusion with change: 'teachers' experience of waves of reform as "flavor of the month" eventually leads them to lose their enthusiasm and/or their ability to sustain changes to practice ... educational policymakers have not learned anything from these decades of research, whose recurring theme has been the complexity (if not outright failure) of educational change and the inadequacy of so many reform ideas' (Bascia and Hargreaves, 2000: 19–20).

3 Mandates that clash with established values. Rowland (2000) mentions a chemist who sees lectures as an opportunity to model ways of thinking that are characteristic of the subject. One consequence is that he does not know exactly what will happen in a class because his commitment is to drawing students into a process of thinking aloud about doing chemistry. Values such as his are threatened where managers expect teachers to have specific, measurable deliverables for each session.

4 The challenge of mass higher education. In some countries older teachers were socialized into an elite system, and those who came into more open systems have seen the make-up of the student body change. Teaching well is more complex today because more differences have to be catered for. Sometimes, the challenge of differentiated teaching can be overwhelming, especially if some students may have the ability to graduate but lack the knowledge needed to succeed on a particular course or module.

5 Structural reforms. For example, in the 1990s many British universities adopted modular programme structures. Blackwell and Williamson (1999) have shown staff dissatisfaction with them, noting that short modules invite undesirable assessment practices and make it hard for tutors to get to know students. In such ways teachers' psychic rewards are compromised.

6 Obsolescence. Dubin (1990) argued that professionals must be constantly learning, as otherwise they rapidly succumb to obsolescence. For example, if web-supported, problem-based learning with on-line conferencing becomes something to aim for, then a lot of faculty are going to feel pretty inept. If they do not update themselves, then they are liable to reduce their commitment to teaching, which allows them to preserve their self-esteem

by saying that they are really good as researchers or administrators, but not as teachers.

7 Inveterate suspiciousness. In institutions where administrators are enemies and where academic freedom needs vigorous defence, attempts to invigorate teaching can be treated suspiciously as if they were managerial initiatives to get more out of staff, or to bring them more firmly under surveillance and control.

8 Better uses of life. Why spend time exploring teaching alternatives when it is easier just to swim in the mainstream? There is a life to be lived outside work: children are to be enjoyed while growing up and then, with them grown up, there is the chance to reclaim the freedoms of one's early twenties.

9 Intensification. This refers to an absolute increase in the amount of work, to a proliferation of roles and demands, and to feelings that many of these demands are peripheral to the four forms of scholarship. The drive to improve teaching by making procedures, standards and practices more explicit has contributed to a significant intensification of teaching work. Calls for teaching improvement may struggle for attention if academic staff feel that teaching is already a greedy activity and not as rewarding as it was when they could concentrate on classroom matters. McInnis (2000) gives details of intensification among Australian faculty, writing that 'it is reasonable to suggest that many (but again, not all) academics have reached the limits of tolerance for change and lack the energy to pursue quality in teaching' (p. 151), while adding that the situation need not be intractable.

confirm, many others' teaching practices have become obsolete. The workshops and courses that might help pass many, perhaps most, of them by. Could things be arranged so that settled teachers are more likely to commit to the processes of teaching improvement?

Informed practices

Although the recent literature we surveyed emphasized quite persuasively the institution's role in sustaining faculty productivity, strategies aimed at developing the individual were mentioned much more frequently. In fact, individual strategies were discussed . . . six times more frequently than institution-level strategies.

(Bland and Schmitz, 1990: 52)

The predominance of advice about how individuals might invigorate their teaching is not commensurate with its quality. Recommendations to read, talk, go on courses and be ready to innovate may be unexceptionable but do little to indicate how to reach established faculty who are content for things to stay as they are. Two things are necessary to influence them. First, they have to be implicated in teaching improvement (and those interested in it need to be kept interested); second, they then need good advice about what to do (Part 2 of this book is a contribution to that). So, although individual faculty members are responsible for how far they choose to engage in teaching improvement, and although there are many things they can do on their own initiative, it is widely recognized that institutions and departments must make a substantial contribution to teaching vitality. Bland and Schmitz's (1990) thorough literature review identified institutional practices that sustain teaching development: teaching must be a priority in mission goals; be reflected in personnel policies, including reward systems; and be supported with instructional and professional development centres and practical support such as libraries, day care and car parking. Wright and O'Neil's (1995) survey of educational development professionals in Australasia, North America and the UK found that they saw teaching improvement as contingent upon institutional actions: upon employment policies and practices; development opportunities and grants; structural and organizational arrangements to support teaching improvement; and the leadership of senior administration. Plainly, it is easier to improve teaching when the institution is geared up to support it but the goals, rewards and facilities are only effective to the extent that faculty choose to do something to improve their work. However, McInnis (2000) reported that only a quarter of his sample of 1554 Australian respondents had some involvement in professional development in teaching methods in the past two years. His survey did not establish what that involvement was but in many institutions it would usually take the form of attending courses and workshops. Alongside claims that they are effective (Rust, 1998), there is evidence that courses and workshops are not too effective as ways of improving teaching practices (Weimer and Lenze, 1991; Kember, 2000), which raises some awkward questions about how best to invigorate the teaching of established academic staff.

Knight and Trowler (2001) argue that change forces operate best in the mid level systems that connect with the macro level of the institution and the micro level of the individual. They argue that subject departments in higher education can be understood as such meso level systems, and reason that attempts to maintain the teaching vitality of settled staff, for example, should be departmental attempts that connect individual and institutional actions. Wright and O'Neil found that the single most important category of improvement practices was not institutional but the leadership of deans and heads of department. Karpiak's discussion of ways of sustaining faculty teaching vitality is redolent of the literature on motivation surveyed in Chapter 4. Her recommendations can be read as advice to leaders in departments and teams. She wrote (Karpiak, 2000: 133) that:

- Academics need to be encouraged to explore new areas, new orientation and new avenues for broadening their perspectives or deepening them.
- Academics have a critical need to feel valued for their influence on the lives of others, to know that they are part of a larger collegial effort, that their perspectives and input can be useful to improving quality in academe and that they matter. Opportunities are needed for administrators and teachers to participate and 'hold hands' in matters of shared university concern.
- Good individual review, mentoring and appraisal practices are important, especially where they are decoupled from the high-stakes, summative accountability of formal performance evaluations and reflect a developmental approach that assumes and nurtures the capacity for continuing growth.
- Where departments and teams operate on the basis of collegiality, respect and mutual concern, the quality that comes from creativity and commitment is more likely to be seen.

Institutional and departmental practices that favour teaching vitality need to be complemented by actions that make teaching quality a matter of continuing concern. There are many possibilities, some mentioned in Table 5.1 and others reviewed in Part 2. The remainder of this section is about an area of teaching practice which is often overlooked in discussions of teaching improvement. The claim is that a promising way of engaging all teachers in teaching improvement is for departments to reflect on the teaching scripts in use.

The idea of making teaching scripts a matter for on-going attention is based on the work of Stigler and Hiebert (1999) who studied mathematics teaching in the USA, Germany and Japan. They found that teachers' effectiveness 'depends on the scripts they use. Recruiting highly qualified teachers will not result in steady improvement as long as they continue to use the same scripts. It is the scripts that must be improved' (p. 134). They found that teachers in the three countries used similar teaching actions but their teaching scripts – the sequential combination of lesson features – differed markedly; hence their claim that better mathematics teaching in the USA did not require teachers to learn new techniques because 'individual features make sense only in terms of how they relate to others that surround them . . . their value depends on how they connect with others' (p. 75). So, 'to improve teaching over the long run we must improve the script' (p. 101). Their scripts resemble what Richard Dawkins called 'memes'. Cohen and Stewart (1995: 358–9) describe a 'meme' as

> a thought pattern that inhabits human brains and replicates by the spoken word . . . every seminar is a device for the reproduction and dissemination of memes . . . [they] range from simple slogans to vast

Table 5.1   Ten ways to tinker with teaching

Action	*Comment*
1 Explore the possibilities of appreciative enquiry (Ludema *et al.*, 2001)	Start with the assumption that some, at least, of what you do as a teacher is good or better. Identify things that go well and appreciate them as indicators of competence. Why do they work? Can you extend these successes and the principles and practices behind them to other parts of your teaching work?
2 Talking with colleagues: for example, teaching circles (Blackwell *et al.*, 2001) and dialogue groups (Qualter, 2000)	'Dialogue is a carefully constructed and monitored process whereby individuals with shared interests come together to talk in a non-threatening, non-judgmental and structured format designed to help establish a common language, probe their practice assumptions, and examine the practice assumptions of colleagues' (Qualter, 2000: n.p.). Tom joined a Dialogue group and spoke of the ways in which others had made him believe that 'I am a very limited teacher'. Nevertheless, he explored with the dialogue group what that limit was and how he could work to best effect within it, saying, 'I can't be any smarter than I am. I can't be any dumber than I am . . . For the first time Tom opened his classroom door and it didn't get slammed in his face' (Qualter, 2000: n.p.). There are obvious parallels with appreciative enquiry in this story of how Tom's teaching began to improve.
3 Playing with similes, exploring ideas	In what ways is teaching like fishing? Gardening? Aerobics? This play with similes can limber up assumptions about how teaching is and how it might be. It can be a good prelude to imagining different ways of helping students to learn, which can lead you to ask what is stopping you and how you might act otherwise.
4 Asking on the web	Post a message to an educational development, professional or subject association list that briefly describes what you do and asks colleagues to suggest one simple idea for making your teaching more enjoyable, effective, efficient etc.

Table 5.1   (Cont'd)

Action	Comment
5 Getting better feedback from students	When evaluating, ask students to identify things that work well with your teaching and topics they enjoy. Invite a group of students to advise you on improving your course, asking them to take account of constraints under which you *have* to work.
6 Freshening up your teaching content	For example, each year drop a couple of stale lectures, replace them with up-to-date material or get students to read and report upon one or two papers that are 'hot off the press'.
7 Putting less emphasis on content coverage. Teach for concept mastery – expose and challenge common misconceptions	The information we assume students have to have is often not vital. Much of what they really need they can get from books, journals and the web. Teaching for understanding – spending half an hour explaining Newton's laws of motion, illustrating them and then playing with popular fallacies – should be more enjoyable than narrating information; more powerful too.
8 Making spaces for students in seminars and other small group sessions	Dull seminars are frequently caused by the students being in awe of 'the prof'. Begin by giving them ten minutes to talk in groups of, say, three, asking each group to come up with three conclusions, reasons, criticisms, questions etc. Then ask them to debate the issue more openly.
9 Reducing your marking load	Set fewer assignments to grade; have students mark solutions in class and then only mark a sample yourself; consider self and peer assessment; set shorter assignments (our students say short essays are harder than long ones); use 'tick forms' for some feedback; etc.
10 Setting more interesting student assignments	For example, tasks that ask students to apply their learning to authentic problems. Encourage group tasks. Consider poster assignments and photo-journalism. Ask them to give you ideas about how to deal with problems in your research. Etc.

interlocking systems of principle and precedent . . . The relationship between memes and the actions they produce is analogous to that between genes and the behavior they produce in the organisms that produce them.

This idea is suggestive because it implies that these taken-for-granteds, scripts or embedded thought patterns could be modified in order to change action, just as gene patterns are altered in order to change behaviour. Of course, attempts to bring about change can be concentrated on actions themselves but if actions are heavily influenced by these underlying 'being a teacher' scripts, it makes sense, as Stigler and Hiebert say, to work on the scripts themselves. This leads to questions about how scripts are acquired, which means returning to ideas set out in Chapter 2. Propositional learning in the form of books, presentations, papers and videos is one way of disseminating memes but some of its limitations were established earlier, when it was argued that a great deal is learned through doing in everyday situations. In the case of teaching, Stigler and Hiebert's work suggests that different memes have infused national cultures so that there are different, unexamined and powerful assumptions about good teaching routines and the proper structure of mathematics lessons in Germany, Japan and the USA. There is a need for pedagogic research to identify these memes in higher education, scrutinize and disseminate them. In so far as this is about raising awareness of memes and their associated action, it is an attempt to raise the metacognitive awareness of communities of practice. In so far as it is a prelude to changing what metacognition knows by modifying or replacing memes, it is memetic engineering. And just as new genes need the right environment in which to flourish, so memetic modifications will fail unless departments are fit to engage with them. An extended view of change and teaching is in Chapter 12.

Higher education needs communities of practice – departments, for example – in which good teaching memes are so much a part of what happens that they are passed on to whomsoever is implicated in those workgroups. As is implied by Figure 2.2, the explicitness of propositional knowledge is connected with the implicit learning of procedural knowings, which implies that the transmission of teaching memes can and should operate in both modes, through propositional knowledge and through the knowings of practice. Stigler and Hiebert conclude that this means that teaching improvement has to be done in context, by and with teachers. As far as higher education goes, the suggestion would be that the task is to strive for departments that are 'learning departments' because there high-quality teaching is taken for granted, while also being a matter for discussion and continuing piecemeal improvements.

All well and good, but what has this to do with maintaining and enhancing the teaching vitality of settled academic staff? This approach, working at the meso level – for example on the memes, scripts or taken for granteds in departments – does three things that traditional approaches to sustaining established teachers' pedagogic vitality cannot. First, it reaches all staff because it is concerned with important systems of which they are a part. They are affected by the dynamics of departmental attention to teaching scripts more than most of them would be by institution-level initiatives supported by workshops and seminars. Second, this community of practice approach is primarily concerned with 'what we do around here'. It consumes propositional knowledge but the emphasis is on using it to make better practice, not on acquiring propositional knowledge as a matter of intellectual curiosity. Third, it has a continuous presence, which is to say there is a continuing concern with establishing conditions under which dynamic human systems – departments – routinely make good teaching. This is not to say that macro, institution-level connections are unimportant, nor that there are no individual issues of teaching vitality. The whole point of the sort of systems thinking contained in Chapter 1 is that they are both significant: for example, the institution may be a source of energy and of constraint, while the individuals may be sources of diversity. The core of this digression on scripts and memes is the claim that departments, or sometimes programme teams, are, for most teachers in higher education, the places in which pedagogic meaning and identity happen and where memes influence actions, reproduce and are passed on, sometimes mutating in the process. As such, normal departmental practices are the key to new teachers' commitment to teaching (Chapter 3) and to the quality of established teachers' pedagogical practices. That leads to the proposition that teaching vitality is most likely to survive and flourish in good departments. Of course, like a tough grass, it can survive and even grow elsewhere. Conversely, even in fertile settings some grasses wilt and others are grazed away. Nevertheless, teaching vitality has its best chances in good departments. Institutional practices can improve the odds and individuals can fix them in their favour, if they are motivated to try (and since departments contribute so much to motivation, trying is itself often an outcome of good departments). If this sounds like common sense, remember that most actions to improve teaching vitality have been directed at individuals and institutions (Bland and Schmitz, 1990) and few at creating departments good enough to qualify as 'learning departments'.

Action points

Although most universities and colleges nowadays would say that they are signed up to the teaching-friendly practices identified by Bland and Schmitz and Wright and O'Neil, it is doubtful whether faculty really feel that institutional practices encourage a commitment to teaching. Action should be taken to find out whether that is the case. Assuming it is, remedial actions are certainly called for at the institutional level. They are likely to involve strengthening expectations and rewards and trying to raise the profile of the official messages about teaching.

Individuals can easily get ideas about teaching better and it goes without saying that this is recommended. Table 5.1 contributes ten suggestions for tinkering with teaching which are intended to help teachers, new and old, to keep reinvigorating what they do. The crucial, prior question asks how, in the first place, are academics to become disposed to commit to good pedagogy? Institutional blandishments and messages help but they are not sufficient because many established academics ignore them. The answer provided here has been that teaching vitality comes from good communities of teaching practice. Good departments sustain and enhance it just by being as they are and doing what they do.

The main action point, then, is that those responsible for teaching quality need to invoke the neglected concept of departmental effectiveness, an effective department being defined as a learning department with good teaching (research and service) memes. It follows that they must identify ways of bringing new memes to dull departments and consider how people learn to lead departments. Two strategies are recommended, each of which can be treated as research and lead to publication. Problem-based learning, principally in the form of action learning projects (Gibbs, 1995; Kember 2000), has a great deal of power but because it can be seen as additional to normal departmental work it may be sidelined. Curriculum review and development is a duty that has more potential for maintaining and increasing everyone's pedagogic vitality (Knight, 1998), and that is where I would start, regardless of whether or not my main aim was to freshen established faculty whose teaching is stale.

The advice is the same for individuals who want to improve their teaching: try to make a difference; get a project, tune a curriculum, grapple with a problem. In all cases, do it with others.

Further reading

A good starting point is the paper 'Fostering instructional vitality and motivation' by Walker and Quinn (1996). Peter Knight and Paul Trowler explore ways in which subject departments can, as a matter of course, be learning departments in Chapter 9 of *Departmental Leadership in Higher Education* (2001). David Kember's *Action Learning and Action Research* (2000) clearly develops the case for action learning projects as powerful and efficient means to teaching improvement.

6

Part-time teaching

A stance

Part-time teaching staff are important in higher education, although there
is a lot of evidence that institutions do not treat them accordingly (for
example, Gappa and Leslie, 1993; Husbands and Davies, 2000). Chitnis
and Williams (1999) estimate that they do about one-half of all undergraduate teaching in the UK and Leslie (1998) reckons they do more in
the USA. This chapter is not so much about what these academic staff do
and how indifferently they are treated as about how being a part-time
teacher can be a source of fulfilment in the workplace. I preview some
themes developed in Chapter 13, which is on career management, but I
put more emphasis on how departments can be considerate of part-time
teachers and what they can do to get the best from them. Since this is very
much the application of principles developed in Chapters 1 to 4 to the
specific case of part-time teaching staff, much of it can be applied to full-
time teaching staff on fixed-term and sessional contracts, although it may
apply less strongly.

Key points

1 The messages about career management and self-presentation in Chapter
  13 apply doubly to part-time teachers and those on fixed-term contracts.
2 Higher education may be the most casualized profession in the UK
  but others are close behind on this post-Fordist path. Turning back is
  unlikely.
3 It is easy for part-time teachers to be poorly connected members of
  teaching systems who are also casually exploited. If only for reasons of
  effectiveness, such distributed, weakly communicating activity systems
  need attention.

4 Part-time teachers can themselves strengthen their links with departments and other activity systems but it is more important for workgroups
to act.

Research

Husbands and Davies (2000: 342) wrote that much of the UK literature on
part-time faculty 'is recondite, or elusive, or unpublished, or if published
appears in ephemeral or exotic publications'. The trend, both in the UK
and in similar countries, is clear. The number of teaching and research
staff on permanent contracts has stabilized or is in decline. The number
on fixed-term contracts has increased, often sharply and especially in the
1990s (Bryson, 2001). Leslie (1998: 6) wrote of the USA that 'Part-time
and non-tenure-track faculty now constitute a majority of all who teach
in the nation's colleges and universities. The proportion of these non-
traditional faculty appears to be far greater than in other sectors of the
economy.'

Part-time teachers are overwhelmingly on fixed-term contracts. Opportunities to move on to permanent contracts are few because 'As staff on
permanent contracts retire, they are replaced (in aggregate) by staff on
casualised contracts' (Bryson, 2001: 7). Stories of abuse are common.
Beckett (2001) tells of problems with intellectual property rights and being
expected to do unpaid work, such as the setting of examination questions.
One teacher told how

> After a long wait. she was finally given a computer, but she gets no
> staff training opportunities, feels insecure in the department, and
> resents the fact that the university owns the materials she has pro-
> duced for them . . . But perhaps the worst thing of all is that every
> single contract lecturer and researcher I talked to was very anxious
> that no-one would ever find out that they had told me how they were
> treated. 'I . . . could not risk being categorised as an "untouchable"',
> said Susan. '. . . I simply would not get any more jobs'.
>
> (Beckett, 2001: 9–10)

Husbands and Davies found that pre- and post-1992 British universities
used part-timers differently. Compared to pre-1992 universities, the older
ones had five times the proportion of postgraduate students and research
staff teaching. On the other hand, newer universities had four and a half
times the proportion of 'occasionals', who made one or two teaching
contributions, and two and a half times the proportion of hourly rate
teachers. To some degree this reflected the different mix of subjects taught
in the two types of university, but other factors were at work, such as the

sheer availability of postgraduate students and contract researchers. The newer universities tended to have more professional and systematized employment practices, although Husbands and Davies mordantly observe that good administration need not necessarily signal ethical and caring practices. In fact they found that 50 per cent of institutions did not pay postgraduate students extra for examination marking, 73 per cent did not pay extra for coursework marking, 88 per cent paid nothing for having office hours and 93 per cent made no extra payment for preparation. Their conclusion? 'The "mere hireling" analogy [for being a part-time teacher] may be limited in a strict definitional sense. However, in terms of general employment conditions, there are substantial indications of its applicability in many cases. Employed in such a way, life really must be "just a horizontal chute"' (Husbands and Davies, 2000: 359).

Where Husbands and Davies differentiated part-time staff by role and contractual status, Leslie (1998) argued that the experience of being a part-time teacher varied by subject area. Those working in liberal arts departments were expected to do more time-consuming essay marking than those working in, say, vocational subjects, were more reliant on their part-time teaching for their income, felt more need to stay up-to-date in their field and tended to be more discontented than other part-time faculty. He also noted that the prestigious research universities relied less on part-time staff (23.4 per cent of faculty) than the more numerous comprehensive universities (38.6 per cent) and two-year public colleges (60.2 per cent). It goes without saying that these broad patterns of difference work out in different ways in different departments.

A number of writers are concerned by the over-representation of women among part-time and sessional staff and their under-representation at senior levels (for example, Caplan, 1994; Morley and Walsh, 1996; Malina and Maslin Prothero, 1998). Bett (1999) reported that 6 per cent of male non-clinical academic staff in the pre-1992 UK universities were part-timers and 14 per cent were on fixed term contracts. Twelve per cent of the female non-clinical academic staff were part-timers and 28 per cent were on fixed term contracts. The over-representation of women in these less favourable grades was not as obvious in the newer universities. There, 40 per cent of male faculty were on part-time contracts and 7 per cent were on fixed term contracts. For women the figures were 50 and 9 per cent respectively. In those universities the mean male salary was some £1500 p.a. greater than the women's. In the older universities the difference was closer to £4250.

The implication is that being a part-time teacher is likely to be complicated by the institutional discrimination present in many organizations. Caplan (1994) attributes much of this gender discrimination, which affects all women, not just part-time teachers, to a series of myths about women academics. To a dozen 'myths about academia' which work against women, she adds eleven about women and four about women in academia. She considers that, together with patronizing behaviour and casual sexism, they mean that women have to do more and better than men of similar academic standing. Women also have a different experience of paid work because many are managing 'double careers' – being a teacher and being a carer (of children or aged relatives). While men may also have 'double careers' it is still safe to say that it frequently costs women a lot more to be up-to-date as academic staff because they do two jobs, not one.

The impact of structural conditions such as these is mediated by people's histories, self-theories, needs and goals. One reason why they experience broadly similar working conditions in quite different ways is because they are doing part-time teaching for a variety of reasons. Some are trying to get established as academics and they, along with others, may be greatly in need of the money. Others, especially practising professionals, may welcome the money but be working out of a sense of duty to the community of professional practice (as with clinical teachers), or because of the opportunities that teaching can offer for professional learning and stimulation. Tait (2002) found that this intrinsic, self-actualizing motivation was strong in her sample of excellent associate lecturers (ALs) in the UK Open University (ALs are all part-timers). For example, she asked, 'What one thing would make you more keen to participate further in . . . [my] research [into ALs]?' The most forceful responses turned out to be variations on themes like 'making a difference to student learning', and 'to have somebody hear my ideas for improvement'. Many part-time teachers need to worry about things I called 'hygiene factors' in Chapter 4, about pay, security, hours of work and resources, but Tait's research is an important reminder that many, perhaps most, part-timers want opportunities for self-fulfilment in their teaching. Strategies for improving their teaching practices ought to be framed accordingly.

Table 6.1, which is my interpretation of the literature, summarizes some of the areas of difference between part-time and full-time faculty and something of the differences among part-time teachers by means of one column for those trying to earn a living and build a career by part-time work and another for professionals and others who teach for the psychic rewards. This is all, of course, an over-simplification.

The column on the left shows 12 aspects of being a teacher which have been derived from activity system theory (see Figure 2.1) and Chapter 4 on motivation. The suggestion is that there are differences between part-time and full-time teachers in their relationships to these factors which can accumulate to make it more likely that part-time teachers will be marginal people, ones who may be formally enrolled in a network or community but who are, in practice, poorly connected and inefficiently mobilized in its service. It suggests that they have less power and less

Table 6.1 Part-time and full-time academic staff

Some factors affecting the experience of work	Part-time, career-seeking	Part-time, working largely out of interest	Full-time, research orientation	Full-time, teaching and research mix
1 Is there free access to tools and artefacts?	Possibly only partial knowledge of and access to available technology		✓	✓
2 Is there easy access to knowledge of the formal and tacit teaching rules?	Likely to have only a working knowledge of main conventions, expectations		✓, but only if interested	✓
3 What is the division of labour? Are they treated as technicians or professionals?	Easily treated as if they were 'mere hirelings', skilled technicians		Professionals, especially when they are associated with high-status research	
4 What is the quality of community as shown by interactions with others in the department?	Interactions often limited by per-hour payment for face-to-face teaching only		✓, interactions and socialization may be limited: faculty may be socialized primarily as researchers or as teachers, or into one of several departmental sub-cultures. Interactions may then be constrained by the boundaries established by socialization	
5 Are they socialized into higher education?	Probably	Possibly not		
6 Are they inducted into the HEI?	Probably	Probably not		
7 Are they inducted into the team or department?	Probably	Possibly not		

8 Power (delivery): is there a choice of teaching methods?	Teachers in schools and HE expect to teach as they think best but some part-timers do not get a choice		✓, usually
9 Power (design): is it easy to innovate, change the givens and cross boundaries?	Not usual, I think	✓, if professional expertise is at a premium	✓, usually and if interested
10 Power (self-determination): do they have control of their own futures?	Little	Generally high but may be limited when it comes to teaching roles	As high as it gets in HE
11 Hygiene factors: what is the likelihood of their being satisfied with basic work conditions?	Low	N/A: teaching for intrinsic reasons	As high as it gets in HE
12 Motivators: what are the affordances for self-fulfilment in this teaching work?	They may concentrate on the fulfilling side of teaching but they may be frustrated by their conditions of work	High – this is why they choose to teach	As high as it gets in HE

knowledge of the activity systems in which they work, are more on the edges and, in the case of career-seekers, less likely to have opportunities for self-actualization through work. Ironically, marginal status can coexist with self-exploitation. Those who are trying to claw their way to a permanent job will feel they have to overwork to get good references. Others will often end up doing far more than they are paid for partly because they may have the time and partly because they can imagine that 'proper' academic staff's teaching practices are far more painstaking than theirs and feel that they must slave to be as scrupulous. These peripheral people are not well placed to find that this is not so and often find it hard to believe that their conscientiousness means that far from being imposters they are, in fact, often better than many of the 'real' academics.

This is most unsatisfactory for part-time, career-seeking staff and for the teaching activity system too. Table 6.1 implies that the system is disrupted because part-time staff tend not to know things that those at the heart of the community of teaching practice know. At its simplest, unless they are paid to learn about new ways of teaching, such as problem-based learning, they will not have what they need to continue to teach in the way the department wants to develop. This disruption can also be bad for the full-time staff who are committed to teaching because they have to do all of the design, innovation, maintenance and administrative work, which they often resent. If a department of ten full-time staff becomes one of six with lots of part-timers, the remaining six end up with much more backstage work to do – and remember this backstage work is seldom a source of psychic rewards for faculty. The department also loses when part-time staff, especially those who are practising professionals, are kept on the edges of the system because it does not benefit as it should by learning from the wider environment through conversations with these boundary-spanning professionals.

If part-time teachers have problems being noticed, heard and treated considerately, and if departments often fail to enrol them properly in teaching systems, then it is not surprising that there are fears that the quality of student learning might be impaired by the widespread use of part-time teachers (Chitnis and Williams, 1999). This is less about the personal and academic qualities of part-time teachers, who can be great assets, and more about what universities and departments do to prepare them for their duties, support, supervise and develop them. This and the other research reviewed in this section can be taken to support the view that being a good (part-time) teacher is something of a personal achievement, while there is also a strong sense in which it is an outcome of the way a workgroup, such as a department, has come to operate – of its teaching memes, values and procedures. These social practices affect all they touch but, as people who may be professionally vulnerable, they can affect part-timers particularly hard.

Informed practices

Chapter 13 distinguishes between extrinsic career management (position-ing oneself to have the best chance of running up the promotion ladder) and intrinsic career management (maximizing the opportunities for self-fulfilment in the workplace). Ali and Graham (2000) give a lot of advice on the extrinsic business of presenting oneself to best advantage, whether the aim is to get a permanent academic post or a job outside higher education. It is reminiscent of books such as *What Color Is Your Parachute?* (Bolles, 1997), encouraging individuals to think about their ideal job, identify what employers would expect from people applying for it, reflect on one's own profile, build good networks in the preferred area, adopt intelligent job search strategies, craft a good presentation of skills, dis-positions and achievements so as to lay a good claim to jobs of that sort, brush up on interview craft and so on. Chapter 13 covers this more thoroughly.

Notice that this sort of sound, accessible general advice presumes that job seekers will be mobile and flexible, that jobs are available and that structural inequalities do not work against women, racial minorities and those from low-status universities. Furthermore, no amount of good career management and self-presentational chutzpah will compensate for the oversupply of good candidates for permanent posts in almost all subject areas in the UK (Bett, 1999). Regardless of what they hope for and what they are qualified to do, many, perhaps most, part-time teachers have little prospect of a traditional academic career. Given these limits to what slick positioning and presentation can do, it is more fruitful to ask what part-timers can do to try to get the most satisfaction from teaching and what academic departments ought to be doing to support them in their efforts.

It is hardly surprising if there is a shortage of advice on the intrinsic business of getting fulfilment while feeling exploited and weakly connected to the network of teaching practice in a department or university. It is hard, perhaps impossible, to avoid the happy-clappy tone of some self-help books and a subliminal invitation to part-timers to exploit themselves for the benefit of a cheapskate institution. Furthermore, because the chances of converting a part-time teaching contract into a full-time job are slim, advice can do very little to ease the stress that many people have as a result of low pay, overwork and insecurity. So, what can be said? Box 6.1 contains 11 suggestions for getting more fulfilment as a part-time teacher. It can be read alongside Tables 4.1 and 5.1.

The suggestions in Table 4.2 for departmental actions to sustain teach-ing commitment apply here as well. The golden rule, to treat others as you would wish to be treated, should govern departmental conduct, although the chances of it applying to payment are slight. As far as pay

Box 6.1 Eleven suggestions for increasing fulfilment in part-time teaching

1 Keep the busy-work under control. Less time spent on marking may mean doing a better job (because it makes you and the student focus on the 'big picture', not on pettifogging detail). Spend less time on lecture preparation on the grounds that new teachers – some more experienced ones too – are prone to over-fill lectures with information at the expense of explaining frameworks, background assumptions and key academic practices. It takes less time to cover less more considerately. Encourage students to ask each other questions before they ask you. And so on.

2 Draw on the advice in Chapter 11 about getting good evaluations.

3 If you have to use centrally prescribed evaluation questionnaires, supplement them with your own that tell you what you are doing well and suggest things to build on.

4 It can be stimulating to work on programme and course design and review.

5 Talk with other teachers; perhaps about teaching matters, definitely about academic ones. I like to ask colleagues about the ideas that are exciting them and what others with different specialisms in the field might learn from them. Blackwell et al. (2001: 41) write favourably about teaching circles for part-time teachers, occasions for them to meet, 'to promote dialogue and scholarship about teaching, to enhance teaching practice and to provide a forum for professional development [through] . . . seminars, online discussions . . . peer observation of teaching [and] . . . open public discussion of teaching.'

6 Ask for a mentor. Chapter 3 outlines things that teaching mentors do.

7 If you have the time and inclination, you might volunteer to do some committee work. Committees are often torpefying but they keep you abreast of institutional developments, they may open up opportunities and what you learn can be helpful if trying to get a full-time job.

8 Network. Join a professional association, if you can afford to and if you can identify an unfossilized one. Otherwise, contribute to electronic lists.

9 Make the most of what you, as a part-time teacher, have that is special. In my part-time teaching career I have been able to: play to up-to-date professional experience with its imperative of coping; use the experience of being a part-time student on a shoddy course while also being a teacher; and capitalize on understanding the assessment system little better than the students I was teaching.

10 Take courses and other professional development opportunities within the HEI. It is likely that you will have to go direct to the teaching or professional development unit to find out about them. If there are course fees, press for your department to pay them.

11 Suggest easy, low-cost ways in which the department could make your working life better.

goes, heads of department should at least ask themselves how much they are exploiting part-timers' goodwill. That means first asking how many hours it takes to deliver a 20 contact-hour module properly and then working to bring payment into line with it. It should also include payment for attending quality assurance meetings, such as course and programme reviews, and for any quality enhancement work, such as planning course revisions and participating in curriculum development. Arguably, part-timers should also be paid for participating in professional development activities.

In the same spirit, departmental leaders should look out for institutional incivilities, ways in which the way the department demeans part-time teachers (and support staff and other junior academic staff). They include not giving part-time staff fair working space, library rights, computer and Internet access; not asking their opinions or informing them about changes; excluding them from teaching and staff meetings, faculty lounges, mentoring arrangements, appraisal and the appreciative acts that matter to full-time colleagues; and problems with crèches and car-parking. These incivilities are roots of discrimination that can be magnified when part-timers are women or come from unfavoured racial or religious groups. The subtle ways in which discrimination is created in systems, despite 40 years of activism and modern equity policies, hint at the complexity involved in trying to reduce it. That, though, is no reason why heads of department should not reflect on what happens and ask whether some people's experiences get skewed by the improper influence of non-relevant factors.

One of the most urgent tasks for leaders is to bring part-time teachers, along with other part-time staff, into the community of practice and particularly into the arrangements for quality enhancement and professional development. Although my stance on professional learning is that good learning happens, first and foremost, in vibrant communities of practice, when it comes to part-time staff I say the opposite and insist on the necessity of planned participation in formal staff development activities. The reason is that part-time staff are liable to be so marginalized that they can effectively lack opportunities to learn by being in an activity system. They need mentors, regular and formal appraisals of progress, professional development plans and formal learning opportunities because they are often weakly connected to the learning system that is the department or programme team.

The Open University's associate lecturers are an example of people in distributed networks. In the Open University module design is done by task forces of leading academics, with professional design help, and delivery is done by course materials which are mediated for the students by ALs. As interpreters of the texts, ALs do not have the scope to put themselves into teaching in the ways that hourly paid teachers can have elsewhere or to be designers of learning sequences. Nor do they have physical access to a teaching community, and the virtual networks of ALs teaching the same module are less like the networks in Figures 1.1 to 1.4 than like the spokes on a cartwheel. In this way Open University networks are prone to seal such inputs within little local systems, with the result that individual students gain from ALs' intrinsic motivation and expertise but the larger system, whether it is a module, an Open University faculty or the institution as a whole, is hardly enriched. In such ways the community itself can suffer from their absence and fail to benefit from what part-timers can initiate out of their identity as boundary-spanning teachers. Tait (2002) found that courses and information-giving staff development workshops provided opportunities for ALs to talk with each other and that engaging them in shared research and reflection was a powerful stimulus to professional learning.

The Open University is unusual but the general point – that the poor connections between part-time staff, departments and teams are bad for part-timers, students, teams and departments alike – holds good for HEIs in general. It is everywhere important that the radial communications between the department and its part-timers are full and effective. It is also important for all departments and institutions to tackle incivilities and make it a priority to talk with and listen to part-time staff and others liable to get marginalized. Actions such as these can improve the activity system twice over; once through better information flows, which are precursors of better system integration, and again by the affective enrichment which comes from a feeling of belonging in a network. Given the recurrent theme that professional, caring, creative work needs people whose interest is groomed by psychic rewards, this affective enhancement is in everyone's interests.

I do not want to lay responsibility for good practice in engaging with part-time staff at the door of heads of department, thereby implying that these issues get solved by capable mid-level leaders with good consciences. The connectionist metaphor is a reminder that power is more likely to be dispersed than concentrated in hero figures. That said, chairs and heads of department do have clear, formal responsibility for student learning and the well-being of those employed full-time and part-time in the department. Arrangements for helping them to learn to lead generally leave a lot to be desired (Knight and Trowler, 2001) and it is hard to suppose that any preparation they get has much to do with issues like those sketched in this chapter. Of course, actions that improve these mid-level systems cannot do anything about the oversupply of people who want to become full-time academic staff but they could do something about unthinking exploitation, indifference and discrimination, perhaps, in the process, improving the way the work feels, teachers' psychic rewards and students' learning.

Action points

Some part-time teachers may be dedicated to teaching improvement and be ready to tackle big projects. For many, though, the best self-help advice for part-time teachers extends a point made in Chapter 2: be *bricoleurs*, tinkerers, who look for opportunities to make further low-cost, achievable changes to the work as it was presented to you. Seek ways to cultivate it into forms more pleasing to you. Needless to say, that advice runs alongside all the career management and self-promotion work that you have to do to extend the range of potential choices you want to have.

Heads of department and those with responsibility for teaching staff are advised to listen to part-timers and explore ways of making the department a more considerate place for them. Table 6.1 could be used to prompt this work.

Further reading

In *The Invisible Faculty*, Gappa and Leslie (1993) reported on the experience of part-time teachers in the USA. They used their findings to advise HEIs on good employment practices and ways of making it possible for part-time faculty to contribute their best. Although there have been studies updating their survey and establishing the position in other countries, their findings and suggestions still hold up well.

Part 2

Teaching practices

The five chapters in this section are about what teachers do. They are organized around distinctions laid out in Table II.1. The implication, fundamental to this part, is that teaching is a selection of activities designed to evoke complex student learning. It encompasses instruction (face-to-face and otherwise), task setting, giving feedback and the design of courses. For some it will include the design of programmes and student learning environments as well. In Cowan's words, teaching is 'the purposeful creation of situations from which motivated learners should not be able to escape without learning or developing' (Cowan, 1998: 47). So, it includes instruction, of which face-to-face performance is a familiar example, but instruction is only a part of it. It is possible to be a superb teacher and a modest classroom performer, or to be a barnstorming lecturer and 'stuck' as a teacher.

Chapters 1 and 2 noted that learning happens, sometimes with an intention to learn, often without it. For simplicity's sake, I propose that it happens through the stimulus of direct instruction, engagement with tasks and simply being in environments of certain sorts. I also assume that intentional learning can be more or less tightly specified. On the one hand there can be well defined learning product outcomes ('scores >80% on a test of Chapter 6 on plant cell cytology'; 'explains the causes of the first industrial revolution in Britain'). On the other, there are less well defined process outcomes ('has experience of identifying problem systems in civil engineering contexts'; 'has shown stagecraft through performance in a public production'). This distinction between product and process learning outcomes is taken from Eisner's (1985) observation that much human learning can be neither specified precisely nor predicted with certainty. A complication is that while I might not have an intention to learn, others might have designed tasks or the learning environment in ways that favour certain non-intentional learning – affordances for certain sorts of learning have been designed into the course, the programme, the institutional environment. For instance, degree programmes can be designed to

Table II.1 Designing for intentional and non-intentional learning

Learning form	Learning stimulus			Educational foci	
	Instruction	Tasks	Environment	Priorities	Concerns
Intentional learning, *product* outcomes	Software packages, coaching, lecturing, distance learning materials, textbooks	Memory, note-making, most examinations, comprehension, problem-solving, well defined experiments, working to someone else's design	Seating arrangements, the organization of time, assessment requirements, workloads and resources can be varied so as to reinforce overt teaching messages and to stimulate covert ones. Hour-long classes on research methods encourage the view that research is technique. Half-day workshops don't. Heavy assessment loads reinforce surface learning approaches and teach people coping strategies. And so on . . .	1 The design of instructional sequences and tasks that reliably lead to the intended learning outcomes	A The mismatch between what we intend as instructors and designers of tasks/environments and what learners perceive and do
Intentional learning, *process* outcomes	Demonstrate-and-practise sessions: how to use a sphygmomanometer, discourse analysis procedures, web page design techniques	Discussions, group work, action learning sets, criticism, appreciation, some essay writing, creating, authentic professional performance		2 The provision of environments conducive to those processes	B Limited reach – most appropriate with well defined learning goals and when educational inputs can be imagined as tightly coupled to learning outcomes
Non-intentional learning	Empirical work can tell us about non-intentional learning in formal educational settings. Hargreaves (1983) said that high school children learn how to endure boredom. People also learn what counts as worthwhile knowledge and good reasoning. Evidence and empathic thinking can help us plan instruction, task-setting and environmental design to afford plenty of opportunities for certain sorts of connecting and learning. This is a probabilistic approach at a group level. It does not guarantee that any person will learn anything in particular, nor does it anticipate all the learning that might happen to him or her			3 The design of environments rich in affordances for learning things that are valued	C How to attract learners to take advantage of the affordances and go beyond compliance by attendance and good-enough task completion

encourage the development of a particular learning culture by means of the messages that suffuse feedback to students, the amount of assessed work required, the sorts of tasks set, the way time is organized, the level of integration or fragmentation of the curriculum, the ratio of core to elective courses available to each student cohort, the technology to hand, the quality of the teaching rooms, the pacing and management of work experiences and so on. Task design also influences learning. Consider the list of 50 assessment methods in Box 9.1. Many of those methods could be used to assess the same product outcomes – knowledge and understanding of a topic – but it is easy to see that different assessment tasks carry very different messages about what is to be learned and valued and how. Where one method encourages non-intentional learning that higher education is about information recall, another is designed to encourage the process outcome of getting to grips with problem-working (not problem-*solving*) and a third also affords opportunities for metacognitive development.

Behind all this is the assumption that higher education is in the business of promoting *complex* learning. Box II.1 illustrates this with three fairly typical lists of sorts of learning outcomes that are associated with undergraduate programmes. I find it helpful to simplify this complexity by saying that undergraduate education is in the business of promoting:

- **u**nderstanding of the subject matter;
- **s**ubject-specific and generic skills (or social practices);
- **e**fficacy beliefs and incremental self-theories that are the basis of the view that we can, by and large, make a difference to what we experience;
- **m**etacognition, the reflection that supports it and strategic thinking in general.

This USEM model of curriculum goals could be challenged by saying that higher education should concentrate on developing advanced understandings of worthwhile subject matter. But even if this rejection of metacognition, incremental self-theories and skills were accepted, it would still be important to observe that learning, teaching, assessment and curriculum experts are liable to argue that good subject matter understanding depends upon a mix of instruction, tasks and learning environments that call for exactly the sorts of qualities – self-motivation, reflection, skill at working with others, self-organization and incremental theories – that this position rejected as curriculum goals. Good understanding entails the use and development of exactly those personal and intellectual practices and dispositions that are simultaneously rejected by critics of complex goals such as those I have summarized with the USEM model. This leads me to claim that complex curriculum goals simultaneously make for good learning and for what is, in the UK, called 'employability'.

Box II.1   Complex learning outcomes associated with undergraduate programmes

- Harvey *et al.* (1997) found that employers want graduates with knowledge, intellect, willingness to learn, self-management skills, communication skills, team-working and interpersonal skills.
- Alverno College, Milwaukee, values eight 'general outcomes': communication, analysis, problem-solving, valuing in decision-making, social interaction, global perspectives, effective citizenship, aesthetic responsiveness (Mentkowski *et al.*, 2000).
- Research reported by Yorke (1999) found that small enterprises especially valued skill at oral communication, handling one's own work load, team-working, managing others, getting to the heart of problems, critical analysis, summarizing and group problem-solving. Valued attributes (part of the *plus* in our skills *plus* model) included being able to work under pressure, commitment, working varied hours, dependability, imagination/creativity, getting on with people and willingness to learn.

Other critics of this position that undergraduate programmes should have complex goals, such as those described by the USEM model, argue that praiseworthy though the goals are, higher education is not able to make a difference. For example, Atkins (1999) has used this line in an attack on the idea that skills are real and that higher education should teach them. It is quite important to be clear about what the implications are. If the claim is that qualities and dispositions cannot be changed by the time people have reached 18, then it is based on an error of fact (see, for instance, Perry, 1997). If it is that higher education cannot teach them, then the situation is more complicated. Direct instruction is not the way to go and it is equally certain that there can be no guarantee that any individual *will* become metacognitively sharp, adept at seeing possibilities for acting efficaciously and skilled in a variety of social practices. Yet it is clear that higher education affects groups of students' subject matter understanding and can influence more complex and subtle achievements as well (for example, Pascarella and Terenzini, 1991; Astin, 1997; Mentkowski and associates, 2000). Interestingly, these substantial US studies argue that students in certain higher education environments – small liberal arts colleges, for example – are more likely to show evidence of such complex and subtle learning than ones in different higher education settings – part-time students in large metropolitan universities. Instruction, understood as direct teaching, may contribute to differences but it is the whole learning environment that makes a difference. Nearly 20 years ago Entwistle and Ramsden (1983) pointed in a similar direction by providing evidence of the importance of the subject department as a factor influencing what students learned and how.

These five chapters consider some implications of the view of learning and its goals outlined here and in Chapters 1 and 2. Chapter 7 is about instruction. Chapters 8 and 9 are about learning tasks and the feedback that arises from them. Together they cover much of what is conventionally known as teaching. Chapter 10 draws these themes together in an introduction to course design. Chapter 11, which is about getting good evaluations, is effectively an extended summary of Chapters 7 to 10 and, to a lesser extent, of Chapters 1 to 6 as well.

7

Instruction

A stance

Being a teacher almost always involves being an instructor, which usually means being a lecturer, which often means presenting students with lots of information. Students need information, but they also need to understand it – to assimilate it to their existing webs of meaning or to accommodate their webs to it. Presentations can be admirable ways of supporting understanding, although it is doubtful whether they are a very good way to communicate large amounts of information. Now that information and communication technology (ICT) is commonplace, it might be said that face-to-face presentation, whatever its purpose, has become obsolete and that being a teacher should now mean being an on-line instructor. I support the idea behind this – that good teaching involves the design of varied learning environments full of affordances for stimulating engagements – but not the claim that modern teaching, learning and assessment should normally be done on-line. We must keep face-to-face learning. That understood, on-line and face-to-face teachers are still in the business of supporting student understanding through sound instructional practices, good task setting and creating plenty of feedback for learners. This chapter contains research findings about instructional practices that students value and/or which correlate with good learning outcomes, with some consideration of on-line instruction. The next two chapters concentrate on task setting and feedback.

Key points

1 Teaching, described in Table II.1 as a combination of instruction, task setting and creating feedback, can be further analysed into a pre-active, interactive and post-active practices.

2 North American students say they appreciate instructors who are personable and technically skilled.

3 Although there are long lists of what skilled teachers do, three themes recur: they make the material clear, they do it with enthusiasm and they involve students, creating some rapport with them.

4 It is easy to put a course on-line in the sense of putting notes, handouts and handbooks on the web and then encouraging students to be autonomous (a.k.a. to get on with it).

5 Good practice in on-line tuition combines the opportunities that ICT affords with pedagogically sound course development.

6 It would be educationally regrettable if on-line tuition destroyed real communities of practice, people connecting in real time in real places.

Research

One communal tie that does bind the *Heeding New Voices* interviewees [newcomers to the academic professions in the USA] is their enjoyment of teaching and students . . . Many reported that they 'love to teach' and that they particularly enjoy 'working with young people, who keep you young,' the personal contact with students, the 'cognitive stimulation' of designing courses and classes, and the potential for influence on others. Said one, 'I love having an impact on students.'

(Rice *et al.*, 2000, 14)

Following Table II.1, I take teaching to be all the actions done with the intention of evoking student learning of certain sorts. I think that the quotation from *Heeding New Voices* points in this direction. So, task setting, for example, is teaching, even if a task is open-ended and we cannot be precise about the sort of learning that will emerge. I do not count it as teaching if students are more or less left to their own devices, although I do count it if we make learning contracts with students so that they independently work on topics of their choice, using methods they prefer in the shared hope that learning of certain sorts will follow.

Complementing the distinctions shown in Table II.1 are distinctions between pre-active, interactive and post-active teaching practices. Table 7.1 illustrates them, although it and Table II.1 run the risk of making the divisions between the faces and phases of teaching look sharper than they are. They are presented as convenient analytical categories to apply to the turbulent dynamics of student, teacher and environment interactions. The distinctions in Table 7.1 echo those between presage, process and product factors in teaching and learning (Prosser and Trigwell, 1998). That triplet indicates that teachers (and learners) come to intentional learning situations (the process) with the presage of background beliefs and experiences

Table 7.1 Practices in three phases of teaching

	Pre-active	Interactive	Post-active
Instruction	Course (and website) design. Planning presentations, workshops, fieldwork, on-line engagements, demonstrations, groupwork etc. Writing the course handbook (course syllabus) and other teaching handouts	Doing demonstrations, seminars and presentations etc. (face-to-face and on-line). Leading fieldwork etc. Facilitating other student activities, e-moderating. Monitoring student performance and acting accordingly. Counselling individual students	Being available for consultation by students, face-to-face or on-line. Revising one's stock of 'lessons in memory' and 'tasks in memory' for future reference. Evaluating the instruction and tasks and then revising plans for next year's version of the course
Tasks	Task design. Writing task briefings and associated materials. Making any necessary arrangements	Setting, explaining and illustrating tasks. Drawing assessment indicators to students' attention and trying to be sure they understand them	
Assessment	Writing an assessment plan. Writing tests. Producing specifications and grading indicators for all assessment items	Advising students on demand. If need be, fine-tuning tasks. Monitoring student progress, formally or otherwise. As far as possible, ensuring formative feedback is created	Getting feedback to students. Reappraising what teacher and students will be doing in the next sessions. Revising own stock of 'assessments in memory'

(about what counts as learning or teaching, for example, or an emotional disposition towards undergraduate teaching). The products for teachers may be those intended (that learners better understand a topic, for example), by-products (that a teacher has a better idea of how to handle this topic in future, or the feeling of a job well done) and unintentional ones (a teacher's judgement that these students are dumb and lazy, or a distaste for undergraduate teaching). Regardless of the distinctions that researchers use to help themselves to understand what teaching and learning involve, it should be understood that they are exploring a dynamic and interactive set of communications, so that post-active thinking affects subsequent pre-active work and presage variables affect the sorts of products a teacher might anticipate because they direct his or her planning into grooves that lead to those sorts of outcomes. This recalls the connectionist insights set out in Chapter 1, in the process reminding us that sets of connections can be resistant to change. As far as teaching improvement goes, the implication is that teachers' beliefs, emotions and practices, as well as their substantive knowledge, need attention, and not just at the interactive stage, because their pre-active and post-active thinking and doing are as much a part of teaching as face-to-face instruction. This casts instructional, educational and staff development as a complex business of helping those who want to become better teachers to align their beliefs, feelings and cognitions with the distinctive concerns of the three phases of teaching (Table 7.1) and the three stimuli to learning (Table II.1).

A further complication is that despite considerable interest in what Boyer (1990) called the scholarship of teaching (Kreber, 2001), there is little agreement in the research community about what teaching is. There are hints of this in the way that I have defined teaching (intentional action to produce student learning) indirectly, in terms of what should come from it. A consequence is that such research evidence as there is about higher education pedagogies does not provide neat conclusions about good teaching in higher education. Although research into schoolteaching cannot escape this definitional fog, as is so often the case it has considerable power to help us think well about what we do in higher education. For example, Bennett and colleagues (1984) treated teaching as the management of classroom task processes and argued that for good learning to take place:

1 Teachers should have well considered learning intentions for the teaching session. Ideally, learning intentions should be suitably matched to the achievements of the different learners in the class.
2 Tasks should be devised to express learning intentions in forms that should fruitfully engage the learners.
3 The tasks – perhaps the learning intentions as well – should be presented so that there is no mismatch between what the learners believe they should do and what the teacher intended they should do.

4 The learners should do the intended task. This may sound obvious but sometimes learners go off task, plagiarize or find other ways of 'faking good'.

5 Learning is assessed so that: (a) teachers get information that can inform what they do next, or what they do next year; (b) learners get feedback to help them improve their thinking and working on tasks of this sort.

6 Teachers form learning intentions for the next teaching session (and, by implication, for the next time they run this course) that are influenced by the teaching sequence that has just been completed.

Stigler and Hiebert's (1999) research, summarized in Chapter 5, showed that improving teaching is more about memetic engineering, improving the fitness for purpose of teaching scripts, than about improving the range of teaching techniques. This squares with the approach taken by one of the most successful attempts to improve adolescents' classroom learning (in this case in science), which put great emphasis on the principled orchestration of teaching techniques and concerns (Adey and Shayer, 1994: esp. 76). Yet those who try to improve teaching have often concentrated upon improving techniques and left alone the teaching sequences and memes that shape them. In much the same way they have also paid little attention to the design of learning environments, despite research indicating that children's learning is a complex outcome of a variety of factors, of which the quality of the experienced learning environment is an important one (Filer and Pollard, 2000).

School-based research shows that teaching is more than instruction and that good instruction is more than a haphazard collection of teaching techniques. The best higher education research finds similar complexity. For Biggs (1999a), good teaching in higher education centres on the presence of teaching/learning activities that encourage 'deep' approaches to learning. 'Low-level' activities such as memorizing, identification, sentence comprehension, paraphrasing, enumerating and describing are necessary but they cannot be sufficient in themselves. In addition, learners need to be involved in intellectual activities such as relating, arguing, explaining; in applying understanding to near problems and far problems; in relating specifics to principles; in hypothesizing; and in reflecting. His list resembles the list of 'epistemic games' that another psychologist, Ohlsson (1996), saw as central to the business of creating understandings, which is what 'deep' approaches to learning are all about. This view that good pedagogy is bound up with activities that encourage 'deep', meaning-making approaches and downplay 'surface' approaches, where the intention is to cram and cope, leads to two other claims. The first concerns motivation. Echoing Chapter 4, it breaks decisively with the naive view that motivation is something, like monosodium glutamate, to be added to 'spice up' teaching. A better simile would be that it comes from the very way that teaching happens, rather in the way flavour comes from the whole process of cooking the food. It is a position that

> teachers might worry less about motivating students, and more about teaching better. When they teach in such a way that students build up a good knowledge base, achieve success in solving problems that are significant, and build up a feeling of 'ownership' over their learning, motivation follows good learning as night follows day.
>
> (Biggs, 1999a: 61)

There are clear parallels between this view of learners' motivation and the account of teacher motivation set out in Chapter 4.

The second claim draws attention to learning climate. Biggs argues that one based on putting the fear of God into students – a blame-the-student model – tends to produce anxiety, cynicism and a stressed feeling about time. This is not helpful for learning, which means it is a sign of poor to indifferent teaching. Biggs writes that the climate in which good teaching happens 'assumes that students do their best work when given freedom and space to use their own judgement' (Biggs, 1999a: 62).

Turning to instruction: there are thousands of studies of student evaluations of teaching which consistently show that instruction is itself a multi-dimensional activity. Box 7.1 lists 35 dimensions identified by Abrami *et al.* (1997: 358–64). They report that these dimensions can be collapsed into four factors, of which two, 'the instructor viewed in the instructional role' and 'the instructor viewed as a person' (p. 355), explain most of the variation in student evaluations of teaching quality. It may seem banal to say that teaching effectiveness is down to skill as an instructor and personal qualities but I do think it worth saying clearly that the way someone interacts with students – the sort of person they appear to be – matters as much as technical competence. That is something to return to in Chapter 11.

The list in Box 7.1 is helpful in drawing attention to the complexity of teaching but it should not be taken too seriously because: (a) some of the categories are open to quite divergent interpretations (their meanings are not fixed); (b) such lists depend on evaluations of conventional North American lecture-and-test courses; and (c) things which please students might not correlate too closely with their learning.

Murray (1997) reports a well designed five-year study with Canadian psychology undergraduates that addresses this third point: although we know much about student satisfaction with instruction, we know much less about the connections between instructional behaviours and student learning outcomes. Observers used the 100-item Teacher Behaviors Inventory to profile 36 instructors' low inference teaching behaviours – behaviours that can be readily and reliably identified. Twelve teaching dimensions were identified from these 100 behaviours. They

Box 7.1 Thirty-five elements of teaching

1 Ability to motivate students to greater effort.
2 Amount and quality of interaction and discussion ('modeled, encouraged and achieved interactive classes': p. 360).
3 Assessment of student learning (appropriateness of tests, fairness and consistency in grading).
4 Availability (outside the classroom).
5 Clarity of instruction ('clear, concise, understandable and accurate instruction': p. 358).
6 Clarity of instructional objectives (communicated performance criteria and assignment/test deadlines).
7 Concern for general knowledge and cultural attainment.
8 Concern for high-level cognitive outcomes ('the extent to which the instructor is promoting ... outcomes such as writing skills, reasoning, meta-cognition, problem solving, etc.': p. 360).
9 Concern for students (concerned and helpful about student difficulties).
10 Degree of stimulation of interest in the course.
11 Dramatic delivery.
12 Enthusiasm for students ('enthusiasm, interest or liking for students as persons': p. 359).
13 Enthusiasm for subject.
14 Enthusiasm for teaching.
15 Feedback (frequency, whether positive or negative, effect on students).
16 Friendly classroom climate.
17 General (something of a 'left-overs' category).
18 Instructor's personal appearance, health, attire (indicators include 'poor posture', 'wore wrinkled clothes', 'very pleasing appearance': p. 362).
19 Instructor's personality characteristics and peculiarities.
20 Instructor's respect for others.
21 Management style.
22 Overall course evaluation (how good/enjoyable was it for you?).
23 Overall instructor evaluation (how good?).
24 Quality of monitoring of student learning (including subsequent matching of work to students).
25 Quality of supervision and disciplinary actions.
26 Quality of vocal delivery.
27 Relevance of instruction.
28 Teacher choice of prescribed learning materials (are prescribed materials and assignments appropriate?).
29 Teacher knowledge of domain ('did not need notes': p. 361).
30 Teacher knowledge of teaching and students.
31 Teacher research productivity and reputation.
32 Teacher selection of supplementary learning materials (appropriate?).
33 Teacher skill at answering questions (includes encouraging students to ask questions).
34 Teacher tolerance of diversity ('the extent to which the instructor modeled, encouraged and achieved tolerance for a diversity of opinion, ideas and viewpoints': p. 364).
35 Teaching preparation and organization (pre-active, not interactive).

After Abrami et al. (1997).

tended to correlate higher with student ratings of the course and instructor (mean $r = .37$) than with measures of student learning (mean $r = .26$) or student motivation (mean $r = .20$) ... the factors that best predicted student achievement ... showed generally weak and non-significant correlations with student ratings of instructor and course. None of the 12 teaching behavior factors correlated significantly with all 6 outcome measures.

(Murray, 1997: 184–5)

There are two important points there: the teaching behaviours that are most strongly associated with student learning are not the ones they like the most; teaching behaviours are not at all neatly related to student learning outcomes. Focusing on the correlates of good student learning (as measured by classroom tests), Murray concluded that the research evidence consistently identifies three general qualities that mark out good instruction (Murray calls it 'teaching'): enthusiasm and expressiveness, clarity of explanation, rapport and interaction. Again, good instruction is represented as a personal and technical achievement, the outcome of qualities such as enthusiasm and rapport combined with clear exposition of the material. Commenting on similar research findings, McKeachie (1997) suggested that the things students value in their ratings of instructor effectiveness could be organized under headings provided by the big five dimensions of personality research: extraversion (teacher enthusiasm), conscientiousness (organization), agreeableness (rapport), openness to experience (breadth of coverage) and emotional stability (teacher personality). So, does this come close to implying that instructional effectiveness is about who you are, not what you know about the subject and teaching it? Not quite, because even if enthusiasm and expressiveness account for 13.7 per cent of the variance in Murray's students' learning outcomes that is not the same as saying that it accounts for 13.7 per cent of their learning. Undergraduate students usually do well and most of their instructors can be presumed to be competent, at least in the lecture-and-test style. Teacher enthusiasm helps to explain the *variation* in performance around this high mean level of achievement. Enthusiasm may enhance learning but it is no substitute for competence in the other dimensions of teaching which are necessary for learning.

On the basis of this I suggest that good teaching can be said to comprise five 'moments':

1 Being and doing. At its simplest, being a good teacher means doing the things that research studies, such as Abrami and colleagues' (1997) and Murray's (1997), associate with student learning *and* displaying the human or personal qualities that they find attractive.

2 Using good instructional scripts. The Stigler and Heibert (1999) research introduces a second form, the memes that chain together individual teaching practices.

3 Planning appropriate learning–teaching sequences. This is about orchestrating instruction, tasks and assessment across the pre-active, interactive and post-active phases.
4 Course design. This is about making decisions about sequences of teaching so that the broad learning intentions for the whole module have the best chances of emerging.
5 Learning architectures. The design of environments with affordances for simple and complex learning to happen over the three or four years of a programme in all of the ways identified in Table II.1. This is mainly a matter of programme design, which, along with course design, is explored in Chapter 10.

Yet even with respect to the first moment, it is striking how limited the direct contribution of research is. In the case of the three most commonly reported factors, enthusiasm, clarity and rapport, research has identified qualities that are contingent and ambiguous. While it is quite easy to see how to advise teachers who are very short of these qualities, it is another matter to see how to help people whose teaching is moderately clear how to be hyper-clear when dealing with the complex subject matter that is the concern of higher education. It might be that students who get poor grades and say the teaching was not clear are simply doing tough classes for which they might not have been well enough prepared. For example, I recently enrolled in a statistics course and found the teaching clear enough, although I recognized that I would have been in difficulty if I had not already got a serviceable background in statistics. It reminded me that clarity is not something that teachers have but something that emerges from the connections between what students know and do, what the teacher does and what the teacher intends to do. So, if instruction is essentially a practical and fluid activity in complex webs of connection and if, regardless of the prepositional knowledge teachers need and the preparation they do, good instruction is expressed in action and often intuitively (Atkinson and Claxton, 2000), then questions should be asked about the value of pedagogic research intended to produce generalizations about good practice. More than in previous chapters, the implications for practice that follow should be read as things to think about, and not taken as Viagra for flaccid pedagogies.

Informed practices

Two areas of practice are explored here: doing presentations (lecturing) and the instructional uses of ICT. Facilitating learning is covered in the next chapter, which should be read with Chapter 9, which is on feedback.

Books such as those by Nilson (1998) and Fry *et al.* (1999) go into more detail and cover other teaching techniques as well.

Presentations (lectures)

> The formal lecture is a refuge for the faint-hearted, both lecturer and students. It keeps channels of communication closed, freezes hierarchy between lecturer and students and removes any responsibility on the student to respond ... students remain as voyeurs; the lecture remains a comfort zone ... the students' unsettling is held at a distance.
>
> (Barnett, 2000: 159)

If lectures are being used as a way of getting learners to write out a text-book in 1500 word instalments, then all the common criticisms hold true: they can be boring; other methods of conveying information – notably books and the web – are more convenient, flexible and effective; the one-hour format defies everything we know about human attention rhythms; and students only remember slivers of what was said. And that assumes that lecturers are competent, although it is known that new lecturers are prone to try to cram too much information into their teaching, some graduate teaching assistants are not easily understood when teaching in their second language and in some disciplines, such as the natural sciences, it is less usual to use techniques that contribute to student learning, such as making the lecture room a site of interaction (Murray and Renaud, 1995).

Technique can be improved. Take clear speaking, for example. It is difficult to do much if the teacher's accent is hard to penetrate but easier when diction is the problem. Speakers can benefit from learning to relax the body and breathe with a soft belly so that breath is not squelched out of the top of the lungs through a tight throat and a hard jaw. Upright posture, which is nothing like the ramrod stance of the parade ground, is important so that lungs and diaphragm can work easily in a balanced body. Filling a large room with voice is quite easy when the breath is easy. On the other hand, those who do not breathe from the belly are likely to try to force the volume and almost shout, which is bad for the quality of delivery (shouting is not pleasant to hear) and bad for the throat. The Alexander Technique, which is widely learned by actors, singers and other performers, attends to the bad habits we have developed in holding and moving our bodies. It arose out of F. M. Alexander's attempts to rectify his own voice problems. Brennan (1992) provides a clear review of the technique. Carrington and Carey (1992) add detail, although there is consensus that reading about the Alexander Technique is no substitute for lessons with a qualified practitioner. Of course, in a well planned presentation that is not stuffed with information, words do not have to be gabbled to fit and there is time to speak clearly, regardless of whether any special voice work has been done or not. Pace, pitch and volume should be deliberately

varied while watching the audience carefully. This implies that the presenter is improvising around key points, which may be projected on-screen
and which are probably in handouts that students have (and handouts are
the proper place for a lot of the detail that tends to clutter lectures). There
is no need, then, to stand at a lectern and in many rooms the presenter
can then get much closer to the students, in more than one sense, than
traditional lecturers do.

People who hold and use themselves easily are rated more highly than
those whose body language bespeaks torpor or fear. It is often written that
93 per cent of communication is non-verbal and, although I distrust the
figure, I accept that it points to something important. Research reviewed
in the previous section established that students are sensitive to the teacher's
enthusiasm, something that is carried by gesture, inflection, eye contact,
posture and appearance, as well as by the words we speak. An implication
is that if we wish to be rated as a good presenter, then we would do well
to work on voice, posture and body language in general. Echoing point 18
in the teaching dimensions shown in Box 7.1, Dr Kate Nobes, a London
research scientist and lecturer, said:

> I wear smart but comfortable trousers and tops . . . Most senior scient-
> ists are male and that does influence how I dress – if I wore anything
> too glamorous, I know they'd view it as frivolous. I don't do the power
> dressing thing but . . . if the audience is male and academic I tie my
> hair back and wear black. I feel if I look like that my science will be
> taken more seriously . . . Perhaps you can't be a good scientist and
> show your belly button.
>
> (*The Guardian*, 22 January 2001)

I want to juxtapose this emphasis on deliberateness and technique with
Palmer's assertion that 'Good teaching cannot be reduced to technique;
good teaching comes from the identity and integrity of the teacher' (Palmer,
1998: 10), which leads to the position that technically 'bad' teaching could
be good if done with integrity and passion. This insistence that teaching,
particularly presenting, is an emotional practice usefully connects thinking about what counts as good teaching with what we know about faculty
motivation to teach, as reviewed in Chapter 4. People teach for the emotional rewards and that invigorates the instructional practices of those who
are reckoned to teach well. There is another side to this, though.

> Asking faculty to modify their teaching style is like asking them to
> change their personality. [So], *The choice of a teaching method is in part
> dictated by one's personality* [and] *people are more likely to adopt alternative
> teaching methods if they provide a comfortable match to their personal
> dispositions.*
>
> (Grasha, 1996: 61, emphasis in the original)

This seems to me to be consistent with research, such as Prosser and Trigwell's (1999), which has linked instructors' teaching practices with their beliefs about what is to count as good teaching and learning. They describe three main views of teaching. The first is the limited view that teaching is about imparting the concepts specified in the syllabus or, more ambitiously, the teachers' knowledge. This is associated with transmission teaching. They see the second set of ideas as intermediate conceptions. These views go with more considerate pedagogies as teachers look for ways to help students to master syllabus concepts or understand the knowledge that they, the teachers, have. In the third set, 'complete conceptions' of teaching, the job involves helping students to develop understandings and change existing ones. It follows that there is little point introducing teachers to new techniques if they clash with teachers' beliefs about the nature and purposes of teaching and learning. For a tutor to make a place in a course for student self-assessment, mini-projects or writing evidence-informed opinion pieces in the style of editorials in *New Scientist, The Times* or *Nursing Times*, he or she needs first to know what the pay-offs are likely to be and have views of teaching and learning that can recognize that meaning-making pieces of work like these are important, arguably more important that some of the activities they would be displacing. Evidently, this is about fundamental change because our often-implicit views of what counts as knowledge (or understanding), how it is to be got (or created) and how teachers are to instill it (or help learners construct it) are very much a part of our professional *and* personal identities. The maxim of no curriculum change without teacher change (Stenhouse, 1975) is an important reminder that instructional improvement involves a lot more than giving teachers a pedagogical toolkit. That said, Chapter 4 referred to situations where people have to take actions they would not have chosen but, even though extrinsic motivation lay behind what they did, clear explanations of the thinking behind the mandates and experience of following them produced acceptance. In such ways, beliefs can sometimes be changed by getting people to change their practices and providing a cogent rationale. The underlying point is that in so far as teaching well is about being as well as about technique, becoming a better teacher is, to some extent, about identity work.

Nevertheless, presentations can be improved by engaging with guidelines such as those in Box 7.2. They should be understood in the context of a consensus that people's attention falls off sharply after 10, 12, 15 or 18 minutes (authorities differ). An implication is that a mix of activities is used to revive attention and so presentations get planned in 10, 12, 15 or 18 minute segments.

Box 7.2 Presentation hints

Presentations are not so much for information giving as providing:
- A conceptual framework for a topic.
- An indication of how key areas of information fit into that framework.
- An indication of the strengths and problems with the framework.
- A preview of implications of a framework.
- A model of the ways in which people in a discipline develop understandings, test and apply them.

Planning questions include:
- Why is this topic, skill etc. important?
- How can this material be connected with issues of significance, especially 'real world', live ones?
- How does this connect to what went before/will come afterwards?
- What concepts or ideas make sense of this topic?
- What illustrates these concepts, procedures etc.?
- What are the strengths, uses, limits and weaknesses of these concepts, skills etc.?

In the presentation
- Preview the argument (which does not mean alluding to the areas you will address).
- Use active learning techniques.
- Make time to use Classroom Assessment Techniques (Angelo and Cross, 1993). For example: (a) provide a part-completed summary chart or figure for students to complete; (b) set a 'one-minute paper' (students have to write 50-word summaries of the presentation).
- Set questions for the students to talk about with their neighbours.
- Provide two-minute 'stand up, stretch and breathe' sessions.
- Include time for students to review their notes (or perhaps to review each other's notes).

Presentational style:
- Do not rush or try to cover too much information.
- Concentrate on the 'big picture'.
- Do repeat yourself but vary your words.
- Use examples, similes and metaphors.
- Make connections with 'real life', if possible.
- When using OHTs, assume students can read. A presentation based on OHTs can be as dull as one in which the lecturer just reads notes. I think that the worst lecture I have attended was a monologue based on about 20 slides and 350 bullet points. A *Powerpoint* presentation in Mandarin looked *much* worse but I can't be sure because I couldn't understand any of it.
- Limit the number of points on each OHT – a *guide* which I seldom stick to is six slides, each with six points. Handouts can carry the detail, slides show the ideas.

Towards the end of the presentation:
- Summarize and connect. For example, ask: How does this contribute to the whole? What are some implications? What does this suggest about the nature of the subject? How does this connect with what comes next?
- Use Classroom Assessment Techniques.

Afterwards:
- There is some evidence that if you give students a test right after the presentation their factual and conceptual recall after eight weeks will be double what it would have been without any test (Nilson, 1998: 77).
- Make notes to yourself about how you can do it differently next time.

ICT and good instruction

Has face-to-face instruction a future when it looks as if ICT-based methods can deliver on-demand instruction cheaply to large audiences anywhere in the world? Traditional lectures can be replaced by on-line notes or slick multimedia sequences that edit together notes, video-clips, sound and graphics, and which provide plenty of hyperlinks to allow students to pursue ideas in greater depth. Group and seminar work can be replaced by a variety of communication strategies: messages can be posted on a bulletin board; 'chat rooms' and webcam-enabled conferencing, perhaps via satellite, support synchronous electronic group conversations; threaded discussion software allows people to contribute at times that are convenient to them (asynchronously) to discussions that may run for weeks; and on-line talk can support learning better than exchanges in seminars because it can be saved, printed and used as a resource for reflection (Lea, 2001). Software can take care of course administration, including on-line evaluation of instruction, classroom tests can be done on-line and assignments can be submitted electronically. Specialized programmes with skill-and-drill sequences designed to build student mastery of content and unproblematic routines can support instruction in well defined areas, such as language learning or anatomy. Many investigative assignments are made easier thanks to bibliographical databases and websites in general, although badly set assignments invite plagiarism or recourse to on-line essay-writing services.

It seems that even with the limited technologies now in use (this is written at a time when broadband communications are more of a vision than a reality and when the bluetooth technology, intended to allow wire-less communication between 'intelligent' devices, is just coming to market), electronic media can do what face-to-face instruction does but more cheaply and flexibly. Professor Michael Vitale, Dean of the Australian Graduate School of Management, is less sure: 'There is no question that technology is and will be increasingly used to enhance learning but it won't replace face-to-face learning' (Vitale, 2001: 9). He said that there are vexatious problems with compatibility, access and convenience which tarnish the sheen of ICT-based learning, adding that the hoped-for economies are elusive: 'developing technology can be 10 times costlier than developing something to be used by an instructor'. He concluded that 'It isn't as motivating or engaging as interacting with other people. We're social animals. We like to do things in groups.'

This last point is worth developing because the cost of substituting e-contact for real contact may be even greater than Vitale suggests. There may also be a teaching cost because instructors are less able to be flexible and adjust their teaching to what they sense as they watch students' eyes and body language. For Eisner (1985), an expert on schooling, teaching needs to be very much like good jazz improvisation, involving real-time reactions to the music of classroom dynamics. Teaching is necessarily fluid and, as such, beyond pre-specification. This does not mean that it has to be equated with free-form jam sessions. Duke Ellington's orchestras played to scores that had space for improvisation and feeling. Gage's (1978) book captures something of this with its title: *The Scientific Basis of the Art of Teaching*. The fear is that on-line instruction loses something important when it loses that improvisational, reactive quality.

There may be another subtle cost, especially where whole degree programmes are done on-line. Recall the claims in Chapter 2 that much learning happens in communities of practice and that face-to-face connections are more complex than on-line ones, that they are more subtle and dynamic, less bounded by the confines of being on-line. Brown and Duguid (2000), proponents of new technologies for learning, say that things get lost when virtual 'communities' replace real ones, arguing that students in virtual universities lose the 'unplanned' or unpredictable learning that comes from having smart people gathered together for broadly similar purposes. (I put 'unplanned' in quotation marks because clever education designers put affordances into environments so that certain types of learning are likely to happen.) The things that get lost may be exactly those 'soft skills' and complex qualities that are so valued by employers and educators alike. In other words, when comparing a degree from a virtual university and a face-to-face one, we might observe a non-equivalence in equivalent qualifications. There are pointers to this conclusion in Astin's (1997) large-scale studies of US students, which showed that part-time students who commute to metropolitan universities got less rich educational experiences than full-timers in small liberal arts colleges. There were subtle differences in learning outcomes between the two groups. This can be extended into a claim that whatever the formal equivalence of two certification routes, when they represent two very different ways of teaching and learning they will lead to noticeable differences in learning outcomes, even if they are equivalent in terms of those outcomes recognized by the award. It is the outcomes that the award does not recognize that differ and the suggestion is that those outcomes may, in practice, matter a lot more than those that can be readily assessed and so get warranted by the award.

So what does informed ICT practice look like in the face of claims and warnings? There seems to be agreement that the technology is a vital supplement to traditional instruction, the implication being that:

1 Courses should have a web page that includes the course handbook (syllabus), files of slide shows, lecture notes, handouts and other non-copyright material, notices and the course schedule.
2 Students will be expected to use electronic media to locate and process information.
3 They will be invited to communicate electronically with each other and the tutor.
4 They may submit assignments electronically and get feedback in the same way.

There is little enthusiasm for using new technologies for 'Peking Duck' courses. (In the recipe for Peking Duck, you inflate the duck so that it cooks crisp. I was told in Hong Kong that information-cramming classes are called 'Peking Duck'.) It is easy to use the new media to puff students up with information and dispense with the costly business of providing face-to-face tuition, but doing it electronically is reckoned to be no better than traditional, much-criticized, dictation-style lectures. A good way of using ICT is to make traditional face-to-face instruction a little more considerate in ways such as the four listed above, but without abandoning other learning media, such as attending real classes. However, the preferred approach to e-learning is to do these things and then to use the technologies to sustain dialogue by connecting students into virtual communities of deliberation. There is some suggestion that this may work best with postgraduate students, particularly those in occupations related to their programme of study, because it helps to have more to deliberate about than what is in course texts alone.

Informed educational application of ICT looks less like direct instruction and more like skilled facilitation of good, active learning through interaction with others (see Palloff and Pratt, 1999, for a North American version of this theme and Salmon, 2000, for a British one). A summary of this view is a convenient way of moving from instruction, the theme of this chapter, to tasks, which is the theme of the next. It also extends the meaning of 'instruction' to accommodate the widely accepted constructionist position that learning is not about capturing information from authorities, but involves the construction of meaning from new information and the reappraisal of old information against a background of socially shared scripts and routines (Wertsch, 1998). Instruction still has a part to play in helping learners to have new information but it also has much to do in helping them to make new connections to and within their webs of understanding. This puts 'e-moderating' or 'e-facilitation' at the heart of good teaching. Salmon (2000) is not the only researcher to report that this makes good teaching very much a matter of good facilitation – prompting, summarizing, encouraging, redirecting, nudging discussion back on track and being an authority of last resort – which is something that can prove tricky for experienced face-to-face facilitators and be a real challenge to others who have a yen to transmit lots of information on-line. There is, of course, still a need for teachers' expertise, perhaps by providing pre-reading or by giving short briefings on particular points during the on-line exchanges. Where students are on professional programmes, this need may be less than is sometimes assumed and the teacher's authority may be shown by the questions she or he raises, the quality of his or her summaries and the tasks set.

A good pedagogic practice is for students to get information, whether from tutor notes, readings or guided research into tutor-set topics, and then work on it or with it. In arts, humanities and social science subjects this 'working on' is frequently a mix of discussion (analysing, criticizing, appreciating, evaluating or synthesizing new thinking and old) and application (problem-working and planning tasks, making recommendations, carrying out enquiries). These activities and other 'epistemic games' can quite easily be organized and supported by skilful on-line facilitation (by the teacher or by other students in a learning set) and there is a case for saying that this is where the new technologies are at their best, supporting higher-level learning activities in ways that are hard to do in the real-time environment of teaching timetables.

Where it is possible, teachers generally prefer to gather students together physically at the beginning of an on-line module and to have regular face-to-face seminars throughout. The electronic communication can be synchronous or asynchronous. The former is when the tutor and students are all expected to be on-line at the same time. For example, tutors may establish a chat room – an electronic discussion space – and require all students to log on to each chat session, perhaps insisting that each also contributes. Some have on-line office hours, when students know that they will get attention, and others insist that all students 'check in' during each office hour, just to provide evidence of continued course 'attendance'. With synchronous communication there can be a sense of event but, as with face-to-face seminars, it can also be a sense of jostling to be heard in a crowded event at which things are moving too fast.

Asynchronous communication is more usual. Its advantages include:

1 More people can participate. Although there is agreement on this point, there are different views about how big asynchronous groups can be. I have not seen anyone suggest more than 20, and half that seems to be the preferred size.

2 People contribute when it is convenient for them. (Tutors are advised to specify the minimum levels of contribution that all students must make – 'post at least two messages a week', for example. Those who go silent may be phoned to find out what has gone wrong.)

3 There is not the clamour to contribute that there can be with synchronous communication and which can lead to a welter of cross-cutting, brief comments.

4 On the web all are equal and people who are less extravert can be more at ease contributing than they would be face-to-face. Asynchronous communication means they are not jostling for on-line time as they could be in a synchronous session.

5 There is time for thought. Other people's messages can be thought about carefully and considered postings can be crafted. Reflection, not loudmouthing, is encouraged. When one or two people seen to dominate a conference, others, writes Salmon (2000), can fall away. Facilitators need to know this can happen and encourage the voluble to continue to engage, but less overwhelmingly.

6 'Students also reported improved contact and increased dialogue with the tutor and other module participants, a finding which is also reported elsewhere' (Lapham, 1999: 19).

On-line learning can be more time-consuming for the tutor – students too – than many face-to-face courses, largely, I suspect, because, done like this, courses are educationally better conceived and more engaging than many face-to-face ones. Teachers are committed to designing good discussion and application activities, responding to a lot of individual enquiries, communicating with the class as a whole, advising on the inevitable technical glitches and building a working community. It is not flashy web design that takes the time – and simpler is usually better because special effects slow everything down and may crash older machines – but the greater commitment to working with students as individuals and as a group. For example, there is a need to help students to get comfortable with the idea of working as a fixed-term community of enquiry, sharing, cooperating, being considerate of others' points of view and feelings, reflecting and perhaps working together in small groups. Part of this means making time for people to introduce themselves and begin to establish some identity. This can be done quite smoothly if students start the course with their own web pages already set up and then, when introducing themselves on-line, include hyperlinks to their home pages so that people can find out more if they want to. Part of it is establishing rules, which may be a mix of things that are not negotiable (minimum posting requirements, netiquette and privacy) and those that are agreed by the whole class. And part of it comes down to the teacher's skill as a facilitator, which resembles skill at face-to-face work (Brockbank and McGill, 1998). Despite similarities

between face-to-face and on-line facilitation, there are at least four important differences:

1 The teacher must understand the software and know what to do when
   the inevitable hard/software failures happen. Given the difficulty that
   even some educational development professionals have using the overhead projector properly, this is not a trivial requirement.
2 On-line work is likely to take more tutor time unless he or she organizes
   the class into small groups from the start and only facilitates groups, not
   individuals.
3 It is more demanding because electronic messages are not suffused with
   all the non-text information available in face-to-face settings.
4 Teachers have to make a way of learning work when it may be doubly
   unfamiliar to many students – it is both on-line and active.

An interesting point, though, is that while it is clear that web-based teaching does demand technical skill, personal qualities still count. Palloff and
Pratt (1999: 20) consider that 'The keys to the creation of a learning community and successful facilitation online are simple. They are as follows:
honesty, responsiveness, relevance, respect, openness, and *empowerment.*' Just as
research into effective face-to-face instruction found that it was a mix of
technique and who the teacher seemed to be, so this identifies the on-line
persona of the teacher as a key factor in successful electronic teaching.
It is ironic that what some take to be a dehumanizing technology may
actually need teachers who use it to be more empathic and considerate.

Action points

In the UK the Learning and Teaching Support Network (www.ltsn.ac.uk)
has 24 subject centres to support teachers in the application of good
instructional practices in their subjects and areas. There are also professional bodies and subject associations. Other countries are different,
although they too have organizations able to advise on teaching well,
generally and in the disciplines. I recommend contacting them and using
web searches to identify other sources of good advice about what counts as
effective instruction in your subject area. I suggest putting such advice
alongside research findings, particularly those saying that effective instructors are clear and enthusiastic and interact with their classes, and then
drawing up a simple teaching evaluation checklist to be applied to your
own teaching. I recommend doing this with the primary aim of identifying
and appreciating *what you do well.* You might ask a friend to watch you
teach with this list as a set of evaluative prompts, you might want to use
it to reflect on instruction you have just done or you might boldly ask

students to use it. Having appreciated your strengths, you might pick something you do less well and work to bring it more into line with the things you do best.

In the end-of-course evaluation ask students to name up to three things that worked well or they liked and up to three specific suggestions for making the course even better next year. I make this an in-class task and leave the room while groups get on with it. I ask for group feedback because I have found that groups filter out sour, unrepresentative ideas. Welcome the news that you do some things well and make notes about how you will incorporate some of the group's suggestions for change next year.

On-line teaching, as described above, has a lot to offer teachers, such as I was until recently, who are in traditional universities and find it difficult to do fieldwork, consult and attend off-site seminars while being committed to regular undergraduate classes. It may not reduce the hours involved but it does offer flexible scheduling. Increasing the amount of on-line teaching means making sure that there is a good blend of information-gathering, discussion and application tasks in a course, getting this good pedagogy into robust and simple electronic form, and learning to be sensitive as an e-facilitator. Teachers might lay a two-year plan to tackle these three demands; inspired heads of department might try to get a group of teachers to form a teaching circle with the intention of together raising the electronic profile of several courses at the same time. Salmon (2000: 106) provides a simple tool to help you to judge how ready you are to work on-line.

Educational developers are well placed to work with teachers wanting to electrify all or part of a course. Besides helping with the technology, this is an opportunity to engage colleagues with good ideas about learning and how to be a sensitive on-line facilitator.

Further reading

I like Grasha's (1996) practically focused work on teaching styles and Ramsden's (1992) general work on teaching in higher education. There are now quite a lot of books on electronic teaching. Good, clear ones are by Palloff and Pratt (1999) and Salmon (2000), although they cannot help much with the usually infuriating business of choosing software, using it, cursing it and learning to put up with it, nor can they be sensitive to the interplay between the technologies' affordances and discipline-specific teaching priorities.

8

Learning tasks

A stance

Wisner (1995) distinguishes between tasks, which the teacher sets, and
activities, which are what learners do. Important though the distinction
is for some analyses, I think it would complicate things too much, so I
am going to refer only to tasks. Whether they are graded by teachers
or not, tasks drive student learning. Tasks by no means always have the
sorts of effects that teachers intend because students understand them
in the light of their own learning histories and in terms of their own
perceptions of the learning environment, a point which is illustrated by
Figure 10.1.

Being a good teacher, then, is very much about being a good designer
of tasks and a sensitive facilitator of student engagement with them. This
is a view that will be extended in Chapter 10, which is all about course
design.

Key points

1 The tasks we set – what we ask students to do – are at the heart of
  their learning. If we want complex learning we need to design tasks
  accordingly.
2 Good tasks provide opportunities for fresh learning, give practice and
  foster metacognition, partly by encouraging students to think about
  transfer of learning.
3 There is a strong case for ensuring that some tasks involve groupwork.
4 Being a skilful teacher involves being a skilful facilitator.

Research

Barr and Tagg's (1995) paper arguing for a shift from a concern with teaching to the improvement of learning brought North American readers an idea that had been influential elsewhere, namely that teachers are in the business of evoking learning. Barnett, who asks about the role of the university in times of 'supercomplexity', concurs, writing that

> A pedagogy for supercomplexity . . . cannot be a matter of passing on knowledge or of acquiring skills, for such definitions reek of certainty . . . teaching for a supercomplex world has to be the generation of disjunction in the mind and in the being – in the self understanding and in the actions – of the student . . . [this] calls for a pedagogical transaction in which the student has the pedagogical space to develop her own voice.
>
> (Barnett, 2000: 160)

That challenges traditional beliefs about what counts as teaching. As was noted in Chapter 7, Prosser and Trigwell (1999) have drawn together a series of studies identifying variations in what teachers take to be teaching (and learning) and argue that these varying conceptions affect their teaching practices. Teachers who see their job as information transmission are likely not to see the point of complex, innovative, well structured and time-consuming tasks, whereas those who are open to the idea that students learn by sense making (which is in turn helped by well judged tasks) will get the most benefit from advice on task setting. Consequently, this chapter on tasks for complex learning will make little sense to teachers who see tasks as something set to make sure that students do the grunt work of learning (memorizing) the information covered in the lectures.

Researchers into schoolteaching, notably Doyle (1983) and Bennett *et al.* (1984), have recognized that the tasks teachers set dominate learning. Instruction and the environment matter and unintentional learning happens, but good teaching is, above all, about engaging students with good tasks. This implies that tasks which do not engage students are not going to lead to much learning, good or otherwise, but good learning *is* likely to follow from engagement with good quality tasks. Doyle introduced the idea of grade/performance exchange to describe a tension between teachers' goal of encouraging fresh understanding and students' preference for straightforward tasks that allow them to get good grades by sedulously using the algorithms they have been taught. Students tend to resist task ambiguity and try to get teachers to convert understanding tasks into algorithmic ones on which success will follow from making plenty of effort. If this holds true for higher education (and I think it does, especially where students 'are bringing to higher education exactly the same consumer expectations they have f r every other commercial establishment . . . they focus on convenience, quality, service and cost' (Levine and Cureton, 1998: 14)), then it warns us that students may resist ambiguous, open-ended and non-routine tasks. Yet if we want understanding and complex learning then these are exactly the sorts of tasks on which they should be engaged. For example, a course concerned to foster understanding must have tasks that call for analysis, evaluation, application etc. Furthermore, they should be feasible and matched to the learners, which is not quite the same as saying that they should be easy or straightforward.

It is useful here to introduce the notion of the 'zone of proximal development' (ZPD), a term used to describe tasks that can be done with help. Help can be provided through the way the task is structured (breaking complex tasks into steps and providing prompts and clues), and by having learners work in groups (the principle here is that together they should be able to do that which they cannot achieve alone). Much of the next section is about helping students to work in the ZPD by working with others, so it is appropriate to say a little about helping them by considerate task structuring. Laurillard and colleagues (2000) studied children learning with CD-ROMs. They 'kept finding a lack of evidence of engagement by the students, and a consistent focus on the operational aspects of the task in hand, rather than its content or meaning' (p. 6). They suggested that the software provided few affordances for the quality of thinking they wanted to stimulate, an interpretation which they explored by designing easy-to-use CD-ROMs with 'features that we hoped would act as affordances for the intended learning activities' (p. 11). As the following list of features shows, these features acted as scaffolding, guiding and supporting students to the point where they could concentrate on thinking purposefully about the subject matter. The affordances, or scaffolding, came from:

- A clear statement of the overall goal – to support generation of a task-related plan.
- Continued reminders of the goal – to support keeping to the learning plan.
- Index of sub-goals – to provide a choice of activities relevant to task.
- Multimedia resources – as alternative presentations of the material.
- Interactive activities – to provide adaptive feedback on actions, to motivate repeat actions to improve performance.
- An editable notepad – to enable students to articulate their conceptions.
- A model answer – as feedback on their conceptions, to motivate reflection on their conceptions (Laurillard *et al.*, 2000: 11).

Although their paper is about on-line learning, the conclusion that if learners are to be intellectually extended by tasks in the ZPD, then appropriate scaffolding and affordances must be provided, can be generalized to face-to-face teaching. This leads to a view of progression in learning as students go through the programme that places more emphasis on teachers taking away the scaffolding and making the affordances less obvious, than upon the rival idea, which is often associated with Bloom's taxonomy (Bloom, 1956), that students should move from simple skills and concepts to difficult ones. There are severe epistemological and practical problems with notions of progression that are rooted in the idea that concepts, skills and understandings can be arranged into general taxonomies (see Hoyles, 1990, for elaboration), so I am going to treat progression as the removal of scaffolding.

It also needs to be said that I assume that students are not bound by learning styles such as 'dependent' or 'convergent' that make them impervious to tasks which call for different approaches, such as collaboration, divergence or independence. Agreed, students do have preferred learning approaches but, in Grasha's words, 'these preferences typically are not rigid and inflexible. *They can be changed and modified depending on the classroom procedures used*' (Grasha, 1996: 171; emphasis in the original). This holds the prospect that well conceived suites of tasks can accustom learners to using approaches that are different from those they would have formerly depended upon.

Questions arise, then, about what tasks might be set and how we might know them to be of good quality. When one is thinking about types of task, the range is as great as the range of imagination. Box 8.1 lists some common ones. Cowan (1998), Nilson (1998), Fry *et al.* (1999) and Salmon (2000) have good ideas to add. An answer to the question about task quality comes from an account of what is involved in learning. It was claimed in Chapter 2 that much learning is non-intentional and arises from engaging with others, which directs attention to the design of learning, which is the subject of Chapter 10. But what about intentional learning? In Chapter 2, I distinguished between propositional or declarative knowledge and procedural or practical knowings. Ohlsson (1996), summarizing psychologists' conclusions on learning, considers that 'practical knowledge' (my 'procedural knowings') is made up of skills. He characterizes skill acquisition as the development and modification of rules of action largely in the light of feedback, which is the subject of the next chapter. Practice is very important, partly because it should produce plenty of feedback but also because practice makes performance faster, smoother and more automatic. It follows that individual teachers should set practice tasks which should be orchestrated through the programme design with the practice work done in other modules. Furthermore, Claxton (1998) argues that complex learning tends to be slow learning, something that cannot be achieved in 'quick-shot' classes. The implication is that tasks intended to promote the development of complex achievements may need to be distributed across a whole three- or four-year programme. I infer that it is hard for any individual to be good at setting tasks that make for

Box 8.1 Some learning tasks

1 Action learning sets (ALSs). These are small groups of students who together tackle problems that are significant to them. It may seem a little anomalous to include ALSs in a list of tasks but some teachers, especially at postgraduate level, will set students the task of forming ALSs to tackle issues arising out of another task, such as a small-scale research project. This requirement puts social interaction into the process, opening learning possibilities that would otherwise only have arisen if students had spontaneously created them.

2 Analysing case studies. Established practice in business studies, quite common in other vocational and near-vocational subjects.

3 Annotated bibliographies. We often want students to research a topic but have no need for them to write yet another report. Instead, ask them to submit a ten-item bibliography, explaining why each reference has been chosen. Why is it significant? How does it connect to the other nine?

4 Appreciations. An alternative to asking students to write critical commentaries, which can be needlessly destructive. Learners identify strengths, ideas of value and points to copy before suggesting practicable ways in which the target report or practice might have been stronger.

5 Case study or problem writing. Instead of being given case studies or problems to deal with, some students have to produce them and others have to do them. The producers give feedback to the students working on the cases/problems while they, in turn, rate the quality of the problems or cases, preferably formatively.

6 Completion tasks. Especially useful for checking understanding of a book, presentation, paper etc. Students complete a summary that contains blanks, or a partly finished table or figure.

7 Concept or mind-mapping (Buzan, 1995). Excellent as a group task towards the end of a course, when it acts as a revision, organizing and thinking task. Best to start with ideas or points written on Post-its (one per Post-it) and then progress to mapping the thinking on two A1 sheets taped together. The posters are then displayed for all to learn from.

8 Criteria writing. Writing criteria by which something could be graded is a tough and powerful activity. Not only does it require learners to identify what counts, it also makes them think hard about what would distinguish excellent, good, acceptable, modest and poor achievements. Make it harder by banning the use of comparatives: 'more', 'clearer', 'poorer', 'less' etc.

9 Design an investigation to . . . Students should explain why their design is fit for the set purpose (and preferable to alternatives that could be imagined). This approach is widely used in many 'production' subjects when students are told to design a product to do . . .

10 Disconfirmation activities. Tell a story or describe a situation. Ask how it may have come about or ask for predictions about the outcomes. Then tell students what the causes or consequences actually were/are. The main value is in getting learners to think more closely about the situation

or story, realizing that what happens is usually one of the possibilities that might have happened.

11 Emotional practices. This is not as much a class of task as a call for tasks that direct attention to the emotional quality of matters in hand. It is a reminder that cognition and affect twine around each other. In vocational and near-vocational subjects it directs attention to all sorts of activities that concern the quality of interpersonal relations. In humanities and social sciences it is a reminder that empathy involves understanding emotion and not just the objective facts of the matter.

12 Identifying safety hazards. A particular and important example of tasks asking students to analyse a complex situation from one point of view.

13 Individual–pair–pyramid seminars. A problem is posed or an issue is identified. Individually, students write four or five points (or four or five points for and as many against). They pair up and agree on, say, the three best. Pairs join to form fours or sixes, which then report the main points to the whole seminar group. I move this activity along quickly. Three minutes for individual work, five for pairs, four or five for larger groups and then five for a plenary. I often handle reporting back by having groups put key points on Post-its which are then all arranged on a wall for all to see and talk about.

14 In-tray exercises. Students face a bunch of authentic problems to be tackled in a limited amount of time. It is usually necessary for them to get the papers or messages into an order of priority, giving minor problems brief attention and concentrating on what they identify as major problems. A good examination format.

15 Lab reports. Well established routine task. From time to time, revisit the requirements for different sections and: (a) tell students to pay especial attention to that section in their next report; (b) grade and/or give feedback on that section alone.

16 Matching questions. One column contains the first halves of a series of statements, each one numbered. The second column contains the second halves, lettered but not in sequence. The task is to match the numbers and letters.

17 Metacognitive reflection. There is a variety of tasks that stimulate reflection, from simple injunctions to reflect, through learning logs, journals, appraisals and evaluations. The distinctive thing about metacognitive reflection is that the tasks direct attention beyond front-of-mind thinking towards less obvious questions to do with what one knows/can do, how it can be used effectively, how one learns and how improvement, which may involve some work on self-theories and beliefs, might be encouraged.

18 Mock press conferences which require students to present a position concisely and then take hostile questions about it. Both the questioners, who may be rewarded for their shrewdness, and the 'press officers' need to be well prepared.

19 Moral dilemmas. These are somewhat like case studies except that they are designed to engage students with moral issues as they try to decide what actions or strategies to recommend.

20 Multiple choice question (MCQ) writing. Students have to write, say, ten MCQs. Others answer and rate them. The teacher adds successful MCQs to a course item bank, which is put on-line to make it available to all students as a learning revision aid. (It may be necessary to control access to the on-line bank. If it is available too early it can make it impossible to write fresh questions.)

21 Observations of (videos of) practice. I try to discourage critical comments because students are far too good at picking holes in anything. First I ask them to identify good things in the performance, to suggest explanations for features that strike them as less satisfactory and then to speculate on practicable ways of doing things otherwise *in the situation as it stands*. Criticism, leading to an overall evaluation comes last.

22 Ranking. Students are given, or generate, lists of implications, causes, effects, evidence that would falsify a position etc. They then have to identify the two or three most important causes, effects etc. I often set this as a seminar preparation task. The seminar then begins with students wrangling in small groups to agree on their shared priorities. Pyramiding follows (see also Box 8.2, point 2).

23 Reducing complex information, identifying key ideas and presenting it all on a poster.

24 Resumé or précis activities.

25 Role playing, which might also be termed 'simulation'. Students take on different, authentic roles. They may be given briefings by the teacher or told to research and develop their own roles from the briefest of descriptions. An authentic situation, such as a law moot, is simulated in the classroom, with students taking on roles. Those not acting become a participating audience, asking questions of the role-players and giving them feedback.

26 Slices of practice: learning how to do a procedure (and demonstrating it in practice or in the classroom).

27 Thinking experiments. To encourage habits of thinking, have students brainstorm answers to questions such as, 'How could you measure the speed of sound?' 'What would falsify Lamarck's view of inheritance?' 'How would you estimate how much oxygen there is in the atmosphere?'

28 Time-constrained individual assessments (examinations). Open-book examinations are an excellent way of getting students to organize and integrate their understanding, of grading complex tasks relatively quickly and of getting grades that should be plagiarism-free. For example, students keep learning logs or portfolios or do a substantial project. They bring whatever they like to an examination room, where they are given two or three hours to answer questions such as 'What were your main findings? Why are these important and to whom? What detailed advice would you give students doing this task next year? What are the strengths and weaknesses of this as a learning task?'

29 Transfer tasks. I distinguish between tasks that get students to practise concepts, skills and understandings (near transfer) and ones that get learners to take them to fresh problems and settings (far transfer). Near transfer

tasks are necessary but developing the ability to apply learning under conditions of ambiguity and uncertainty is a primary concern of higher education. Examples include: using ideas about the US War of Independence when trying to get the measure of communist success in China, 1945–9; bringing complexity metaphors to the analysis of change in primary health care practice; or facing an engineering problem that depends upon recognizing the usefulness of algorithms learnt last year in another course. Far transfer tasks are characteristic of more advanced courses.

30 Virtual performance of real-life tasks. For example, simulated surgery, CAD and test routines.

31 What didn't the book/presentation/paper tell you? Students have to identify gaps, perhaps as a prelude to doing an evaluation of the book, presentation or paper or to some pair or small group work on how the gaps could be filled.

32 Writing position papers or executive summaries. Make this life-like by putting tough word limits in place (this does *not* make it easier for students) and saying whom the paper is for.

the development of complex skills because they, unlike simple, determinate skills, come from sustained sequences of well conceived tasks that are ordered with progression in mind.

Ohlsson's analysis of the development of understanding (propositional or declarative knowledge), though, has more immediate relevance to course-level task setting. He argues that it is driven by distinctive learning processes which comprise seven 'epistemic tasks' or games:

- describing;
- explaining (events or states);
- predicting;
- arguing;
- critiquing (evaluating);
- explicating (concepts);
- defining.

This leads to the tentative definition of 'the study of higher-order learning as the study of how people learn to perform epistemic tasks' (Ohlsson, 1996: 52). I suggest that a corollary is that teaching for understanding means engaging learners with tasks that have them define, explicate, critique etc. Some of these epistemic tasks will be better suited than others to some material and some purposes at some times, but course teachers could still make a point of checking the tasks they plan to set against this set of epistemic games in order to satisfy themselves that coverage is both wide and appropriate to the material. Programme designers should certainly satisfy themselves that all seven are regularly present or that there are good reasons for absence or unevenness.

Given that there is an underlying intention to set tasks that provoke learning which is liable to be used in novel situations, it follows that setting tasks that engage the learners in the seven 'epistemic games' (Ohlsson, 1996: 51) is a necessary but not a sufficient condition for good learning. Something needs to be done to make it more likely that learning associated with a particular task is abstracted and stored in memory in ways that make it probable that it will be available and used in other situations, including ones that may appear to be quite far removed from the task in hand. There is a view that this concern with generalization for transfer is what distinguishes education from training and non-intentional learning: education is concerned to promote generalized, transferable learning. Unfortunately, there is a great accumulation of psychological research showing that transfer is not a simple matter and might best be described as a battle, with reports of attempts at transfer described as 'war stories' because 'knowledge doesn't market very easily' (Brown and Duguid, 2000: 215). Levine and Cureton (1998: 17) report research in US universities showing that

> more than half of today's students perform best in a learning situation characterized by 'direct, concrete experience, moderate-to-high degrees of structure, and a linear approach to learning. They value the practical and the immediate, and the focus of their perception is primarily on the physical world.'

There is an uncanny resemblance here to descriptions of concrete operational thinking, which is characteristic of pre-adolescent children and, it should be noticed, of many older people for much of the time. The point is that if we want declarative or practical knowledge, propositional or procedural knowledge to transfer, we need to do something to make it more likely. It is naive to run a first year module on good academic practices and expect it to have a tonic effect on everything that follows. 'Most investigators nowadays', writes De Corte (1996: 101), 'share the standpoint that in order to achieve cognitive transfer in learners, it is necessary to teach explicitly and intentionally for transfer.' At the heart of this are tasks that stimulate metacognition, tasks that encourage learners to reflect on what they are trying to do, to call to mind experience of working on somewhat similar problems and relevant knowledge, and to monitor themselves and the strategies they use as they work on the problem. Instruction is necessary, whether through books, on-line tutorials or face-to-face classes, in order to inform learners about the importance of transfer and metacognition. So too are tasks that:

1 '[P]rovide a temporary support for learners that allows them to perform at a level just beyond their current ability level' (De Corte, 1996: 104), mainly by decomposing complex tasks into manageable steps and by

giving prompts and hints so that students can work, when appropriate, in the ZPD.

2 Encourage students to frame novel tasks as ones that can be tackled by applying already-learned practices, concepts and understanding. In order to foster 'far transfer' it is necessary to set problems that promote the habit of searching widely for tools. The 'near transfer' tasks that are so widely used may please students-as-commodity-consumers but do little to develop habits of far transfer.

3 Get them to reflect on what can be learned and abstracted – on what can be added to their metacognitive awareness – from the tasks they have just completed. In other words, set tasks whose aim is metacognitive enrichment. (See Box 8.1, point 17.)

It will be evident that the individual tutor who tries to set these tasks in a department which has not heard of metacognition and which has only a vague understanding of the importance of programme-level planning for the development of complex learning is likely to become frustrated by student resistance and a lack of success. Nevertheless, while we should appreciate the limits to what any one course tutor's task-setting practices can contribute to complex curriculum goals, an awareness of the potential helps teachers to tinker with what they do in order to diversify intentional learning engagements.

Informed practices

Box 8.1 carries much that I have to say about informed practices. This section touches on four other matters that bear upon task-setting practices: the social context of tasks; problem-based learning; task design; facilitating learning.

The social context of tasks

Good tasks, ones that stimulate an interplay between the task, existing understandings and new information, are often designed to be done by individuals. However, learning can also be encouraged by directly involving others, whether teachers, other students or friends: by getting advice from them (they support us in stepping into the ZPD); by getting feedback from them (they help us to see what is working well and what else might be done); and by interacting with them (having to explain our reasoning helps us to clarify it, while having to defend it tests, modifies and consolidates it). In fact we interact with 'others' when we work alone and come across books advising us on problem-working strategies, use self-diagnosis software and read ideas that are contrary to our emerging

constructions. There is, though, a case for making these quasi-social processes of support, feedback and challenge fully social by setting tasks
that compel interaction, whether it be face-to-face or computer-mediated
communication (CMC). It follows that there is a strong educational case
for organizing tasks so as to create social interaction. Sometimes teacher–
student interaction, as with tutor feedback or in tutorial conversations, fits
the bill, but there are good reasons for making a wider range of group
activities central to the curriculum. Moshman (1999: 39) puts this rather
well:

> Social interaction is a context where one is particularly likely to face
> challenges to one's perspectives, and encounter alternative perspect-
> ives. In explaining the effects of such experiences, it is helpful to
> distinguish *symmetric* from *asymmetric* social interactions. Asymmetric
> interactions involve individuals who differ in knowledge, authority
> and/or power. In such situations, the lower status individual may
> learn what the higher status individual teaches without this having much
> impact on the rationality of either. Symmetric social interactions,
> in contrast, involve individuals who are – and perceive themselves
> to be – comparable in knowledge, authority and power. In such inter-
> actions, neither individual can impose his or her perspective on the
> other, and neither is inclined simply to accept the other's perspective
> as superior to his or her own. Symmetric social interactions are thus
> especially likely to encourage individuals to reflect on their own per-
> spectives and coordinate multiple viewpoints.

Lincoln University in New Zealand has a Teaching and Learning Services website containing a summary of research evidence about the impact
of groupwork (http://learn.lincoln.ac.nz/groupwork/why/research.htm).
It shows that groupwork can: benefit higher-order practices, such as synthesizing, problem-solving and critical thinking; increase persistence;
foster positive attitudes to work; enhance understanding; and improve
metacognition. It is also important to appreciate that employers frequently
expect graduates to be able to make strong claims to being skilled in
working in groups.

There are three main objections to group tasks.

1 *Motivational issues.* Groupwork may be a licence for less committed students
   to take it easy. Slavin (1996) recommends setting tasks that produce
   individual marks from group activities: this may address the extrinsic
   motivational issues but it creates assessment difficulties.
2 *Assessment issues.* It is hard to get reliable assessments of individual contributions to group achievements. One answer is not to assess group
   tasks summatively, which sidesteps the reliability problem. (The general
   case for not trying reliably to assess achievements that resist reliable

assessment is outlined in the next chapter.) Those who do not contribute to these group tasks penalize themselves by missing the chance
to get feedback on improving their work. However, that is contrary to
Slavin's advice. There are complicated systems for getting individual
marks from group activities (Knight *et al.*, 2000) but I find them trouble-
some and try to avoid them. If it is really necessary to get individual
grades from group tasks, the easiest way is to have a formative group
task as preparation for an individual summative task.

3 *Equity issues.* Some might say that groupwork may be good for the average student who learns a lot from those who understand the material
better, but not for those excellent students who are held back by having
to explain things to the others. Although this has some common-sense
appeal, research with young children (Perret-Clérmont, 1985) suggests
that the maxim 'to teach is to learn twice' applies. The more advanced
gain by having to explain to others and help them.

Box 8.2 summarizes seven group activities that can be used in seminars
and presentations. I find they work best if:

1 I break activities down into well defined steps and take beginning students through them one step at a time.
2 I ride the students to work fast on the assumption that the returns
diminish sharply after a few minutes on any one stage of an activity.
3 I avoid the tedium of routinely having groups report back to the whole
class. (I would rather they give me their main points on slips of paper so
that I can type up a summary sheet to discuss at the beginning of the
next seminar/presentation.)

Sometimes there is a problem because some people say too much, others
too little. If so, consider giving each student five 'talk cards'. Each time a
person speaks, a card has to be laid down. When someone has used up
their five cards, they have to stay silent. This quietens the megaphonic,
encourages the less forthcoming and prompts people to wonder whether
what they are about to say is worth the price of one talk card.

Putting tasks first: problem-based learning

Problem-based learning (PBL) is a radical way of putting tasks at the
centre which is firmly established in some medical schools. Practices vary
but generally students are given authentic, complex tasks to solve. The
tasks are written to get them to get new information, understand it
and apply it. Any formal presentations are, like seminars and lab classes,
arranged to cover material that bears upon the week's work. So, rather
than study separate aspects of medicine, such as anatomy, haematology,
pharmacology and clinical practices, knowledge from the specialisms is

Box 8.2   Seven group and collaborative learning activities

1 *Buzz groups, pairs or triads*. Give a question on whatever the topic or reading you are working on to subgroups of two to four students. Before you ask them to 'buzz' for five minutes, insist on a couple of minutes of individual thought. Once the five minutes is up, have groups report one or two *key* points to the class.

2 *Pyramids*. As above, but have students buzzing in pairs or triplets. Pairs/triplets then join with another pair or triplet and decide which are the best two points out of all those they bring to the new group of four or six. Now pyramid those groups into eights or twelves. Stop the pyramiding either by asking these groups to report their main agreed points or by trusting the process by not expecting that anything much would be gained by getting students to report back to the whole class.

3 *Debates*. Divide the class into groups of four or five. Half the groups work on the 'pros' and prepare a rebuttal to the 'cons', while the others do the opposite. After about ten minutes, move into whole-class debate. While many students don't get to speak in the whole-class part, the real work and active learning took place in the groups.

4 *Crossovers*. Both pyramids and debates hit reporting back problems when classes are medium-sized or large. Unless you are in a tiered lecture theatre, try cross-overs. Small groups reach a position on an issue, problem or whatever. Each person in a group has a number (1–4 in groups of four, 1–5 in groups of five and so on). All number 5s assemble in one part of the hall, all number 4s in another and so on. They re-form into new groups of four or five. The new groups rework the original question. In effect, each student is reporting back to a few people who constitute an informed and perhaps sceptical audience.

5 *Silent brainstorming*. This is variation of the more well known brainstorm activity. In this one, students are in groups of four to six and each has a sheet of paper. They are given a common problem to solve or issue to expand. To start, they write one idea or solution on the paper. Once done, they pass the paper to the left and take the person's paper from the right. They read the person's idea and must add something to the page. They can 'hitchhike' if it is an improvement or development of the idea. Continue until the students are almost drained of ideas.

6 *Poster tours*. Have students in small groups work on a poster or concept map to illustrate the most important points of their discussion of a set topic. Display them. Have one student stay with the poster to answer questions as the others make the tour of the rest. The students who stood by the poster then have their tour and each group puts comments or questions about what they have seen on Post-its, which they stick on the posters.

7 *Jigsaw*. Students are formed into 'home groups' of four or five. They immediately leave their home group and go to topic stations in the room and work there in newly formed groups to become 'experts' on a sub-topic that you have set. They then return to the home groups and each 'expert' teaches the rest about their sub-topic.

Based on Knight *et al*. (2000).

brought to students' attention as affordances for working on authentic problems. PBL is valued because:

1 Students cover much the same material as previously but it is organized and 'delivered' differently. In PBL courses the information coheres around life-like problems so as to get students thinking like practitioners from the first.
2 It is relevant, in that the problems students face tend to be those encountered in practice and not textbook curiosities.
3 It emphasizes understanding, problem identification, problem-working and action: it is about praxis as opposed to the memorization of information emphasized in traditional curricula.
4 It raises organizational matters (for example, how does a hospital clinic work?) and social issues (for example, why do the poor people in some regions have such poor diets?) that were marginal in traditional courses.
5 These medical students have to be client- and practice-focused, from the start. There are reports from Britain and North America that doctors who have graduated from PBL programmes have 'bigger hearts'.
6 It requires students to become more independent *and* collaborative learners, which is a good basis for life-long learning. It also enhances professional employability.
7 There is a change from transmission pedagogies (lectures and multiple choice tests) to what is often called 'active' learning. (A nice position is that learning must, by definition, be active.) The seminars in which students report their enquiries, suggest solutions, talk about implications and prepare themselves for the next week's problem are the new pedagogical core, and assessment has moved from memory testing to more authentic assessments of diagnostic and problem-working.
8 *Once substantial start-up costs are covered,* PBL is reckoned to be cost-efficient.

Problem-based learning, which can be seen as the height of a task-focused approach to teaching, has considerable potential in most vocational and applied subjects. It can also bewilder students and annoy teachers accustomed to other ways of doing things. Six things needed for success are:

1 Great clarity about goals, learning outcomes, sequence and progression.
2 Massive, sophisticated planning.
3 The skill to write good, authentic cases.
4 The nerve to align assessment practices with PBL. Taken-for-granted practices are often upended.
5 Plenty of start-up resources (consultancy, development and validation time, materials, administrative support).

Table 8.1 Course EDS 232: assessed tasks and learning outcomes

Task	O1	O2	O3	O4	O5	O6	O7	O8
Coursework 1: literature review	✓	✓	✓		✓	✓	✓	
Coursework 2: designing a research enquiry	✓	✓		✓	✓	✓	✓	✓
Coursework 3: evaluation of a published research paper	✓	✓	✓		✓	✓	✓	
Weekly bullet point lists (not graded)	✓				✓		✓	
Examination: Q1 note-making	✓							
Examination: Q2 designing an enquiry	✓	✓		✓				

Note: This table links these outcomes to the main pieces of work students do. The columns refer to *course* learning outcomes 1–8, which are a subset of the outcomes in the *programme* specification. The table is elaborated in Box 9.2.

6 A lot of professional development so that teachers, including part-time teachers, understand the theory and practice of PBL. Many find it hard to facilitate without turning seminars into lectures.

These points come mainly from evaluations of programme-wide approaches to PBL but they also speak to the teacher interested in course-level change. Problem-based learning unequivocally puts instruction at the service of learning and characterizes teaching as the design and facilitation of sets of good learning tasks. Single PBL modules have interesting possibilities but PBL programmes of three or four years' duration have a potential to transform students that is hardly matched by any other pedagogical innovation. Reynolds (1997) provides a good review of the issues, combined with an account of her PBL practices.

Designing tasks

There is a background assumption that good tasks address worthwhile and authentic problems. Thereafter, tasks should, taken as a set, address all of the course learning outcomes. Table 8.1 illustrates this with reference to one undergraduate course. It is considerate to publish the criteria by which task performance will be judged, even if there is no formal summative assessment directly arising out of it. For example, students taking EDS 232 (see Table 8.1) submit bullet point summaries of their reading for classes. The course handbook specifies the form they should take and says that, from time to time, the teacher will give feedback on the quality of note-making that they show. They are not graded. This example points to another feature of a good set of tasks, namely that they should not all lead to a piece of continuous prose. Sometimes evidence of engagement is enough; other task products include notes, charts, posters, short talks and sets of questions.

Even so, tasks can turn out to be harder than teachers imagined and can produce quite unexpected divergent responses. There is no sure-fire formula for designing good tasks but good tasks are more likely to emerge if three common pitfalls are avoided. One is setting tasks that are too long. It is easy to over-estimate what the average student can do. I am humbled when I re-read my own undergraduate maunderings on the antebellum USA. The second is designing over-complicated tasks. It is good to set complex tasks when students know how to work them into a manageable form. Until then it is a good idea to provide scaffolding, more for first year students, little for final years. The third is particularly associated with trying to set authentic tasks. It is easy to set life-like tasks that can only be successfully done by people who have a wide contextual understanding. These tasks fail because they are too authentic.

Facilitating learning

Good tasks need good facilitation, which may take the form of: monitoring progress; adding structure in the form of hints, references or questions; seeing drafts; counselling or coaching; and managing group interactions. Suggestions for facilitating on-line learning were made in Chapter 7, so this is mainly about facilitating face-to-face seminars. Well facilitated seminars give students a model on which to base their own group learning practices, especially when the potential is pointed out to them.

There needs to be well designed tasks and activities that invite learners to do more than receive information. Obvious though this is, it is not easily done, partly for reasons mentioned in the treatment of PBL – it needs skill, attention and some degree of bravery to put students at the helm of learning – and partly because it is likely to take longer. Teaching for understanding may take longer than transmission teaching but it should also be more efficient because the evidence is that understanding tends to last, whereas bits of information, lodged in memory as facts to be remembered, decay fast.

Good intentions and good design are likely to be undone by group dynamics, especially when the teacher is part of the group, as in seminars. Galton and Williamson (1992) showed in their research that school children are prone to see group activities as something to use up time until the teacher cracks and tells them the right answer. This helps to explain why asymmetries of power can limit the learning potential of groups; it is because those who feel they lack power – students, for example – adopt cue-seeking behaviour, looking to the powerful – teachers – to tell them what matters and what is right. Worse, these are high-stakes situations because the invitation to students to contribute to discussion is also an invitation to give the wrong answer and lose face. (It is less clear what counts as 'the wrong answer' when equals are talking and when the stakes are usually lower.) So, good facilitation includes:

1 Resisting the subliminal pressure to take over and do the talking.
2 Managing the seminar so that there are plenty of low-stakes chances for talk.
3 Reducing the stakes by encouraging trust and ease.

Some tutors go into seminars determined not to do all the talking and fail (it is sobering to have someone keep a tally of who talks for how long), while others succeed by dint of toughing out long silences that ratchet up tension to a counterproductive degree. The quickest way to get students talking is to ask a question, get them to work on it in pairs or triplets, give them five minutes to come up with an answer and three reasons/causes/effects/criticisms/whatever, and leave the room for a minute or so while they forget to be self-conscious. Then pyramid (see Box 8.2) or get quick reports from each pair and then move the seminar on to the next sequence. Each of these elements is important: symmetrical power relationships; protection against looking, personally, a fool when reporting back; manageable, tightly focused thinking tasks; restricted time; and not hovering at students' shoulders. A seminar can be planned as a set of two or three sequences like this. The students do a great deal of talking and thinking and the teacher manages the process, ensuring that good ideas and key points are recognized and noted.

Easy interpersonal relationships help students to feel it is fairly safe to take a risk by asking or answering a question. As many writers have noted, this means that teachers should thank students for contributions and not respond in ways that suggest that they are dumb. This means being mindful about speech and about body language. Brockbank and McGill (1998) recommend a SOLER listening style: Square-on to the speaker, Open posture, Lean a little towards the speaker, make Eye contact, look Relaxed. Although the teacher might then rephrase some student contributions to check that they have been properly understood, the trick is to draw others in, keeping conversation flowing until it makes sense for the teacher to summarize what has been said, perhaps adding material to enrich the work the students have done.

This works best when there is a shared understanding of what seminars are for and agreement on basic rules of procedure. The following elaboration of those two points applies equally to groupwork in general. My answer to the 'purpose' question is that presentations are ways of introducing frameworks, themes and key concepts. Reading and work on the web are common ways of fleshing out those skeletons, while seminars, small group work and many tasks are occasions for thinking about what has been learned through 'higher order' activities such as explaining, predicting, arguing, critiquing, explicating and defining. A story like that helps to make sense of the rule in some universities that lectures are optional but seminars and tutorials, the hard thinking sessions, are compulsory.

Bolton writes that the key principles of groupwork are 'Respect, shared responsibility, confidence and confidentiality' (Bolton, 2001: 59). In seminars it will be the teacher who must work hardest at making it possible for students to believe that this is how things will be. One of the first things that many groups do is to set some ground rules, which often include:

1 Do the reading and other preparation for group meetings.
2 Follow safety procedures.
3 Expect to speak.
4 Don't speak when someone else is talking.
5 Try not to criticize others. Feel free to disagree with their words and deeds, though.
6 Try to use open language: for example, instead of using 'but', prefer 'and'.
7 Take it in turn to chair, keep notes and take on other roles such as critic, manager, pragmatist, creative thinker.
8 Aim to make time to end sessions with a summary of what has been said and a review of what is to be done before the next session.
9 Use people's names.
10 Reflect on yourself as a group member. What do you add to the group? How do you do it effectively? Is there anything you do that disturbs group effectiveness?
11 The group should review its functioning. Have irritating or ineffective practices developed? Do people feel that they are getting what they want from the group? Are the rules working? How could things be better?

Some rules will not apply (number 2 is not relevant in most seminars) and others will need to be added (for example, ethical practices must be observed when real people are being discussed in professional practice seminars).

It has been suggested that good learning is stimulated by good tasks which are often done with others. A surprising amount of care may have to be taken to help people to feel comfortable working with others. Some teachers resent that and see it as stealing time that would be better spent on learning more about the subject. They have a point because the emphasis that complex curricula put on students being skilled in processes such as groupwork, locating and evaluating information and metacognition leaves less time for the traditional concern that they should know a lot and be fluent in a number of subject-specific routines. Although some teachers try to cram it all in, others know that surface approaches to learning result and prefer to encourage understanding by identifying the most powerful concepts, debates and practices associated with the material, concentrating on them and cutting the clutter. In this way good teaching, in the sense of designing good tasks, depends on good teaching in the sense of artful course design.

Action points

A good way to apply the ideas surveyed in this chapter is to choose one course and review the student learning tasks. Five questions might guide the audit:

1 Is a good range of tasks used? (See Box 8.1.)
2 Are the tasks clearly related to module and programme learning outcomes? Do students know? (See Table 8.1.)
3 As a set, do the tasks call for describing, explaining, predicting, arguing, critiquing, explicating and defining?
4 Are tasks considerately structured? Are the affordances clear and appropriate to the level of study?
5 Are there tasks to be done in groups? (See Box 8.2.)

Further reading

Good learning tasks are described by John Cowan's thoughtful and friendly book *On Becoming an Innovative University Teacher* (1998). Linda Nilson's *Teaching at Its Best* (1998) is a strong North American compendium of advice on most aspects of teaching, tasks included. There are also useful ideas in some of the chapters in Parts 1 and 3 of *A Handbook for Teaching and Learning in Higher Education*, by Fry *et al.* (1999).

9

Creating feedback

A stance

The single, strongest influence on learning is surely the assessment
procedures . . . even the form of an examination question or essay
topics set can affect how students study . . . It is also important to
remember that entrenched attitudes which support traditional
methods of teaching and assessment are hard to change.

(Entwistle, 1996: 111–12)

Summative assessment, or grading, is part of a teacher's work but, following
the line taken in Chapter 8, so too is formative assessment, or the creation
of feedback to help learners to do better. Noting some often unrecognized
problems with summative assessment, I concentrate upon assessment that
has formative purposes. Not only has it great potential to improve learning but it is much easier for teachers to be creative when the purposes are
formative and low-stakes than it is if they are summative and high-stakes.

Key points

1 High-stakes, summative assessment has limited reach because grades
  cannot be reliably and affordably attached to many valued but complex
  learning outcomes.
2 It has been shown that good formative assessment practices can lead to
  greater learning gains than almost any other educational innovation.
3 Good formative assessment is a product of careful thought about the
  relationship between instruction, tasks and assessment at the course and
  programme levels.
4 In general we want knowing students, ones who know our expectations,
  learning intentions and the rules of the game. It is essential where
  assessment is concerned.

Research

It is usual in books such as this to have a chapter on assessment which provides a quick summary of alternatives to multiple choice questions (MCQs), essays and lab reports. I am not following custom, partly because there is no shortage of books on assessment techniques (Brown and Knight, 1994; Banta *et al.*, 1996; Hounsell *et al.*, 1996; Brown *et al.*, 1997; Walvoord and Anderson, 1998; Heywood, 2000) which are more helpful than a chapter-length treatment can be and partly because I am becoming convinced that assessment questions, especially questions about high-stakes assessment, are mainly leadership and system questions that are fundamentally about programme-level practices (Knight and Trowler, 2001). The concept of high-stakes assessment needs to be explained before the point can be developed. Table 9.1 associates it with related concepts. It distinguishes between local and general audiences for low- and high-stakes assessment in order to make the point that the ways in which we go about assessment are affected by whether the information is to be locally used, by you and your students, or fed out to others who will read the information without understanding the subtleties of the context and the circumstances of assessment.

High-stakes assessment is close to what many books call 'summative assessment', and low-stakes could be labelled 'formative assessment'. There are many reasons for believing that high-stakes assessment is nothing like as reliable, objective or useful as is widely assumed. In Broadfoot's (2000: 208) view, 'it is a frail and flawed technology which, although it has its range of legitimate uses, needs to be cut down to size'. In a substantial review of theories and research bearing on high-stakes assessments, Pellegrino *et al.* (1999: 332) suggest that

> It also appears that as assessment development and use moves away from the classroom teaching and learning situation, validity issues seem to take a back seat to issues of reliability and generalizability. In contrast, when assessments are integral parts of instructional practice, validity appears to be the primary issue and very often the major technical criterion by which assessments are judged.

Highly reliable assessments can be had, often at great cost, although they frequently turn out not to have measured what they were supposed to be measuring (Pellegrino *et al.*, 1999) and it is always a problem to know exactly what the results signify. Low-stakes assessments tend to be more meaningful but their folksy nature means there are reliability and generalizability problems. Teachers have some room for manoeuvre when assessment purposes are summative (Box 9.1 lists 50 assessment methods to choose from), but there is a lot more that individual teachers can do when tasks have formative, low-stakes purposes, when they are intended to

Table 9.1 Assessment contexts and purposes

	Local audience who appreciate the assessment context	*General audiences whose understanding of the information is limited because they do not appreciate the assessment context*	*Issues*
High stakes			
Examples	Classroom tests	Exams and other assessments for warranting purposes	The emphasis is on judgements or measurements that sum up achievement – the
Typical consumer	Instructor	Employers, graduate schools etc.	purposes are summative. The more these judgements are
How fixed are assessment judgements?	Student has no appeal but this grade will soon be overtaken by new test scores	Judgement is fixed and public	aggregated and reported in numbers to the world at large, the harder it is to know what they *signify*. Meaning becomes a problem
Low stakes			
Examples	Assessment conversations	Learning portfolios and other claims to achievement not warranted by the institution	The emphasis is on judging to help better learning – the purposes are (in)formative. Meanings are closely bound up with the
Typical consumer	The learners	Employers, graduate schools etc.	specific contexts of particular tasks. People make their own sense
How fixed are assessment judgements?	Conversations are fluid and judgements contestable	Claims to achievement are public but open to legitimate revision by the learners who make them	of what arises in low-stakes assessments and recognize that generalizations will be subjective

provide feedback for learning, not feedout for certification, selection and accountability. Creating feedback is central to formative assessment and, since Chapter 8 had much to say about task design, this concentrates on how feedback on task performance can be stimulated, heard and understood, and, all being well, can foster better learning. The critique of assessment for summative, warranting purposes is first developed a little more

Box 9.1 Fifty assessment techniques

1 Artefacts/products, especially in fashion, design, engineering etc.
2 Assessment as gatekeeping: students gain entry to classes only on production of bullet point summaries etc.
3 Assessment banks. Students have access to a question and answer bank. They learn how to answer all of them but are assessed on a sample.
4 Assessment of work-based learning (in a variety of ways, many times, by a variety of people, for different purposes).
5 Bidding for funds or writing responses to invitations to tender. The quality of the briefing you give students greatly affects the quality of their responses.
6 Book, website or program reviews.
7 Classroom assessment techniques. They are *brief* tasks that tell the teacher something about the *class's* grasp of the material (see Angelo and Cross, 1993).
8 Completing structured summaries of readings, debates etc.
9 Computer-based self-assessment.
10 Concept maps. An excellent way of seeing how students understand complex content and relationships.
11 Contribution to threaded electronic discussions.
12 Design and build (similar to point 2 above)
13 Dissertations and theses.
14 Electronic monitoring of web searches, program use and communications.
15 Essay writing: one 5000 word piece (make harder/easier by varying amount of tutorial guidance, range of reading expected, novelty of the topic/ problem, time available, conceptual complexity etc.)
16 Exhibitions of work, posters, products. History students have curated museum exhibitions in lieu of doing a dissertation.
17 Field work and lab work assessment (traditional and well established).
18 Formative assessment of logs/journals/portfolios. (When the purposes are formative, students identify areas for discussion. *If* summative, sampling within the logs etc. is recommended, especially if students know in advance the areas that are likely to get closest attention.)
19 Games and simulations.
20 'General' assessments, drawing together learning in several modules.
21 Glossaries. Easy to plagiarize but valuable tests of understanding under examination conditions.
22 Making annotated bibliographies for next year's students.
23 Making models (literally, in some subjects, conceptual models in others).
24 Multiple choice questions (they do not have to be only tests of information, although it is a lot quicker to write MCQs like that. See also point 3 above).
25 New tests in which learners use old software/programs/notes.
26 Objective structured clinical examination (OSCE), which is where students move between some 10–20 'stations', each of which engages them with a problem, task or activity representative of the clinical field being

examined. Similar techniques can be used to test students' laboratory skills.

27 Open-book, end-of-course exams.
28 Orals and vivas.
29 Peer assessment. Some try to use it summatively but it is a lot easier if done for formative purposes.
30 Performances. Vital in the assessment of competence. Note massive problems assessing complex performances fairly and reliably. Simulations are sometimes possible.
31 Personal response assessments. Usually done in classes where each student has an electronic response pad. Teachers ask questions and they press a key to show their answers. Can be used for classroom assessment or test purposes.
32 Posters.
33 Production of structured logs of project/dissertation progress and reflection on it.
32 Projects.
35 'Real' problem working, which involves defining 'fuzzy' situations, bringing some order to ill-defined issues, analysing the problem and suggesting solutions.
36 Replication of published enquiries.
37 Role-playing.
38 Self-assessment. Skill at self-evaluation is valued by many employers, which is a reason for having self-assessments. Easiest when used formatively.
39 Seminar presentations (in or out of role, with or without use of video, OHT, Powerpoint etc.)
40 Short answer questions (MCQs *plus* some explanation of the thinking; limit to 100 words per response?)
41 Evaluations (short) of target papers (both appreciative and critical).
42 Small-scale research or enquiry.
43 Statements of relevance, which are short pieces of writing, 1000 words, perhaps, making claims about the relevance of a workshop, article, field observation etc. to another task or activity (see Bourner et al., 2000).
44 Submission of claims to achievement with reference to portfolio (if this is to be summative, I suggest grading on the claim alone *provided that* sufficient evidence supports the claims).
45 Takeaway papers/questions/tests.
46 Terminal, unseen examinations and other individual time-constrained assignments.
47 Two-part assessments. Elements of a task are formatively assessed but the final product is summatively assessed.
48 Web page creation.
49 Writing (i.e. devising) exams/tests/assessments to tutor specification.
50 Writing memoranda, executive summaries or newspaper reports.

Prompted by Brown and Knight (1994) and Hounsell et al. (1996).

in order to make the point that if some learning goals are not covered by low-stakes formative assessment, then it is hard to see how they can be covered at all. Given the mantra that students learn what is assessed, then that would lead to a significant narrowing of the curriculum at a time when governments and employers want higher education to promote more complex and ambitious learning outcomes.

The limits of summative assessment

When people talk about assessment they are frequently talking about assessment which has the summative purpose of producing a grade, mark, classification or prose description summing up someone's achievements. Plainly, summative purposes make for high-stakes assessments, and when the stakes are high it is important that the judgements are reliable, that they are as objective, thorough and dependable as possible. Desirable though reliability is, achieving it is another matter. Consider a common question: how can we *reliably* assess a complex skill, such as communication? It is barely possible in a single course, although a programme can be planned and resources allocated so that tolerably reliable judgements can be made about some aspects of communicative competence *in the programme as a whole*. Again, how do we assess critical thinking? It is certainly possible in a module to set tasks that involve critical thinking, along with other academic practices, but that is not enough to sustain bold claims that this student has reliably shown a certain level of critical thinking skill. Any such claim should come from programme-wide evidence that has been purposefully accumulated through systemic assessment practices. Even so, I am sceptical about the underlying belief that reliable measurements of human achievement are possible if only we work hard enough to deploy the right assessment techniques. Biggs's (1999b) SOLO taxonomy is a good example of an assessment guide. The taxonomy has four main categories:

1 Extended abstract thinking: theorizing, generalizing, hypothesizing and reflecting.
2 Relational thinking: comparing and contrasting, explaining causes, analysing, relating and applying.
3 Multistructural thinking: enumerating, describing, listing, combining and doing algorithms.
4 Unistructural thinking: identifying and doing simple procedures. Failed attempts at more ambitious thinking also come into this category.

Although this taxonomy appeals to many, I have always found it and others like it difficult to use *summatively*. With criteria there is always a problem of meaning, which shows itself as uncertainty about what would count as suitable evidence of, say, algorithmic problem-solving as opposed to problem-solving through relational thinking. For example, how is one to judge whether something is an example of hypothesizing or just feeding back someone else's hypothesis read in a book? Apart from being familiar with the official meanings of the criteria and of the rules to be used when judging achievements against them, markers need to know the curriculum well in order to make a good judgement about what any particular performance meant, and hence how it should be graded. Working with schoolchildren, I also had severe problems deciding on the amount of substantiation I needed before judging their responses to be multistructural rather than an interesting whimsy. Finding that some 7-year-olds could be judged to be relational thinkers on some tasks made me uneasy about using SOLO for high-stakes purposes when information about the context of performance easily gets lost. I do value it as a prompt for thinking about task and assessment design and when the purposes are formative.

Another example of the problems with summative, high-stakes assessment concerns peer assessment of learning. It was noted in Chapter 8 that learning can be better in social situations where there are symmetries of power. One implication is that peer assessment can influence learning in ways that less symmetrical tutor assessments cannot. Add to that the fact that peers are best placed to judge things such as groupworking and contribution to team tasks, and quite a compelling case for it emerges. However, as the steady flow of journal articles on the reliability of peer assessment shows (Lejk and Wyvill, 2001; Li, 2001; Magin, 2001), teachers try to use it for high-stakes purposes and then find themselves spending a lot of time devising ever more elaborate arrangements to reassure themselves that students are judging each other objectively, informedly and thoroughly. Arguably, the only way to get reliable, high-stakes peer judgements is for the teacher to grade the work as well, but that raises questions about why students are being used as judges if their verdict only stands when it matches the teacher's. Things become much more straightforward if peer assessment and self-assessment are used formatively.

There are many other objections to trusting that valued learning outcomes can all be reliably assessed at an affordable cost (Knight, 2002a). Taken together, they suggest the principle that the further we move from the assessment of simple achievements, like information recall, the less feasible it becomes to make reliable judgements. The significance is that I have already claimed that higher education is in the business of promoting complex learning.

Teachers as creators of feedback: the case for formative assessment

Formative assessment does not have a tightly defined and widely accepted meaning. Askew and Lodge (2000) distinguish between three accounts of feedback.

- The dominant one treats it as a gift from the teacher to students to help them learn. Learning is seen as an individual affair involving 'increased understanding of new ideas, memorizing new facts, practising new skills and making decisions based on information' (p. 4).
- The second is a constructivist view of learning which emphasizes 'making connections between new and old experiences, integrating new knowledge and extending established schema' (p. 4). The teacher is not seen as such a dominant power in the process and feedback is more descriptive than judgemental and more conversational than didactic, helping to 'draw out' thinking and 'motivate pupils and develop their commitment to the values and norms of the organization' (p. 9). 'Power still resides with the teacher . . . because the agenda for the feedback is decided by them' (p. 10).
- The third version assumes a more equal distribution of power between teacher and learner, with the teacher being a part of a discourse about learning and how to learn. 'Feedback is a dialogue, formed by loops connecting the participants' (p. 4).

The first is a good description of teaching and feedback processes that are common in higher education when grading is the name of the game, although it is charitable to assume that much of what is given as feedback in this style actually does improve learning. This chapter has little to say about it. The second is consistent with teaching approaches intended to evoke 'deep' learning approaches in students (Hounsell *et al.*, 1996) and with beliefs that both teaching and learning are about students making joined-up sense of the materials with which they engage (Prosser and Trigwell, 1999). Since Askew and Lodge's typology is based on research into primary schools, it is not surprising that they reckoned the third form of feedback is rare. In higher education, though, this emphasis on conversations and symmetries of power fits well with the ideals of peer assessment and with the concept of the teacher as a facilitator (Brockbank and McGill, 1998).

A review of 681 research publications on formative assessment showed 'conclusively that formative assessment does improve learning. It was suggested that if best formative assessment practices were achieved in mathematics on a nationwide scale that would raise "average" countries such as England and the USA into the top five' (Black and Wiliam, 1998: 61): the possible effect size of 0.7 is 'amongst the largest ever recorded for educational interventions' (1998: 61). There is a good case for seeing formative assessment as an extremely powerful contributor to student learning. You could almost say that makes it *more* important than assessment for high-stakes, warranting purposes. The implication is that formative assessment is much more than something to do when complex outcomes have to be assessed (because accountability systems expect outcomes to be assessed) and there is no reliable way of producing high-stakes data. As Chapter 2 indicated, learning theories place great importance on feedback to the learner, irrespective of whether the theories have derived from Skinner's behaviourism, Piaget's genetic epistemology, Vygotsky's dialectical materialism or Gagné's cognitive psychology. Laurillard's (1993) conversational model of teaching is an attempt to explain the central place that purposeful feedback has in learning in higher education, and her more recent work on learning with new technologies (Laurillard *et al.*, 2000) emphasizes the construction of meaning through interactions or 'conversations' between the learner, courseware, other learners, the teacher/facilitator and the feedback they create. Apart from helping the construction of meaning, there are also grounds for saying that considerate feedback can be emotionally important, particularly when it builds learner confidence and sense of achievement. This is not to say that feedback should be uncritical but that when problems are found feedback should presume that learners will be able to tackle them through a combination of smart thinking and effort, and it should offer suggestions to help them do better next time.

Understood in this way, 'it is hard to see how any innovation in formative assessment can be treated as a marginal change in classroom work' (Black and Wiliam, 1998: 16). It shapes and generates learning activity and defines what is learned and how (Perrenoud, 1998). However, its promise depends on meeting a number of conditions. For example, Black (1998) concluded that formative assessment is best when it relates to clear criteria and where the comments are not accompanied by marks or grades. Brown and Knight (1994) identified more than a dozen conditions that should be met if formative assessment is to work well and Torrance and Pryor's (1998) research confirms that the benefits of formative assessment depend on appropriate pedagogic practices being in place. The next section brings together their recommendations and spells out what needs to happen in courses if 'the formative dream: interaction and involvement for all' (Black, 2001: 73) is to become more than a fledgling idea which is 'in need of nurture' (p. 82).

Informed practices

Much of the excitement about on-line learning comes from a growing appreciation of its possibilities for generating more feedback involving more learners. Palloff and Pratt (1999) write that a major advantage of on-line courses is that students get a great deal of feedback from many sources (other students, tutors and, in reflective moments, themselves). They imply that the technology enhances the feedback by capturing it for later consideration, whereas much face-to-face feedback is too fast to be captured or too complex to be properly appreciated either there and then or later. Students get feedback and learn to give it, which is helpful in several ways. It certainly compels their attention to the subject matter and it can encourage them to understand assessment indicators better, which then helps them to judge their own achievements and reflect upon their own learning. As they become better at giving useful and sensitive feedback to others, they improve their interpersonal practices. However, good quality formative feedback has to be worked for, regardless of whether learning is face-to-face or computer-mediated. First, students need to understand that some familiar academic practices are being challenged; second, teachers need to ensure that the right conditions are in place for good formative assessment.

Knowing students: being explicit about the learning culture

Students come to your class with learning histories that have shaped their beliefs about the rules of the academic game, particularly about what learning is and what teachers do. Many innovative teachers have found that students resist academic practices that do not conform to those expectations, partly because they do not understand the thinking behind them and partly because some firmly believe that they have paid to be instructed and then graded on what they remember. If low-stakes assessment is made a central feature of a course it is necessary to explain at least four things very clearly.

The first of these is why there is such an emphasis on formative assessment. Students need to appreciate that you hope to assess all learning outcomes and recognize that it is not feasible to assess them all summatively. Formative assessment is a way of paying serious attention to those that escape high-stakes assessment. There is also compelling evidence that it can be very good for learning, which is why some learning outcomes that are summatively assessed are also formatively assessed. The course assessment plan, a part of which comprises Box 9.2, shows how formative and summative assessment are dovetailed to give sustained attention to all course learning outcomes.

The second is why students should expect to do peer assessment and self-assessment. Formative assessment works well when teachers give thoughtful feedback on improving performance, especially when feedback is related to assessment criteria that are known, understood and used. (They might, for example, be printed on assignment cover sheets that are distributed when assignments are set.)

It also works well – perhaps better – if feedback comes from other students, when those giving feedback and those experiencing it can *both* benefit. Here students must appreciate that the feedback will often relate

Box 9.2   A course assessment overview (see also Table 8.1)

Students are told that by the end of the course they should:

1 Demonstrate knowledge of mainstream educational and social research methods – see programme specification learning outcome 10.2B(2).
2 Be able to engage critically with issues concerning the relationships between research and knowledge, and with the fitness of different research methods for different purposes 10.1A(2).
3 Be comfortable reading and evaluating research reports – see programme specification 10.2A(1), 10.2B(1).
4 Be able to design a feasible, small-scale research enquiry 10.2B(1, 2), 10.2C(3).
5 Take responsibility for organizing and managing much of your own learning 10.2C(2, 4).
6 Work effectively with others, to both their benefit and yours 10.2C(5, 6).
7 Treat the Internet as a mainstream learning resource 10.2B(3).
8 Present your conclusions orally to an audience 10.2B(6).

The following table links these outcomes to the main pieces of work they do.

Assessment tasks	O1	O2	O3	O4	O5	O6	O7	O8
Coursework 1: write a 2000 word literature review (Summative)	B	B	B		C	C, E	C	
Coursework 2: designing a research enquiry (S)	A, B, E	B, E		A, B, E	C	C, E	C	A, E
Coursework 3: write an evaluation of a published research paper (S)	B	B, E	A, E		C	C, E	C	
Submit bullet point lists related to each week's set readings (Formative)	D				C		C	
Examination: Q1 note making (S)	A							
Examination: Q2 designing an enquiry (S)	B	B		A				

Key: A, Learning outcomes that will be deliberately and summatively assessed.
B, Learning outcomes that are assessed as a group. For example, many written assignments make simultaneous demands on information-handling, critical thinking, synthetic and analytical powers and so on. These achievements are not directly and individually assessed but they are collectively assessed in the sense that grades are affected by shortfalls in performance on any of them.
C, Important learning outcomes, such as skill in writing accurate prose or using a referencing system properly, that are only assessed if a background assumption of competence is disturbed by evidence to the contrary. For example, poor punctuation would be noticed and remedial action required, but accurate punctuation would not be remarked upon, the assumption being that this is something students do.
D, Learning outcomes that get formative feedback from the teacher.
E, Learning outcomes that attract feedback from other students or that should be assessed through self-assessment.

to 'fuzzy' learning outcomes, such as 'independent working', 'skill at work-ing in groups' or 'persistence', and that one reason why those outcomes get low-stakes attention is that they are too fuzzy for reliable summative assessment. The criteria used in making judgements will also be fuzzy. (I prefer to describe them as indicators, rather than as criteria, to suggest that they are prompts for professional judgement, not rules that elimin-ate it.) The upshot is that formative assessment conversations cannot be expected to be 'accurate' in the same way we assume – often wrongly – that summative assessments will be. So, when the stakes are low and judge-ments will be fuzzy, then peer assessment is perfectly appropriate. It is still worth having feedback from other students when learning outcomes are well defined and accurate judgements are possible because those doing the assessing can benefit from having to think hard about what criteria mean, how to apply them and how to defend their judgements. Those getting the feedback are more likely to ask for judgements to be explained and more likely to argue about them – see Chapter 8 on symmetrical power relationships – which is good for learning.

In low-stakes formative assessment what matters is how useful and stimu-lating feedback is.

Not only can formative assessment improve the quality of learning but the habits of judgement learned through assessing other students (peer assessment) and then through evaluating one's own achievements (self assessment) contribute to student employability and are a basis of life-long learning.

Third, it may be hard for some students to appreciate that an emphasis on formative assessment is accompanied by a change in tutor role. Teachers are no longer the authoritative judges of achievement, nor is assessment just about grades. Teachers design learning sequences that contain plenty of opportunities to create and get comments related to course learning outcomes. Then they encourage everyone to engage fully with the afford-ances in the course, sometimes lecturing but sometimes expecting stu-dents to work independently; sometimes grading but sometimes expecting students to appraise themselves or each other. This is not idleness and dereliction of duty, as some students suppose, but necessary behaviour if learning is to happen on the intended lines.

Fourth, formative assessment obviously will not work unless students and teachers take it seriously. And obvious though the point is, students need to be told that low-stakes assessment is not a skive. Indeed, in some on-line learning environments, participation in discussions, which could be understood as creating feedback, is compulsory for course credit. Teachers might want to extend the principle to face-to-face work as well, perhaps requiring students to provide evidence that they con-tributed criteria-related feedback to others on x occasions during the course.

These explanations should go in the course handbook and, ideally, be closely related to the course assessment plan.

Many teachers do not believe that modern, consumerist students who treat education as a commodity and course credits as currency will take low-stakes assessment seriously. Where students have little idea why they are doing it and where teachers are lax about requiring engagement, then these sceptics have a point. Yet there is evidence, most famously from Alverno College, Milwaukee, that students can learn to value formative assessment and become adept at sensitively giving criteria-attentive feedback to others, receiving it, acting on it and, in time, becoming skilled and reflective in self-evaluation (Loacker, 2000; Mentkowski *et al.*, 2000). Alverno is exceptional in having a campus-wide learning culture but they are not the only ones to have found that academic practices can be changed through programme-wide learning cultures. Low-stakes assessment practices can also make some difference to learning at the course level if seven main points are heeded.

1 Sufficient tasks are provided. Obvious, but programme assessment reviews often show that some programme learning outcomes get scarcely any attention – the 'key skill' of numeracy is a case in point in many arts and social science programmes. This failing can also be seen at the course level where it is quite common to find that there are not enough tasks to create decent opportunities for getting feedback on all course learning outcomes. In some cases that is because there are too many learning outcomes. (I found a course of 30 contact hours and another 170 student learning hours which had 19 learning outcomes. Needless to say, most were neither addressed nor assessed.) I tend to see this as a programme design failing more than something to blame on the course team. In other cases the problem is that teachers are so busy telling that there is no time for tasks that get students thinking and doing.
2 Students engage with these tasks. This can be understood as a point about motivation, which means designing tasks that students recognize as important and worthwhile. It is also a point about the teacher's authority, indicating teachers needing to require students to participate in the scheduled learning activities.
3 There are criteria or indicators of achievement. Many teachers have spent too much time trying to write unambiguous statements of learning outcome that can then be objectively used in the measurement of achievement. I have already said that this is philosophically suspect, pyschologically misconceived and practically impossible. However, it is very useful to have some indicators, even 'fuzzy' indicators, of the sorts of performance that could be considered as evidence of appropriate achievement. Without indicators it is hard for students and other assessors to have a sense of what could be counted as evidence of achievement.

Indicators do not replace skilled judgement; they support it by providing a rudimentary language in the form of broad-brush reference points for all to cite in arriving at and justifying assessment judgements. Without them students have little idea of what acceptable performance looks like and assessors rely on their individual experiences.

4 Learners and assessors know and understand achievement indicators. Where criteria exist they are usually published in programme and module handbooks and posted on the web for good measure. This is not enough. First, students have to realize that these indicators are the name of the game, that they describe what is going to be valued and that it might be quite different from what they expect to be valued. I remain puzzled that I still get final year students dripping, 'I hadn't realized that I'd get a third if I didn't cover those two criteria.' It happens less when programme learning cultures are well formed. Second, they need to understand what the indicators *mean*. Small group discussion helps, especially if it precedes as well as follows attempts to apply the criteria to make judgements on examples of student work. It also helps to get students to look closely at marked work that has had all identifying features stripped out. Ideally, they would first see it without knowing the grade and comments, try to judge its quality themselves and then reflect on the indicators once the grades and comments had been disclosed to them.

5 Tasks are appropriate to (matched to) learners. Matching means having a sense of pacing so that there is time for consolidation as well as for new learning. It is not a science. Psychology is full of reports of tasks that logically ought to have had certain levels of difficulty turning out to be psychologically quite different. In general, though, tasks are easier when learners are given more scaffolding or guidance; when they are asked to work with a restricted amount of information; when concepts, problems and solution strategies are both well formed and well known; and when others contribute. Good feedback helps learners to understand what they will have to do in order to succeed as they go on to tackle tasks that are less well defined and relate to larger amounts of less well organized material.

6 Feedback is created that is:
   - Purposeful. Purposes might include correction of errors, development of understanding, promotion of generic skills, development of metacognition, maintenance of motivation.
   - Related to the achievement indicators. Some work calls for comments that lie outside the criteria associated with a task, but when learners have been working with indicators in mind and where teachers want to give advice about future improvement, it is likely that the criteria will set the boundaries within which most comments lie. Criteria-referenced comments can also help learners to see the goodness of fit

between judgements and their work. By the same token, they can help teachers to be fair and consistent in giving feedback.

- Developmentally useful. This is the most important of these messages about feedback. Many teachers take pride in the amount of content-related feedback they give and in the number of errors they correct. Yet the whole idea of formative assessment is that learners get good suggestions for improvement. Since they are seldom likely to do the same task again, the implication is that feedback should be general, directed to similar but different problems in the future, not specific. The most useful advice gives concrete advice about *getting better*.
- Understood. This essentially repeats the last point. However well inten-tioned the teacher's advice, if students do not understand it, then the potential of formative assessment gets lost.
- Timely. Good feedback is fast so that students can respond to it with the work fresh in their mind and in time to act on it before tackling another task of a similar sort. Higher education practices, especially in modularized systems, generally compare poorly with the same day turnaround common in many primary schools and the one week turnaround in secondary schools.
- Appropriate, in relation to students' conceptions of learning, know-ledge and the discourse of the discipline. This point is intended to indicate that good feedback can only be effective if learners and teachers share the same underlying ideas about the rules of the game. Some good feedback fails because the teacher has not spotted that students are playing the academic game by different rules.

7 Feedback is received and attended to. There are plenty of stories of students checking the mark and then ignoring all the carefully crafted feedback that goes with it. This may be less likely with peer assessment and self-assessment that produces comments but not marks. When grades are involved some tutors return the work and feedback but withhold the marks for a couple of days. Students are probably most likely to attend to feedback when they work within a programme-wide learning culture that has convinced them of the power of low-stakes, formative assess-ment and of feedback in all its forms.

It becomes clear that to take formative assessment seriously is to make a commitment to look closely at the whole instruction → tasks → assessment sequence. Here it should be understood that the workload involved in reappraising instruction → tasks → assessment sequences can be consider-able, although in good departments this design work can be a collaborative venture, spread over an academic year and supported by educational devel-opment professionals. Box 9.3 lists ten ways of managing the subsequent operational workload of creating plenty of formative feedback, while the next section addresses the more strategic issues in assessment planning.

Box 9.3 Faster feedback

1 In good learning cultures, ones in which they know the 'rules of the game' and understand the criteria to be applied, students are less likely to make a complete mess of assignments, meaning that there are fewer occasions when massive feedback and coaching are necessary.
2 So too when students have worked collaboratively on projects and conversed with one another about drafts.
3 In good learning cultures, students know the grading criteria because they are printed on assignment cover-and-feedback sheets. Again, this helps to reduce the incidence of badly wrong work.
4 Cover/feedback sheets can speed up feedback when students have to identify the indicators that best describe their work (when they have to assess themselves). Sometimes the teacher need write little more than 'I agree'. Having an idea of the student's judgement of an assignment can also make it easier to give feedback because it precisely identifies any gap between the teacher's and the student's judgements: feedback can be concise because it is targeted.
5 Limit what you say. Most people find up to three major suggestions enough to deal with. Cover/feedback sheets can encourage concision by restricting the space for comment.
6 Consider creating a bank of the feedback statements that you frequently use and then draw on it when you give feedback.
7 If there are lots of errors, mark only the first page and then return the work for correction. It saves your time and it forces students to think about how to do better.
8 Sometimes, rather than explaining exactly what's wrong, it is better for student learning to direct them to sources where they can find out for themselves,
9 How far can peer assessment be substituted for tutor assessment? (But bear in mind the time it may take to set up the peer assessment in the first place.)
10 Can self-assessment replace routine second marking?

Doing a course assessment audit

A course assessment audit is a good way of becoming clear about the relationship between current assessment practices and course learning intentions. If the assessment arrangements for all the modules in a programme are mapped in this way, then the programme manager is able, often for the first time, to see what is emphasized and assessed, how and when. Maps like these can be quite discomfiting, as when the head of history found that students who had reached Part II of their course then needed to write 27 3500 word essays and 36 $\frac{3}{4}$ hour essays to get an honours degree.

A course audit may produce a diagram like that in Box 9.2. This exercise should be complemented by checking the whole set of module assessment arrangements against the good formative assessment practices listed in the previous section. The first five apply as much to high-stakes as to low-stakes assessments. The last two should be taken seriously when it is possible to do so – it is often hard or impossible to give feedback on summative assessments such as terminal examinations. An outcome of the audit and good practice review is a profile that provides a good basis for deciding on a couple of priorities for attention in the next semester or year. The same technique can be used in the programme assessment reviews which are really necessary if there are to be serious and credible claims that slowly developed learning outcomes are deliberately and systematically fostered.

Action points

1 Develop learning indicators or criteria and make sure that students understand them and use them.
2 Introduce or increase opportunities for peer assessment and self-assessment, explaining to students why peer assessment and self-assessment are important.
3 Audit your course assessment practices and identify priorities for development.
4 Look for opportunities to work on assessment reform with colleagues. Educational development units may be able to link you with people in other departments but the greatest gains are to be had by looking at these issues on a programme-wide basis.

Further reading

I know of no good study of feedback to learners in higher education. It is well covered by a research report on practices with young children (Torrance and Pryor, 1998). 'Assessment and classroom learning' is a comprehensive analysis of the research literature on formative assessment in schools and colleges by Paul Black and Dougal Wiliam (1998).

Another way to supplement this chapter is to look in the general literature on assessment in higher education. As good an introduction as any is Brown *et al.* (1997). A crisp and sharp account of some ways of assessing better is Gibbs (1999a).

10

Designing for learning

Designing scripts and programmes

This chapter on the pre-active phase of teaching (see Table 7.1) assumes that student learning is shaped by the ways in which programmes, courses and session scripts have been written. I am concentrating on course or module design because individual teachers have to do it but it is not a straightforward business.

Chapter 7 touched on the design of good presentations and Chapter 8 upon seminars. I have also introduced the concept of teaching memes, or scripts, to refer to the ways in which we habitually put teaching techniques together to form a stereotypical lab class, problem-working class, asynchronous on-line discussion, presentation or seminar. Scripts identify the techniques we will most commonly use, their sequence and the amount of time each gets. Scripts ideally contain a developed notion, to be shared with students, of what this sort of learning engagement is for: I say that lab classes are for consolidating ways of working; problem-working sessions are for modelling an approach and teaching for transfer, especially far transfer, of understanding; on-line discussions are for the application and development of understanding; presentations are for establishing frameworks and identifying issues; and seminars are for working on information. There is a case for investigating the scripts that teachers in different subject disciplines typically use and for looking at the relationship between these memes and student learning. This should then lead to the development of protocols to help people to reflect on how they design teaching sessions and explore ways of bringing the most effective memes to their practices. For the present it will have to be enough to say that it is worth thinking about the basic assumptions we design into our teaching sessions and talking about them with interested colleagues.

The more that we expect undergraduate programmes to evoke complex learning, such as that necessary for convincing claims to graduate employability, the more important becomes programme design and its concern for coherence, progression and slow learning. I have tried to establish through Figure 2.2 and Table II.1 that learning happens and that what happens is related to the environment in which people are; that is, to conversations, social practices, rules, expectations, resources and artefacts. I brought these ideas together in the form of a sketch of elements of a teaching and learning system (Figure 2.1). Figure 10.1 rearranges and extends the ideas behind those figures and Table II.1 in order to show better the range of influences on student learning. Most of it should be easily recognizable in the light of the previous nine chapters and much of it is easily related to recent work done by Noel Entwistle and his Edinburgh colleagues (Entwistle, 2000). Notice, though, the shaded cross which represents the mediating influence of individual dynamics such as motivation, self-theories and perceptions on approaches, environments and the curriculum. Their connective influences will vary, especially when it comes to particular engagements, but they will consistently have a considerable effect on the ways in which tasks, for example, are transformed into activities and on the ways in which the turbulent interplay of the four principal influences on learning (approaches to learning and studying, environment and curriculum) creates learning. If this is a fair model, then there is a clear case for considering what can ethically be done to help students to use the malleable self-theories that succour persistent intrinsic motivation and help them to perceive the potential in situations rather than being fixated by seeming impossibilities. Additionally, it follows that those concerned with complex learning outcomes, such as those listed in Box II.1, should be skilled in the design of affordances in the learning environment, as well as in devising formal curricula that promote this complexity and help students take up the approaches to learning and study that improve their chances of success.

At this point it is necessary to go beyond Chapter 2's invitation to understand affordances as opportunities or possibilities. Gibson, who created the term, writes:

> The *affordances* of the environment are what it *offers* the animal, what it *provides* or *furnishes*, either for good or ill. The verb *afford* is in the dictionary, but the noun *affordance* is not. I have made it up. I mean by it something that refers both to the environment and to the animal ... they [affordances] have to be measured *relative to the animal* ... They are not just abstract physical properties ... an affordance is neither an objective property nor a subjective property; or it is both if you like ... It is equally a fact of the environment and a fact of behavior. It is both physical and psychical, yet neither. An affordance points both ways, to the environment and to the observer.
>
> (Gibson, 1986: 127, 129; emphasis in original)

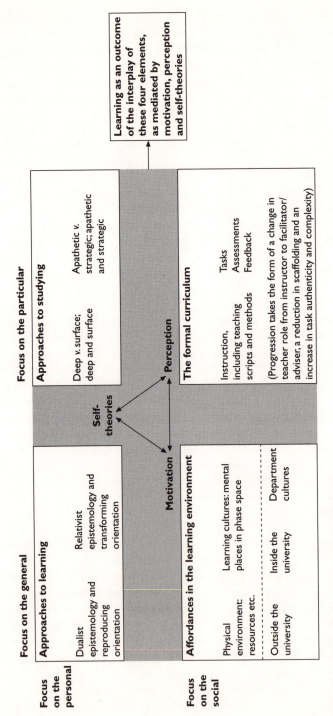

Figure 10.1 Elements of learning architecture

This opens up the possibility that we can design into environments features that have the potential to help with learning or performance tasks. Seen like this, programme design is akin to architecture. In the words of one commentator,

> What appeals to me particularly about architecture as a source of ideas for creating convivial, productive on-line learning spaces is that architecture is about the *crafting of affordances.* Architecture (built space) does not *determine* activity. Bad architecture endangers some kinds of valued activity. Good architecture can nurture it. But the users of built space have proper scope for autonomy.
>
> (Goodyear, 2000: 14–15; emphasis in original)

This depends on programme designers trying to maximize the chances that learners will experience:

1 *Coherence.* Modules and other learning affordances should relate to the programme learning outcomes in such a way that it is probable that students who take advantage of them will have achieved what the learning outcomes specify. There should also be a consistent learning culture, which is to say that students should understand what the programme is trying to achieve and expect that feedback from teachers and the messages in what is sometimes called 'the hidden curriculum' – the messages embedded in daily social practices – dovetail with those goals.
2 *Progression.* The programme should do more than add information to students' stock. There should be some sense in which it is transformative, evoking new ways of understanding or working, new beliefs, perhaps new self-theories and metacognitive formations. Progression has at least three sources.
   - One involves introducing learners to progressively harder concepts, although it was noted in Chapter 8 that this approach is problematic.
   - Another involves modifying self-theories, metacognition, beliefs about learning and studying etc. This can be promoted by learning cultures that are saturated with messages about more robust self-theories etc. and which avoid teaching and assessment practices that so overload students that they resort to the coping strategies that are associated with unproductive beliefs and habits of thought.
   - The third, reducing the scaffolding so as to help learners to become more independent, has been explained in Chapter 8.
3 *Slow learning.* This has two faces. One is making sure that there are sufficient affordances distributed across the programme to support the development of complex achievements such as autonomy, skill in oral presentation, incremental self-theories (see Chapter 4) and problem-working. The second is metacognitive, to do with making sure that students know what they are learning and why it matters. This should involve them in reviewing their achievements in respect of these complex and

Box 10.1 Programme level actions to encourage incremental self-theories and internalist attributional dispositions

1 Make sure that students are told about the learning culture that you are trying to encourage and its significance. Even at Oxbridge there are students who believe that they are impostors who will sooner or later be exposed. There are also people there who believe that brains and charm have got them there and will suffice, come what may. In both cases, work on self-theories and attributions is a key to good learning and employability. All the more so with students who have modest academic histories.

2 Involve study advisers, careers service staff and others in thinking about how your programme can, with their help, best help students to develop the desirable cell A beliefs (see Figure 4.1).

3 Look for ways of building some personal (or professional) development planning (PDP) into your programme. It is an obvious occasion for encouraging students to reflect on programme learning outcomes and their career plan.

4 Are there enough other opportunities in courses and programmes for reflection, metacognition and planning for improvement?

5 Look at the ways in which feedback on performance is given to students. What messages does it send out? (Ones favourable to learned helplessness in many cases.) What specific and useful advice does it give for improvement? (Often none, so there is no contribution to metacognitive or strategic thinking from this source.)

6 Programmes that teach students how to find, shape, work and (perhaps) solve problems are likely to be teaching a great deal about how to learn by showing the power of persistence and strategic thinking in academic life. Problem-based learning programmes keep on showing students' approaches, ways of thinking and ways of acting that can be successful in most circumstances *if* enough mindful effort is put in. What is very clear is that unless they know about the intended learning culture, understand what it means and regularly have to engage with its key ideas, then nothing much will happen. Departmental learning cultures have to be foregrounded, headlined and celebrated.

subtle learnings, identifying directions for development and organizing evidence to support their claims to achievement. A lot of this metacognitive work can be done by getting students to create and grow learning portfolios similar to the teaching portfolios described in Chapter 13.

Box 10.1 gives a glimpse of what this thinking means with its suggestions for promoting learning cultures that encourage malleable self-theories and internalist attributional dispositions (see Figure 4.1). Programme design, though, is something done by teams and, as such, not central to a book on the work of individuals. Course design is.

Designing courses

Figure 10.2, which could also apply to programme design, depicts course design as a complex activity. Reworking Figure 2.1, it shows that the task will be easier or harder according to the helpfulness of the mediating artefacts (concepts and skills are treated as special sorts of artefact), the quality of rules, norms and expectations, the expertise distributed through the community and available to the designer, and the division of labour. It will also depend upon whether this is an incremental change to an established module or a brand-new course and upon the teacher's expertise in module design. The job may be simpler when an experienced teacher reworks an established course than when a new teacher plans a new one, although there is a case for saying that it would be good if established teachers, who may be grooved into some indifferent practices, learned to do redesigns as mindfully as 'blank sheet of paper' designs. The subject matter and the general characteristics of the students likely to take the course will also complicate or simplify the design work.

Regardless of the complexity of the task, course design involves choosing learning outcomes, instructional arrangements, tasks and assessment and orchestrating them so that they work symbiotically.

Teaching, learning and assessment

Enough has been said in Chapters 7 to 9 to make this a short section. The main issues are to do with selecting methods that are fit for the purposes

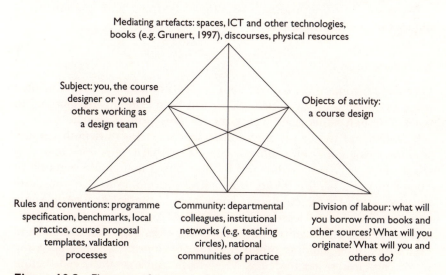

Figure 10.2   Elements of a course design system (after Engeström, 2001)

expressed by the learning outcomes, that are appropriate to the students and that can be squared with resource and time constraints. When it comes to programme design, a lot of attention needs to be paid to ensure that, across the set of constituent modules, there is enough variety of teaching, learning and assessment methods to make it likely that students will meet the goals expressed in the programme learning outcomes. It is still sensible to be concerned about variety at course level but, just as course learning outcomes will be a severe selection from the 20 plus programme learning outcomes, so the methods used will also be a selection from those mentioned in Chapters 7 to 9 and recommended by other books. Too much variety in a short course can give it a restless feel and leave students feeling that they have to skim over things because there is insufficient time for them really to get to grips with, for example, peer assessment, novel summative assessment techniques, participating in presentations or concept mapping. Now, since these methods and others like them are not recommended just as interesting ways of freshening up your teaching – they are quintessential in the development of skills and metacognition – it follows that overcrowding and the superficial learning that follows would be something to worry about. 'Deep', full appreciation of the learning outcomes that can be supported by approaches such as these means making time for students to become easy with them. Of course, in a well constructed programme it may be that you are confident that certain techniques have already been mastered and that students can use them automatically. But in that case it would make sense to consider introducing them to a new teaching, learning or assessment technique as a contribution to the set that constitute the programme.

Use a variety of appropriate assessment, learning and teaching techniques but avoid being too busy.

Learning outcomes

Learning outcomes say what you want students to understand and be able to do by the end of the course. Some will be specific to the material in hand, although rather than use a rather fatuous formula such as 'students will understand the causes and consequences of the thirteenth century scientific revolution', you might consider saying that as they come to understand the subject matter they will be developing their understanding of one or two of a handful of key principles or propositions that constitute the structure of your discipline. For example, the substantive learning outcomes for a history degree might be reduced to statements about change and not-change, the nature and complexities of causation, clock time and lived time, understanding others and the relationship between surviving sources and historical knowledge. An in-depth course on the decade before the American Civil War might engage with the second and fourth, whereas one on 'crime and control 1500–2000' might give priority to the first and the last.

However, the USEM model of curriculum that was introduced at the beginning of Part 2 says that programmes are usually expected to enhance students' subject-specific and general skills, to stimulate their efficacy beliefs and self-theories and to improve their metacognition. Where are learning outcomes associated with these aims to come from?

If you are lucky, they will come from the programme specification or plan. Table 10.1 shows the learning outcomes for a degree programme, and which modules concentrate on which of them. A new module would probably touch upon many, perhaps all, of the 16 programme learning outcomes but the programme director would insist that its designer take two, three or four and give them thorough attention. Notice again the operation of the principle that modules should not be cluttered with learning outcomes. So far from being impressive, the module I saw with 19 of them made me suspicious about the quality of the course and programme teams behind it. Which outcomes are chosen would depend on the designer, although the programme director might say that it would be very welcome if the new course could contribute to numeracy (outcome 10.2C(3)), or to one of the other less well covered outcomes. Of course, 'numeracy' is too vague a term to be much use to a module designer, who will expect to be able to refer to a glossary that briefly explains how it is understood in the context of this programme. (In this case the department said that students should be able to 'read intelligently data summaries based on a range of standard descriptive and inferential techniques, which means being able to understand what the numerical data mean and interpreting them for the purposes at hand'.) The programme plan says what the programme is trying to do but it should not stop individual teachers from adding their own learning outcomes. When there are no programme specifications to help then teachers can usually find suggested learning outcomes in subject associations' or professional bodies' publications or, in the UK, on the subject benchmarks web page (http://www.qaa.ac.uk/crntwork/benchmark/benchmarking.htm).

Identifying a handful of learning outcomes for sustained attention is not the end of the story. How will we know when an outcome has been achieved? This question, much beloved of those who want answers so that they can then use summative assessment data as, they suppose, valid and reliable indicators of teacher, department and institutional performance, needs quite a complex answer. First comes the matter of level of achievement. Common sense says that first year critical thinking ought to be different from final year critical thinking and that some kind of statements can be written to capture the difference. Then comes the matter of quality of achievement. Having described final year critical thinking, we may want to introduce differentiation because we grade on a 1–5, A–E or first-fail

Table 10.1 The contribution to programme learning outcomes made by key courses

Skill outcomes (programme specification, section 10.2)	100 T1	100 T2ª	100 T3	200	205	211	225	227	228	231	232	234	235	236	300ª
A1 Critical capabilities	✓*	✓	✓	✓	✓*	✓*	✓*	✓*	✓*	✓	✓	✓	✓*	✓*	✓*
A2 Argumentation	✓*	✓	✓	✓*	✓*	✓	✓	✓*	✓*	✓	✓	✓*	✓*	✓	✓
A3 Open-mindedness	✓*	✓	✓	✓*	✓	✓*	✓*	✓	✓	✓	✓	✓	✓*	✓	✓
A4 Tolerance of ambiguity	✓	✓	✓	✓	✓	✓	✓*	✓	✓	✓*	✓*	✓	✓	✓*	✓*
B1 Information-handling	✓	✓	✓	✓	✓	✓	✓	✓*	✓*	✓*	✓*	✓	✓	✓*	✓*
B2 Research skills	✓*	✓*	✓	✓	✓	✓	✓	✓	✓*	✓	✓	See left	✓	✓	See left
B3 ICT	✓*	✓*	Students go to ICT workshops if they need to uprate their knowledge. World wide web used in most courses							✓*	✓*	See left		✓*	See left
B4 Number	✓*	✓*	Students read and make sense of numerical data in all courses												
B5 Conventional	✓*	✓*	✓*	✓	✓	The expectations laid down in the first term are reinforced by normal course practices									✓
B6 Presentational	✓*	✓*	✓*	✓*	✓	✓*	✓*	✓	✗	✓	✓	✓*	✓	✓	✓
C1 Reflectiveness	✓	✓	✓*	✓	✓	✓	✓	✓	✓	✓	✓	✓	✓*	✓	✓
C2 Independence	✓	✓	✓*	✓	✓*	✓	✓	✓	✓	✓	✓	✓	✓*	✓	✓
C3 Problem-working	✓	✓	✓*	✓*	✓*	✗	✓	✓	✓*	✓	✓	✓	✓	✓	✓*
C4 Work organization	✓	✓	✓	✓	✓	The expectations laid down in the first term are reinforced by normal course practices							✓	✓	✓
C5 Interpersonal	✓	✓*	✓	✓	✗	✓	✓	✓	✓	✓	✓	✓*	✓	✓	✓
C6 Groupwork	✓	✓*	✓*	✗	✗	✗	✓	✓	✓	✓	✓	✓	✓	✓	✗

Notes:
✓: skills that are likely to be instantiated when students engage with the module's set of learning, teaching and assessment activities. Whether they actually are used or developed depends a lot upon the individual student's construction of the module and prior learning achievements.
*: skills that will get particular attention in a module. Students wishing to improve a skill are advised to use this information when choosing modules.
✗: skills that are not identified as learning priorities in a module.
ª: learning opportunities in these two cases vary according to students' option choice.

scale and need to be able to identify five excellent, good, modal, passable and poor quality critical thinking, even if critical thinking is only assessed as one element in the assessment of a complex piece of work, like the evaluation of a journal paper. Both cases – producing level descriptors and then differentiating within levels – call for descriptors, criteria or indicators, arranged taxonomically, in a hierarchy, to allow us to:

1 Remind ourselves what we are trying to achieve.
2 Tell students what they need to do to succeed.
3 Tell them which sorts of achievements are going to be best rewarded and which will be disdained.
4 Judge student achievements.

It is hardly surprising that there is considerable enthusiasm for decomposing learning outcomes into taxonomies describing levels and qualities of achievement. As far as the course designer is concerned, if you are lucky someone will have done some or all of the work for you. The UK subject benchmark statements, mentioned above, say what the learning outcomes would look like at first year, final year and master's levels. However, if you want to do your marking with close reference to these benchmarks, then you will need to develop statements explaining what good . . . useless performance would look like. But there is also a view, foreshadowed by comments in Chapters 8 and 9 on taxonomies and performance criteria, that challenges the assumptions that learning outcomes can be specified this precisely and that they can be used to make fine-grained judgements. Broad statements, such as the one above, which described how the numeracy learning outcome is to be understood, are extremely useful as 'fuzzy' indicators – they help us to judge and provide a language for conversations about learning and achievement. But attempts to get greater precision run increasingly into three sets of problems:

1 *Philosophical.* Many learning outcomes do not describe 'real' things but practices that are social, contexted and changing. People get into all sorts of trouble because 'the skill of whatever' is only a name for a shifting and varied set of social practices that will resist all attempts to bring them within unambiguous rules.
2 *Psychological.* Psychologists repeatedly find that small changes to the wording or design of tasks designed to measure human performance can produce quite large variations in the results. We cannot be sure that performance on any one task is more trustworthy than performance on another, which is likely to be different.
3 *Practical.* Writers of level and quality statements often use comparators like 'better', 'more developed', 'greater knowledge' and so on. These woolly words have to be interpreted and they, and outcome statements in general, will be applied in different ways by different assessors (Wolf,

1997). Attempts to reduce diversity often lead people to write longer and longer criteria in order to reduce ambiguity. They fail because ambiguity is inbuilt and very few people have any patience with the long, wearisome documents that result.

I interrupted the practical advice on course design with swift deconstruction of the idea that precise statements of learning outcome are possible because the way you see learning outcomes relates to the ways in which you think courses should be designed. That is the subject of the next section.

Rational curriculum planning and other design approaches

Table 10.2 presents five approaches to course design:

1 *Content-led planning*, which is a traditional and simple way, still widely used, even by schoolteachers in the UK who are supposed to be using method no. 2 (Knight, 2002b). The great snag is that once the content is sorted everything else can get casual treatment, leading to spurious claims, unfocused teaching and poor assessment practices. In practice the content, learning intentions, pedagogic and assessment practices are not orchestrated as they should be.
2 *Rational planning.* This is how we are supposed to do it, although Gibbs (1999b: 13) recalled that 'My experience of developing the design of this course was of a series of lurches and insights, rapid progress and being "stuck", wondering what to do next. Ideas about class sessions, assessment and reading material built up in a symbiotic way as I thought my way through it . . . I find it hard to imagine being able to be creative in a systematic way.' Not only does this treat the learning outcomes far more seriously than they can possibly deserve (see the previous section) but people don't work like that (Knight, 2001, 2002b).
3 *Assessment-led planning.* The intention here is to fix a common weakness, namely the tendency to leave assessment issues to last and then to treat them casually. I like it but think it is open to the criticisms that I make of rational approaches, perhaps more so, since it invites designers to suppose that the learning outcomes can be precisely measured.
4 *Fuzzy planning.* This is a continued to-and-fro process of deliberation which starts with an interplay between the designer's values and his or her store of teaching, learning and assessment techniques. Once worthwhile learning and assessment sequences have been imagined as possible learning affordances, it is usually quite easy to set them alongside the programme specification and see two or three learning outcomes that could be honestly appropriated. Knight's (2001) paper on a process approach to curriculum-making contains more details.
5 *Planning for PBL.* The advantages and disadvantages of PBL were reviewed in Chapter 8. It is hard to devise authentic problems to cover the ground,

Table 10.2 Five curriculum planning models

1 Content-led planning	2 Rational planning	3 Assessment-led planning	4 Fuzzy planning	5 Planning for PBL
Identify the content to be covered	Identify learner needs	(Identify learner needs)	(You have a view, often implicit, of what counts as worthwhile learning)	Select or write LOs
Slice it up according to the time available	Select appropriate LOs from PS, or write new ones	Select or write appropriate LOs ↔	Recall learning, teaching and assessment methods that you think make for valuable learning and . . . ↔	Identify topics to be covered
Choose teaching and learning methods	Identify relevant student characteristics and their diversity	Decide how you will assess achievement of LOs	. . . imagine how they could be affordances when with the material you expect to cover ↔	Imagine a series of problems that, as a set, would require students to cover all the material
Decide how you will assess students	Choose course material and pedagogical methods accordingly	Choose course material	Consider what sorts of learning you could reasonably expect to follow ↔	Write problems to fit in a standard sequence (typically one week per problem)

Table 10.2 (Cont'd)

1 Content-led planning	2 Rational planning	3 Assessment-led planning	4 Fuzzy planning	5 Planning for PBL
Consult programme specification (PS) and identify learning outcomes (LOs) that you can claim to have, or write your own	Sequence the materials and methods	Choose teaching and learning methods	Lay claim to three or four fuzzy learning outcomes	Devise a standard pedagogical sequence for this set of problems
Secure resources and implement	Choose methods with which to assess achievement of LOs	Sequence the materials and methods	Review the interplay of pedagogy and material in the light of those claims	Check problems and pedagogy against LOs and topics to be covered
Use evaluation instrument	Secure resources and implement	Secure resources and implement	Sequence, secure resources and implement	Decide how you will assess achievement of LOs
	Use evaluation instrument and revise the course for next year	Use evaluation instrument and revise course for next year	Ask students for suggestions for making next year better	Sequence, secure resources and implement
				Use evaluation instrument and revise the course for next year

while staying faithful to independent group learning methods. Its supporters (Reynolds, 1997) say how good it is when it works.

Course structures

The default design is a weekly cycle of lecture(s) and seminar and/or lab class. This is simple, which means there is little reason for anyone to forget what they should be doing in any week, and it can be efficient (see below). There are alternatives. For example, in one of my courses there are nine presentations in the first five weeks and one seminar in which students form into learning groups and begin to plan how they, as individuals and groups, will tackle the assignments to be done in the next five months. The next three weeks are a mixture of presentations, seminars, which I facilitate in the way I described in Chapter 8, and group meetings, which I do not attend. A workshop takes up the last two weeks of the Christmas term and the first of the Easter term. In these weeks students meet and work where, when and as they please but they keep consulting me by email or calling into my office. This model is easier on my time, quickly gets students in a position where they can undertake complex and authentic tasks, and supports learning outcome 10.2C(6), groupwork. The presentations + seminars + group meeting → workshop cycle is repeated in the Easter term, although there are fewer presentations, and leads to an end-of-term course conference.

A variant of this would extend the three week workshop, add more structure to it and use asynchronous computer-mediated communication (CMC) to underpin it. It would be as well to put one or two face-to-face meetings or synchronous on-line sessions in. Another course design shares this thinking but applies it to the case of a core course taken by students with three different areas of interest. The first weeks are common to everyone and involve a lot of input on the new procedures they will be using, the organizing concepts and essential information. They then join one of three workshops in which they apply the understandings from the first part of the course to authentic issues in their area of interest. After four weeks they come together (face-to-face or on-line) as a whole class for a couple of weeks to rework the ground covered at the beginning of the course, before returning to workshops. Again, the course closes with a conference. The last example of course design is problem-based learning, which typically involves a seminar at the beginning of the week which is attended by three or four student workgroups. (The weekly cycle could, of course, become a two-, three- or four-weekly one.) The week's problems are explored, with the tutor facilitating discussion about the affordances for tackling them (these often include presentations, lab classes, dedicated software, websites, drop-in consultations, clinical opportunities) and about how best to go about the task (supporting the development of metacognition). Groups report back in their end-of-week seminars, getting instant feedback from each other and the teacher, while also submitting a report which may or may not be graded. The cycle may be varied towards the end of the course when a review, consolidation and needs identification session may be provided.

The reason for noticing these five course designs is that they show that courses can be designed in any ways we can imagine that are fit for the purpose and that if the purpose includes really engaging students with procedures, concepts and information, then there is a good case for designs that break from the default model. Two words of caution. First, recall that ICT-based courses may reduce teachers' face-to-face commitments but increase their overall workload. Second, students accustomed to the default pattern may see alternatives as cheapskate devices to take their tuition fees and provide little in return.

Checking

There are more than four things to look at when checking a provisional course design but these four are emphasized because they are easy to miss.

1 *Costs.* The most important cost is teacher time. Good student learning does not have to be expensive. For example, some teachers aim to keep seminar groups small to counterbalance large lecture groups. However, if a seminar is defined as a time to work on information, rather than in terms of the size of the group, then it is possible to run seminars with 20 students and still get plenty of engagement with the task, talk and learning (see Chapter 8). And it is little harder to learn the names of 20 students than it is to learn ten. Likewise with assessment. Each week I ask students to submit summaries of the reading they have done (and that reading replaces information-presenting lectures) but I do not mark them, although I look at them to make sure they have been done seriously, I get students to comment, *briefly* and orally, on each other's and they know that the file of summaries will be used as supplementary evidence should they end up on a grade boundary. Ideas for faster feedback can be found in Box 9.3.

2 *Considerateness.* Consider how students might experience the course. As I just said, those who think that your job is to lecture will need to be won over to novel features of your design. That is a reminder that you will need to write a good handbook so that students can become knowing students, knowing what you are trying to do, how, why and when. Ask too whether students are likely to come to the course well enough

prepared to succeed; what arrangements you envisage for students who experience difficulties; whether you are expecting students, many of whom will have part-time jobs, to do too much themselves; if you want them to work together, whether you have designed tasks that require and help them to do so; whether you have put so much in that students are likely to use coping strategies that lead to superficial short-term memorization of information; whether tasks are too complicated; and whether tasks are framed so that good students really could get top marks (I see lots of tasks that effectively call for description but have grade indicators that reserve top marks for analysis, critical thinking and evaluation, which the tasks do not really call for).

3 *Student motivation.* A considerate course design will contribute to student motivation but it is also worth checking it in the light of the approach to motivation taken in Chapter 4, where it was said that motivation is not a sticks-and-carrots additive but something to be designed in. Emphasis was put upon choice, opportunities for flow experiences and success, good interpersonal relationships and enjoyment. Unrealistic goals, excessive workloads, impersonal environments and oppressive control were identified as demotivators, which in this case will make for disengagement and/or the surface learning that comes from coping.

4 *Psychic rewards.* Assuming that your design is not so inefficient that it could be a source of stress, consider how it might contribute to your own sense of well-being. Have you designed something that plays to your strengths, or to things that you expect to become strengths? Does it provide a challenge that lies within your ZPD? Is there enough variety in it? Can you see yourself writing about it with pride in your teaching portfolio (see Chapter 13)?

Redesigning a course

Previous chapters have taken a continuing quality improvement approach to being a teacher, recommending *bricolage* or tinkering. The implication is that courses will get naturally redesigned when you keep on responding to feedback from good student and peer evaluations, when you experiment with new techniques, tasks and assessment arrangements or when you buy into new technologies by using a website as a course library or introducing CMC tasks. Programme-level changes will also call for some course redesign. For example, a department decides to be more systematic and explicit in its approach to enhancing student employability. It began by doing a skills audit and an audit of learning, teaching and assessment (LTA) methods. Tables 10.1 and 10.3 show audits that gave no great cause for concern. It is more usual for audits to show that:

Table 10.3 Learning, teaching and assessment methods in the key modules of an undergraduate programme

Teaching, learning and assessment activities	100 T1	100 T2ᵃ	100 T3	200	205	211	225	227	228	231	232	234	235	236	300ᵃ
1 Lectures	✓	✓		✓	✓	✓	✓	✓		✓	✓	✓	✓	✓	
2 Seminars	✓	✓	✓	✓	✓	✓		✓		✓	✓	✓	✓	✓	
3 Tutorials	All modules offer students opportunities to consult tutors on a one-to-one or small group basis, according to student preference														
4 Workshops		✓	✓				✓		✓			✓			
5 Problem-working	All modules engage students on problem-working activities, which vary within and between modules in complexity and the amount of scaffolding provided. EDS 300 is the capstone, involving complex problems that are typically identified and defined by students														
6 Structured work in peer groups	✓	✓	✓	✓			✓	✓			✓	✓	✓	✓	✓
7 Self-directed peer group work	✓	✓					✓			✓		✓		✓	
8 Group projects	✓	✓								✓		✓	✓	✓	
9 Structured independent study			✓	✓	✓		✓	✓	✓	✓		✓			✓
10 Self-directed learning					✓		✓	✓		✓	✓	✓	✓	✓	✓
11 Web-enhanced teaching	?	?	?				✓			✓	✓	✓	✓	✓	✓
12 Web searches	?	?	?				✓	✓		✓	✓	✓	✓	✓	✓
13 Practical work	✓	✓	?							?	?				
14 Critical commentaries						✓	✓	✓	✓	✓	✓	✓	✓	✓	✓
15 Essays	✓			✓	✓	✓	✓	✓		✓	✓	✓	✓	✓	
16 Set reading	✓			✓	✓	✓	✓	✓		✓		✓	✓	✓	✓
17 Analysis of target documents	✓			✓	✓	✓	✓		✓	✓		✓			
18 Interpreting data	✓						✓			✓		✓	✓		
19 Student presentations	✓						✓	✓		✓		✓	✓	✓	✓
20 Written examinations	✓			✓								✓	✓		
21 Making a bibliography		?												?	
22 Concept mapping	✓													✓	✓
23 Literature review		✓											✓	✓	
24 Research design/strategy		✓									✓	✓	✓	✓	✓

Note: ᵃ: learning opportunities in these two cases vary according to students' option choice.

1 Some LTA methods are over-used when judged against the LOs (learnng outcomes) in the programme specification.
2 Some LTA methods that need to be used if some of the LOs are to be developed, especially ones conducive to the development of good claims to graduate employability, are hardly there, if at all.
3 Although most modules claim to touch on most LOs, when tutors are asked to identify those that get particular attention a disturbing pattern emerges: some get little attention, others are done to death.
4 There are issues of progression. Some LOs get particular attention in year 1 and never again; others in the final year, when some earlier preparation might have made sense.

This picture is likely to be confirmed if a third, much trickier audit is done to see which LOs are assessed (formatively or summatively) in which modules. The upshot is usually that the programme team goes about tuning the curriculum by asking individual tutors to add a new LTA method or two and remove some hackneyed ones so as to support a couple of LOs that need more attention, while downplaying those that have had too much. These tuning processes are inherently collaborative in that the course redesign comes from an overview of the programme and involves colleagues, especially the programme director, offering advice on how best to respond to the needs identified by the audits.

Further reading

There is surprisingly little written on design work. It is not easy to lay hands on good books by Graham Gibbs (1992) and Alan Jenkins (1998). I value Judith Grunert's 1997 book entitled *The Course Syllabus*, which is really about module design. The North American practices of which she writes are not identical to those elsewhere, so her suggestions need some adaptation and extension. Susan Toohey's *Designing Courses for Higher Education* (1999) is a thoughtful and helpful guide written from an Australian base.

There is a need for advice on programme design, although I think that different national expectations mean that books would need to be written for specific national markets. I admire Boyatzis and associates' (1995) account of the development, evaluation and refinement of an MBA programme at Case Western Reserve University, as a model of how to go about programme development if you have world-class experts, such as Boyatzis and colleagues, and plenty of resources.

11

Getting good evaluations

A stance

Bad evaluation practice is manifest in ways of evaluating teaching quality that use an institution-wide questionnaire to get ratings of some surface features of teaching. Good evaluations, whether they come from students or other teachers, are sensitive to specifics of what teachers do in the planning, active and post-active stages of teaching in order to stimulate complex learning. I suggested in Chapter 7 that this meant looking at five moments of teaching:

1 Doing the things that research studies associate with student learning while being someone students relate to.
2 Using good instructional scripts.
3 Planning appropriate learning–teaching sequences.
4 Designing courses.
5 Designing environments with affordances for simple and complex learning.

Students are well placed to evaluate some parts of these five moments, while other teachers from inside or outside the workgroup judge others. This chapter looks at how to get good teaching evaluations from students and other academic staff, finishing with some words on creating a justifiably good estimate of oneself as a teacher.

It does assume, though, that being judged a good teacher is something that matters. In some institutions student evaluations are used summatively in annual work-planning and performance reviews, so there is some extrinsic reason to make sure that the scores come out right. In most there is some connection between promotion and teaching quality, although quality tends to be judged on the basis of a teaching portfolio (see Chapter 13) of which evaluations are only a part. However, repeated calls for promotion and tenure committees to take teaching more seriously suggest that in most cases teaching quality is not the main factor in promotion decisions. So, why try and get good teaching evaluations, especially when status still comes mainly from the scholarship of discovery and the grants and publications that go with it? Rather than answer in terms of extrinsic motivation – pay and promotion – I prefer to see good evaluations as an intrinsically important part of being a teacher. Although we teach because we have to, it is also a source of psychic rewards (Chapters 1 and 4). Acceptable and good evaluations from students, others and ourselves are feedback that gives us permission to accept, even enjoy, those rewards. Done well, evaluations are an embodiment of the appreciative enquiry that encourages us to improve areas that lag behind those that the enquiry has confirmed as strengths. This points towards a subsidiary meaning of getting good evaluations, which is getting ones that are good in the sense of being useful; and by 'useful' I mean that they affirm our intrinsic motivation to teach, while inspiring us to continue to tinker at doing better. Those are truly good evaluations.

Getting good evaluations from students

A great deal has been said, especially in Chapter 7, about what students like, which is a mixture of technical competence (described, for example, in Box 7.2) and the teachers' persona – in the words of Palloff and Pratt (1999: 20), 'The keys to the creation of a learning community and success- ful facilitation online are simple. They are as follows: *honesty, responsiveness, relevance, respect, openness,* and *empowerment.*' Chapter 8 gave guidance on setting clear, varied tasks within the ZPD and Chapter 9 talked about the sorts of feedback students value, with Box 9.3 advising on how to give them the speedy feedback they want.

Chapter 10 made explicit a theme that runs through Chapters 7 to 9, that good teaching is considerate of students, which particularly means helping students to know what you are trying to help them do, why it is valuable and how you will support them if they hit problems. This is extremely important if you want to get good evaluations and your course is out of the ordinary because although, for example, you know why you will not dictate notes to them, some will assume that you are just lazy. If students do not understand your thinking you cannot complain if they misjudge you. Let me make it clear that I am not saying that good teach- ing means never leaving students puzzled. Commenting that 'teaching audit is a peculiarly British disease', Law (1999: 9) writes 'that one way of failing in [British] university teaching is to be unclear about the purpose of what one is doing. Or to leave students with undefined questions in their minds . . . [But] I believe that they [audits] render complex thinking – . . . thinking that is lumpy or heterogeneous – difficult or impossible.' I value teaching that shares with students the uncertainties of scholarship and I recognize that precise learning outcomes are often unavailable or inappropriate. Students, though, should understand why it is that I will not tell them 'the answer' but make time for them to talk together to see what senses they can create out of lumpy and heterogeneous materials.

This can be developed into the suggestion that good evaluation practices are contoured to the course being evaluated. One-size-fits-all questionnaires are defective because they are not able to recognize good teaching unless it fits the default type (usually didactic information transmission), so they end up penalizing fresh, student-centred teachers because their work hardly registers. In these cases it is like trying to appreciate a sunset with a light meter. Good evaluation practices have been designed to appreciate what a course is intended to do, pick up shortcomings and be sensitive to unanticipated outcomes. Appropriate designs might begin with a survey of students taking the course. The most sophisticated institutions tell teachers they must include some, perhaps half-a-dozen, core questions and invite them to select another ten to twenty from an institutional item bank. They expect data to be reported back to a central unit but in terms of making a difference to teaching and learning it is more important to feed it back to students and ask for their comments. I ask them to help me to interpret the figures (I want to know why have they only rated the course handbook at 83 per cent when I cannot see how it can be improved) and for suggestions about what I could do by way of response (I always treat the three lowest-scoring items as matters for discussion, even if they have scores of >80 per cent). Subsequently I tell them what I am going to change and what I will not change and why. I usually have evaluations in weeks 6 and 14 of 20-week courses, which lets me act and be seen to act on student feedback, explanations and suggestions. These seem to me to be particularly good evaluations because they benefit the students who did them.

Getting good evaluations from other academic staff

Trigwell (2001) writes that good teaching is related to high quality student learning and is scholarly. However, given the endemic unreliability of measures of student learning in higher education (Knight 2002a), it would be unwise to say that students get good grades when taught by good teachers, or even to take the more sophisticated 'added value' line that we can calculate whether students learn more than expected on this teacher's courses. This means that we have to make indirect judgements of whether teaching is contributing to high quality student learning. Student evaluations of the first two teaching moments are proxies for direct measures of learning. Other teachers' judgements triangulate student judgements and extend to the third and fourth moments as well. Ideally, colleagues' evaluations, like students', will be sensitive to the specifics of the course. In this section I will concentrate on two of the ways in which other teachers judge teaching quality. I am deliberately not considering how to get good teaching evaluations from national quality agencies, partly because of the diversity of quality control, assurance or enhancement regimes, and partly because political changes make national practices so unstable that any advice would swiftly date.

The observation of teaching quality

Classroom observation is the obvious way to evaluate teaching quality but this common-sense position has its limitations, as Knight (1993: 22) writes:

> Teaching takes many forms and may not always be observed. Researchers studying primary school classrooms . . . have drawn attention to a host of methodological and procedural problems which mean that even observing something as apparently unproblematic as a lecture is fraught with problems, requiring the skill of a well-trained observer. Such a person will beware of observing in a way which, unwittingly, imposes a preferred model of what counts as good teaching: we have already said that no such model exists . . . Nor can observations be simply translated into points on a scale to allow fine comparisons between tutors and departments . . . There is not space to go into details about the problems with the observation of teaching: suffice it to say that they are many. While this should be no bar to peer visits to colleagues' lectures as a part of a social negotiation about teaching quality (formative assessment), there are clear implications for any institution which chooses to use teaching observation as a part of a top-down, summative system.

In all of this it is important to remember a point made in Chapter 9 about reliability, namely that several observations are needed before it is wise to claim that the judgements made are fairly reliable ones. Books on social science research methods add the point that all observations are driven by some theory, even if they are just the observer's tacit theories of what matters, and that it is important to be sure that the theories used are fit for the observational purpose (for example, Knight, 2002d). What, then, should be said about collegial teaching observation practices which have the low-stakes purpose of enriching conversations about teaching improvement? It makes sense for observers to look out for the things which students regularly say they value and to try to read the body language of the class to get a sense of the felt quality of teaching. Observers may use a set of prompts to help, although because there is the likelihood that prompts which work for a presentation that explores fresh theory will not be suitable for a lecture that informs students about something, they must be treated as prompts, not as criteria of good classroom practice. Observers from the same department as the teacher being observed are able to complement this student-focused observation with some judgement of the quality of the treatment of the subject matter.

Teaching portfolios

Portfolios have become the preferred way of getting an overview of teaching quality and of making claims to take a scholarly approach to teaching. Chapter 13 has things to say about creating portfolios. These notes are about using them for evaluative purposes. Trigwell (2001) argues that there is enough research to show that 'one way of conceiving of university teaching . . . is more likely to result in high quality student learning than other ways of thinking' (p. 67). This is a student-focused way, manifest as a concern to help students to 'develop and change their conceptions or world views' (p. 67) and aligned, in that teaching strategies are fit for this purpose. He says that good teaching has four elements:

1 It shows adaptiveness: the teacher shapes what he or she does to environmental or contextual circumstances – to particular students, subject matter and learning environment.
2 (a) It is student focused, with matching conceptions of teaching, learning and their concomitants. (b) It shows good pedagogic content knowledge, which is good knowledge of the subject and of ways of engaging students with it so as to make it likely that good, complex learning will follow, together with a commitment to reflection and learning.
3 'Good teachers draw upon the literature of their discipline, their knowledge of student learning and a student-focused conception to design a learning experience for students that is aligned with their learning objectives and assessment' (pp. 70–1).
4 It involves the use of good teaching strategies to inspire good learning.

These elements can be judged qualitatively, through observation and portfolios, and set alongside more quantitative data from student evaluations and grades to give a complex picture of teaching quality. However, given that educational developers seem to be attracted by Boyer's (1990) idea of the scholarship of teaching, there is also a need to explore how the scholarly quality of teaching might fairly be appraised: what should we look for? Scholarship can be inferred from evidence of the thinking processes associated with practice, which is typically done by the teacher making claims to scholarship through a portfolio that describes a range of practices and sets out the good, scholarly thinking behind them. Glassick *et al.* (1997: Chapter 2) recommend judging the claims on six counts:

1 Goal clarity. Are goals realistic, achievable and important?
2 Preparation. Shows understanding of existing scholarship and command of appropriate resources and skills.
3 Appropriate methods. Methods are fit for the purpose and effectively used.
4 Significant results. Were goals met? Does this scholarship contribute to pedagogical understanding?
5 Effective presentation of material. This speaks for itself.
6 Reflective critique. 'Does the scholar critically evaluate his or her own work? Does the scholar bring an appropriate breadth of evidence to his or her critique [and] use evaluation to improve future work?' (p. 36).

Indicators of quality, such as those suggested by Trigwell and Glassick *et al.* help to make the evaluation of teaching quality more consistent and less arbitrary. But, to repeat a point made about grade indicators in Chapter 9, indicators can only guide judgement of the variegated evidence of teaching quality presented to assessors operating in communities of practice subject to their own contingencies and expectations. This ought to be a warning against assuming that evaluations are sufficiently comparable for it to be possible to produce a teaching quality league table. Even were that to be a sound idea, it is not clear what the value would be. Although there will be a few cases when the evidence all points towards bad teaching practices, as far as the majority of teachers – perhaps 85 per cent – are concerned, the evidence will point to good practice with room for improvement. Following the line taken by Patton (1997) on good evaluation practice, I suggest that this calls for teaching evaluations which are, in his words, 'utilization-focused'. This means that before any evaluation is done the question 'How can we use evaluation to support teachers in improving their own and others' practices?' gets asked, with everything else following from it. It directs us to the evaluation of teaching quality as a low-stakes activity designed to create feedback that leads to conversations about how one aspect of teaching might be developed over the next six to twelve months. My stance is clearly that the evaluation of teaching quality is almost always a developmental matter and evaluation practices are worthwhile only to the degree that they stimulate good professional learning. If evaluation practices are based on the assumption that there are a lot of bad teachers who need to be identified and disciplined (high-stakes assessment), there is a danger of inquisitorial procedures that obstruct the low-stakes, collaborative evaluation for development that I reckon to be far more valuable.

As with getting good student evaluations, this section suggests that getting good teaching evaluations is primarily about getting ones that are useful, which partly depends on your department having systems that are developmental rather than regulatory and, where such systems are in place,

on your willingness to engage openly with colleagues in assessment conversations that help you to tinker better with what you do. Where evaluation is used for accountability purposes, then it makes sense to know the
evaluation criteria and play shamelessly to them. It is an iron law of assessment that what you measure in high-stakes ways is what you get. Those
leaders who dislike the consequences of assessment should change the
ways they assess.

Good self-evaluations

Academics often treat critical thinking, the ability to deconstruct anything,
as a great virtue, much to the irritation of policy-makers and practitioners
whose need is to act, not to dither. One result is that we are often poor at
evaluating ourselves appreciatively, especially as we can always name plenty
of colleagues who publish more, write better, win more research grants
and get invited to first division conferences. This does not seem to me
to be very healthy. How might we legitimately groom our self-esteem as
teachers?

I have mentioned appreciative enquiry in previous chapters. It starts
with what is good and can have a 'feelgood effect' where other evaluation
methods can be depressing. For example, imagine what might be said
about you, as a teacher, at a farewell speech. What would people say
you do well? What do you bring to your work with students? Beginnings
like these can lead to more systematic thinking about strengths. Other
people are more likely to evaluate your work positively when you play to
the strengths that you identify through this easy start with self-evaluation.
Temper this appreciation with an appraisal of the appropriateness of
your strengths – in terms of the programme learning goals, for example.
Second, although those goals are likely to be quite fixed, your personal
expectations are not. It might be worth reviewing them. As a beginning
schoolteacher I used to get depressed when my teaching was insipid or
a little ragged. A senior colleague said that he was happy if he did 31
adequate lessons and an excellent one a week. Others said much the
same. My expectations, which were out of line with theirs, had been bringing me down and stopped me appreciating that I was doing well in a high-
achieving school. Third, it is a good idea to check priorities. Most teachers
are committed to working with students, face-to-face or on-line, and also
see the value of creative course design. These priorities tend to be associated with good student evaluations as sources of psychic rewards. Getting
good evaluations from students and feeling good about what you do are
likely, then, to be related to the degree to which you make frontstage, not
backstage, work your priority.

Fourth, good self-evaluations should be getting you to identify and rein in aspects of the work that you have been finding dysfunctional: Tables 4.1, 4.2 and 12.1 contain suggestions. However, your self-theories and attributional tendencies also contribute to the ways in which you experience teaching and it makes sense to consider how far problems are fuelled by the ways in which you have come to perceive things. I find the ideas in Figure 4.1 thought-provoking and there is no shortage of 'pop psychology' books that encourage us to reflect on the ways in which we have learned to limit ourselves. This leads to reflection as the fifth theme in good self-evaluations. I made my unease with the concept clear in Chapter 2 but I do think there is something useful about trying to identify things that we might do better, deliberating on how to improve them, talking with others about our intentions and then beginning to tinker. Reflection for practice that is sensitive to the literature and involves talking with others can contribute to how to see problems, to the solutions we can imagine and to the steps we take to make a difference. This 'wriggling' reflection is a part of good self-evaluations.

There are two other things that I do to turn evaluation into something that enhances what I do and how I feel about it. One is to look at what I plan to do in a course and do a 'fun check'. How could this module be more enjoyable for me and for the students? I get a lot of help here from student evaluations because they are always geared to identifying things I could do differently or better. Second, I try to look back on each day and find a couple of good things about it, no matter how small they might be. It brings to mind the student who was pleased to get five minutes of skilful attention, the smooth handling of a seminar, although it didn't fizz, the way that assignments were returned quickly to students, even though marking them was a chore, or the colleague who said, 'That's a good idea. I'll look at it and get back to you.'

Lastly, I draw attention to the discourses of derision directed at the public sector and the remorseless increase of surveillance based on the premise that public sector professionals are short of commitment or competence, or both. They make it hard to have a sense of worth: after all, what value is success in a system that opinion-makers denigrate? They also make it hard to identify priorities for development and think well about how to improve. Yet these are discourses, not objective accounts of the way things are. Consider, for example, the Anglo-American belief that achievement depends on long hours of work. Not so in Sweden, write Campbell and Neill (1994). There schoolteachers who worked as long as English ones would be seen as rather ineffective – good teachers do not need to work 54+ hours a week. Or consider the views of a French woman speaking on BBC Radio 4 on 25 August 2001. She said that her employers are lucky to have someone of her calibre working for them, adding that this is common thinking among professionals in France. Hers is normally a

35-hour week. My argument is that we can evaluate ourselves better (in all senses of the word) if we can disturb Anglo-American background assumptions of the sort that say that if we were any good we would have real jobs. Good reflection wriggles into the assumptions embedded in public discourses, just as it wriggles into our self-theories, assumptions, practices and other taken-for-granteds.

Further reading

The books listed at the end of Chapter 7 all say a lot about what teachers do that results in good evaluations. The best account I know of how the scholarship of teaching might be assessed is Glassick *et al.* (1997).

Part 3

Times of change

These three chapters bring together Part 2's concern with the work of teaching and Part 1's attention to the conditions that make it easier or harder for older and newer academic staff to value teaching, while keeping the idea that good teaching is an individual *and* a social achievement very much to the fore. These themes need to be brought together in order to get some purchase on the dynamism – turbulence, if you prefer – of teaching and the activity systems or communities of practice in which teachers work.

There is a sense in which the first 11 chapters have already dealt with this pervasive change by identifying ways in which individuals, acting in activity systems and communities, can change what they do and reappraise the ways they experience the work of teaching. The figures, starting with Figures 1.1 to 1.4, tables, such as 4.1, 4.2 and 5.1, and most of the boxes are full of ideas for change, ideas that are more often than not aimed at the individual teacher and which imply small-scale, ongoing change rather than root-and-branch upheaval. (Of course, anyone who took them *all* on would experience considerable upheaval.) However, I do not think that it is reasonable to offer recommendations for self-initiated change but say nothing about coping with the external change forces which have such a strong influence on the ways we are able to be teachers. Unless we have ways of keeping other people's change mandates from taking control of our time we cannot be in any position to enjoy working away at improving what we do in ways that suit us and are fit for the contexts in which we work. It might seem ironic, then, that there is a short section in this part on ways of influencing others to change their teaching practices, and I rather wish that I could say a lot more about being an 'organic intellectual' or academic change agent. This is not, I argue, hypocrisy, because whereas mandated changes are driven by power-coercive strategies that try to make us do what others think to be best, my treatment is about normative–re-educative approaches to inviting people to think differently and to engage in local actions to make local differences.

This part also deals, in Chapter 13, with change in the form of career management. The first dozen chapters explored ways in which we might try to take control of what we do now but this one is about how we might act so that we have the best chances of being in positions in a few years' time that afford us recognition as teachers and support for continuing to be the best teachers that we can manage to be in the circumstances. It is emphatically about career management, not about getting promotion and moving on, although it will certainly be useful for those who want to manage their teaching careers so as to get promotion.

Chapter 14 is an upbeat rendition of the theme that it is still possible to be a good teacher in higher education and get the intrinsic rewards that connect teaching so strongly with the personal identities we achieve.

12

Change, experiencing change and making change happen

A stance

Governments and higher education institutions publicly value teaching more than ever before. They insist that new faculty members have some teacher training, invest in teacher development, finance teaching improvement projects, give teaching performance indicators more respect than they deserve, take course and programme approval too seriously and keep trying to freeze artful practice with documentary demands. Professor John Cowan wrote me a letter in which he took a positive stance towards the revaluation of teaching: 'I wish I were 15 years younger, and more able to move into mid-career at a time when teaching in higher education is more and more challenging, more and more rewarding, more and more valued. Maybe the situation is not yet ideal, but it has greatly improved and it is still improving.' Others are less positive about the changes, although I think that John is right to appreciate the positives. My stance has two sides. The first is that we gain by understanding change forces because change will continue to happen, and our success as teachers and as academics will be related to how we manage to experience it. The second is that structural changes, such as the spread of quality assurance practices, will affect but do not dictate our professional identities. We need to beware of imagining that we are forced to do things when choice is actually possible. That is not to say that it is easy to choose to do things we value in the ways we enjoy, but choosing depends on recognizing that choice is possible.

Key points

1 Change gets changed by people as they participate in making it happen. Change may have its victims but many changes have also been the victims of those they have been intended to change.

2 People create their responses to change. Some of the variation in our responses is attributable to differences in the ways we are accustomed to understand ourselves and the world. Sometimes reactions to change can be lightened by taking hold of alternative self-theories.
3 Those who want change teaching on any scale larger than their own practice might remember that systems are often beyond the control of any one person (see Chapter 1).
4 Organic approaches to improving teaching and student learning are preferred.

Research and informed practices

Limits of change

Chapter 1 introduced the idea that system dynamics may be wobbled by change but they none the less are attracted into persistent change-resistant patterns. Change often doesn't change things (Eisner, 2000; Farrell, 2000). It also said that it may be misleading to talk about causes and effects in complex systems and it is certainly unwise to imagine that they are so tightly coupled that a change in one place will have a determinate effect, and only that effect, elsewhere. These two points help to explain why change agents, such as governments, are so regularly frustrated by their inability to bring about changes to which they are committed. Commenting on a considerable international literature on attempts to change schooling, Bascia and Hargreaves (2000: 20) write that

> educational policymakers have not learned anything from these decades of research, whose recurring theme has been the complexity (if not outright failure) of educational change and the inadequacy of so many reform ideas . . . we have so little evidence that anyone has learned anything new about the processes of teaching and schooling beyond the confines of their own personal locations.

This reminds us that people in systems that are subject to change forces will often be less affected by them than change agents had intended. Trowler (1998) has shown how innovations in higher education may be taken up more or less faithfully but may also lead to: compliance and nothing more (change without change); resistance; and subversion through indifference or indolence. Figure 12.1, which is informed by Trowler's research and 1970s literature on externally prompted curriculum change in schools (MacDonald and Walker, 1976), reworks this important point that planned changes are seldom faithfully implemented and that it is naive to imagine that faithful implementation is normal (Trowler and Knight, 2001). Figure 12.1 says that attitudes to externally mandated

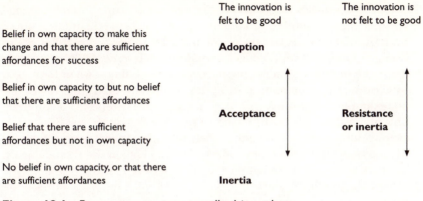

Belief in own capacity to make this
change and that there are sufficient
affordances for success

Belief in own capacity to but no belief
that there are sufficient affordances

Belief that there are sufficient
affordances but not in own capacity

No belief in own capacity, or that there
are sufficient affordances

The innovation is
felt to be good

The innovation is
not felt to be good

Adoption

Acceptance

**Resistance
or inertia**

Inertia

Figure 12.1   Four responses to externally driven change

changes are a combination of their perceived attractiveness, individuals'
beliefs about their capacity to do what is asked and the setting's capacity to
support the planned innovation.

Seen like this, change forces are not as all-conquering as structuralist
analyses of professional work imply. There is no intention here to deny
that it is disturbing to be expected to add key skills teaching, for example,
to a module that you already teach well and students appreciate. Nor
can imposed accountability, quality assurance and inspection initiatives
be ignored, and even changes that fail can make enormous demands
on teachers' time. Yet individual teachers may often find space to avoid
accommodating their existing practices to new mandates and find ways to
assimilate change to what they already enjoy doing. The trick, as some
schoolteachers in the UK have found after years of being repeatedly
assaulted by new government mandates, is not to panic but to look instead
for ways of making the mandates fit what they value and feel easy doing
(McCulloch *et al.*, 2000). There is no doubt that government initiatives
intensified their working lives, led many to become stressed and rather
more to feel less fulfilled in their work and emphasized backstage work
which few teachers valued at the expense of the face-to-face work with
children, which was the main source of their psychic rewards. Having read
that evidence no one could say that government-driven changes do not
cause turbulence. However,

1 Not all changes have equal impact and some, especially those that do
not have valued rewards or significant penalties attached, only reach
enthusiasts. Unfortunately, teaching improvement initiatives have tended
to fall into that category, although some countries, provinces and states
have seen no shortage of sharp-toothed accountability initiatives intended
to push teaching into approved forms.

2 One reason why schoolteachers in England were so oppressed by change was that they responded so conscientiously to change mandates, doing far more than was necessary or intended by some of the architects of change (Campbell and Neill, 1994; McCulloch *et al.*, 2000). I suggest that in higher education too people contribute to their own unhappiness by allowing innovations to take up far more time than they are worth. For example, if you think that teaching appraisal systems are a con trick, how much time is it worth taking to prepare for your own? Enough to avoid trouble, yes, but any more than that? To Americanize the point: whereas it is often enough to concentrate on being in the right ballpark, teachers tend to worry whether they have covered all the bases.

3 Schoolteachers lost control of some aspects of their work but school-teaching, like teaching in higher education, is a loose-coupled system. Despite considerable attempts by the British government to control teachers' work, those we talked with (McCulloch *et al.*, 2000) said that they had essentially managed to preserve their control of how they worked with children in the classroom, which was what really mattered to them. Teachers in higher education should also be able to preserve spaces for working with learners in ways that matter to them and on material they care about. Mantz Yorke and I have been illustrating this in our work on employability, a British government priority that some faculty take to be toxic to academic values.

Here is a view that does not deny that change can hurt, particularly when it comes in the form of unavoidable intensification, but it insists that change agents have less power and influence than people tend to suppose and that what may, on first sight, seem unavoidable often turns out to be less compelling once we look for ways of treating it as such. An implication, which will be followed up in the next section, is that being alert to ways of domesticating change is an important part of being a teacher who enjoys choosing the best ways to work.

Experiencing change

In his account of human systems, Luhmann (1995: xliii) writes:

> Of course, one can still say that human beings act. But since that always occurs in situations, the question remains whether and to what extent the action is attributed to the individual human being or to the situation. If one wants to bring about a decision of this question, one must observe, not the human being in the situation but the process of attribution.

Dweck's (1999) work, which has been mentioned above, takes a similar line. She wonders 'Why some people fall prey to depression and loss of self esteem when setbacks occur . . . Why some people display self defeating behavior in social relationships' (pp. xii–xiii) and 'Why do some students react to an obstacle as though it's a painful condemnation, when others see the same obstacle as a welcome challenge?' (p. 15). Her response is that, 'Contrary to popular opinion, confidence, self esteem and past success are not the keys to adaptive functioning' (p. xiii). Instead, 'adaptive and maladaptive motivational patterns . . . are fostered by people's self-theories' (p. xii). It follows that knowing people's

> implicit theories and goals . . . can tell us who, in encountering difficulty in their lives, will maintain and who will lose self esteem or a sense of worth; who will feel hopeful and who will feel devastated or depressed and who will not. As with achievement, it is ironic that those who care most about proving themselves often act in ways that are least likely to bring it about.
>
> (Dweck, 1999: 50)

This extends the connectionist thinking of Chapter 1 by saying that professional identities happen in activity systems or networks of which structural conditions are parts, but those conditions do not determine professional identities. Boyle and Woods (1996), Halford and Leonard (1999) and Webb (1999) have developed the point with respect to schools and public sector work in general. It would be fair, then, to suppose that professional identities and experiences of change might themselves be open to change. Dweck agrees, claiming that dystopian attributional habits and the learned helplessness that accompanies them can be altered. Attributional retraining, which was mentioned in Chapter 4, is one way of doing this. Despite the rather sinister overtones of the word 'retraining', it would involve stimulating teachers to be aware of the extent to which they create their own world through their own assumptions, habitual priorities, associations and beliefs by using techniques such as those listed in Box 1.2 and Table 4.1. Table 12.1 adds fresh advice inspired by the literature on change.

A parallel strategy for modifying the experience of change concentrates on workgroups rather than individuals. The discourses – languages and practices – they use contain community self-theories which shape the way groups interconnect with their environments. Just as Dweck's work implies that an important part of teaching is the creation of learning cultures favouring incremental self-theories (emphasizing strategic thinking and effort as keys to success), so a valuable concern for communities of practice is the displacement of learned helplessness about the group's capacities by the incremental theories that emphasize possibilities and presage learned optimism (Seligman, 1998). This lies rather outside this book's emphasis on being a teacher, although group discourses about change, action and capacity connect to the ways in which it feels to be a teacher.

Table 12.1 Advice on dealing with change

Advice	Explanation	Stances (see Figure 12.1) to which it is most applicable
1 Don't panic	Panic reactions and feelings that things are overwhelming produce helplessness. Unpicking the change into do-able bits – or unpicking resistance into do-able steps – makes coping easier	All
2 Remember	You have survived changes in the past. What helped? What could you have done better? Did the change turn out to be as all-consuming as you first thought?	All
3 Helicopter	Imagine looking at the change from afar – from the perspective of someone elsewhere, or as if you were two years in the future, looking back. This can cut the change down to size and highlight what matters	All
4 Try not to be in the first development and adoption wave in the system as a whole	Sometimes the first wave innovators get extra resources. They are also the first to reveal the problems with the change's inevitable impracticalities and have a hard time trying to cope	Acceptance. Adoption is easier in the second wave than in the first
5 At the local level, try to influence the nature of the change by being involved in its working out	Having some influence on what happens can itself make change feel better, as well as softening objectionable features. The alternative is becoming the victim of what others have decided is to be done	Adoption. Acceptance, especially if you are open to adoption
6 Look for help outside your activity system	If you are not in the first wave of innovation, people, websites, books, newspapers and journals will have advice	Adoption. Acceptance when there is no good help in the department. Resistance

7 Copy	The 'not invented here' syndrome is a major source of needless stress and overwork	Acceptance, adoption. Resistance, too
8 Assimilate change to existing practices as far as possible.	It often looks as though changes require existing practices to be accommodated to them. This is seldom so. There is a lot to gain by guarding against a tendency to change more than is needed	Adoption, acceptance
9 Simplify and tinker	It is easier to begin a change by starting with one or two big but simple points and taking time to develop from there	Adoption, acceptance
10 Remember: changes change as they are worked out in a setting	This is permission to be more relaxed about change. Fidelity of implementation won't happen and might not be a very good idea anyway	Acceptance, adoption
11 Think collegial within your activity system	Feelgood, reassurance, shared labour, safe challenges and shared knowings are some of the benefits. Collective subversion or resistance, like collective adoption, feels better and may also be better	Adoption, acceptance, resistance
12 Make a cost–benefit analysis	Changes can be time monsters, taking far more effort than they are worth. Decide how much time a change is worth and then restrict your effort within it	Acceptance. Adopters may get intrinsic rewards that negate calculations
13 Encyst the change	Create ways to shrink and isolate the change into something that can be complied with quickly and with detachment	Inertia, perhaps acceptance
14 Get out	Reappraise your career thinking (see Chapter 13), asking whether the costs, benefits, goals and possibilities are still in tolerable alignment	Resistance, inertia, acceptance

Of course, community discourses may be fractured and even if they are coherent they do not determine how individuals feel, but group discourses do connect to the ways in which individuals' feelings happen, are identified and evaluated and have (e)motive force. The suggestions made in Box 1.1 and Table 4.1 can also be profitably explored.

Making change happen

In many ways this is a book about how individual teachers can keep on making small-scale changes to their practices without pushing against the structural boundaries marked by timetables, workloads, programme structures, institutional assessment arrangements, colleagues' priorities and so on. When change is on this bounded scale, then the main limits to what can be achieved are personal limits: the amount of time we are prepared to commit to teaching improvement, the richness of our educational imagination, our own efficacy beliefs and suchlike. However, people who enjoy that side of working in higher education often find themselves helping their colleagues to design for better student learning. What has the literature to say about trying to bring about change on a departmental scale?

Much of the research is concerned with change in national, state or institutional practices, whereas my concern is with the small-scale work of being a teacher. There is agreement, though, that one source of change is change in the shape of the networks with which individuals connect (see page 27 above; Callon, 1999). Other structural changes that can induce individuals to alter what they do include change in the division of labour (seen in the rise of managerialism), rules (e.g. for quality assurance), mediating artefacts (such as the world wide web) and objects (principally, change in the quality of student learning). Activity systems assimilate many changes but others produce conflict or dissonance which can either impair the system's working or lead to changes so that the system accommodates to them (Engeström, 2001). Change agents, then, need to look for ways of disturbing systems enough to create the dissonance which leads to action without sparking such turmoil that the system is harmed. Research in schools says that in change-friendly activity systems teachers feel that they have space to learn; there are formal occasions for learning; tasks are rotated or shared; there is 'tolerance for divergent points of view'; 'tolerance for strategic failure: valuing failure as a source of learning'; and 'speculative thinking' (Leithwood *et al.*, 1999: 216). In these cases they tend to feel that rather than change being their master, they can domesticate it to their own purposes. The claim is that workgroups which are accustomed to learning together by people talking and tinkering will, by definition, see plenty of change but it may not feel overwhelming. In such settings, externally driven changes may still be intrusive but the professional ethos inclines faculty to see how the change can be assimilated to their practices and priorities or, if it cannot, how it can be encysted through minimal compliance that does not much disturb the community's valued discourses. The experience of change in vibrant communities of practice is different from the experience of change of the same objective sort in sclerotic activity systems.

In fact there is evidence that those trying to improve the quality of teaching, learning, assessment and curriculum would do better to work with communities of practice than to rely so much on top-down power-coercive strategies, a point developed by Knight (2002c). Kember (2000) evaluated the contribution to improving the quality of teaching and learning made by quality assurance and quality enhancement approaches. *Quality assurance* has dominated government thinking in most countries over the past 20 years. Despite its popularity with managers, good evidence of impact on the quality of teaching and learning is hard to find. Quality assurance can become 'a game played to a set of formal and informal rules . . . academics learn how to play the system and pass the test rather than improve teaching' (Kember, 2000: 192). Effects on teaching quality are at best indirect (Harvey and Knight, 1996) and subject to diminishing returns, because 'extra effort and more rigorous systems involve more costs, but little extra return and eventually over-intrusive systems result in disillusionment and resistance' (Kember, 2000: 193). Quality assurance procedures were identified in Chapter 1 as contributors to the intensification of academic work, part of the problem of change, not part of the solution – at least as far as academic staff are concerned.

A staff development industry has grown up over the past 20 years to provide the courses and workshops that are the mainstays of one approach to *quality enhancement*. Kember notes uncertainties about their effectiveness in higher education. On the one hand there are problems with the models of learning associated with workshops. If professional learning is defined as that which evokes a change in performance in a context, then the learning theories outlined in Chapter 2 cast doubt on the belief that workshops are necessary, let alone sufficient. The difficulties are profound, well analysed by philosophers and well documented by psychologists. For example, Dreyfus writes that 'rules "discovered" in the detached attitude [in reflection, for example] do not capture the skills manifest in circumspective coping' (Dreyfus, 1991: 86). Even if they did, rules can guarantee neither appropriate learning nor suitable change to practices. Besides, as was noted in Chapter 5, new members of staff attend; established faculty, by and large, do not.

Kember (2000) commends action learning projects as an alternative approach to quality enhancement, arguing that they reach beyond new staff (unlike workshops) and directly improve teaching and student learning (unlike quality assurance), and that his Hong Kong experience is that they are good value for money. Similar thinking can be seen in the establishment in the UK of a Learning and Teaching Support Network which has funded many small-scale projects and which aims to work sensitively with subject departments to negotiate and facilitate changes in pedagogical practice.

There is perhaps a danger here of making change seem like something special, whereas my intention is to suggest that it is normal in vibrant activity systems and that change agents are people with enquiring minds at work. Or, as Fullan wrote,

> I define change agency as being self-conscious about the nature of change and the change process . . . The individual educator is a critical starting point because the leverage for change can be greater through the efforts of individuals, and each educator has some control . . . over what he or she does, because it is one's motives and skills that are at question . . . I am not talking about leaders as change agents . . . but of a more basic message: each and every educator must strive to be an effective change agent.
>
> (Fullan, 1993: 12–13)

Further reading

I enjoy Michael Fullan's work and recommend his short *Change Forces: The Sequel* (1999). His analyses, which I find stimulating, are really about change forces in schools but the messages carry easily into higher education. Paul Trowler's well received *Academics Responding to Change* (1998) is about higher education and shows that change forces do not have things all their own way.

I keep coming back to Carol Dweck's *Self-theories* (1999) because it is consistent with the upbeat, positive thinking messages in pop psychology and self-help books but comes from someone known as an important social psychologist. I often respond to good theoretical works with some disappointment at the recommendations for practice and I do not feel completely comfortable with Dweck's suggestions for helping people to try on other ways of seeing and thinking. Much the same is true of Martin Seligman's *Learned Optimism* (1998).

13

Managing your career

A stance

The notion of 'career' formerly meant a life time of progress in the workplace, marked by greater seniority, salary and status. This assumption was disturbed in Chapters 5 and 6. Nowadays, when the idea of lifetime careers has faded in the face of fixed-term contracts, part-time work, life-long learning and portfolio careers, 'career' cannot be supposed to be a linear progression. Plainly, people will not end their careers where they started and professionals are likely to have more authority and to earn more at the end than at the beginning. However, for many people, especially now, the rise will not be as great as the linear model of a career implied and the pathway from start to end is less likely to resemble a climb straight up the side of the career mountain than strolls along the woodland paths on its slopes. For many people careers are shaped by life decisions that lead to career breaks and sideways moves, which were typically viewed with suspicion in the old model of career. Yet sideways moves are opportunities to consolidate learning by trying to transfer it to new contexts, or to extend learning by adding new routines, refining old ones and gaining new insights. Career breaks, of which motherhood is the most common, are often said to be times of self-appraisal and mothers tend to remark on how much the experience of caring for babies and children improves their job-worthiness. And sometimes career development is considerable but hidden in the form of on-the-job learning and experimentation, as when a teacher moves from competence to excellence but, because promotion is not based on teaching excellence, the development is easily overlooked or discounted. What, then, does career management mean when some faculty are disillusioned or disengaged, many older ones realize they are stuck midway up and others choose, more or less happily, to enjoy the foothills and woodland paths?

Chapter 4 referred to the work of Herzberg and Maslow which emphasized the importance of opportunities for self-fulfilment, satisfaction and self-actualization. These ideas invite us to see career management as attempts to identify and work for conditions conducive to growth and satisfaction. For some people at some times, the quest for satisfaction through work might mean getting into a more senior position (although senior academics are often wistful for times when they were researchers and teachers), but the view of career as a search for psychic rewards does not presume that recurrent promotion is a necessary condition of satisfaction. Finding space for learning, development, satisfying experiences and pleasure does not depend on 'getting ahead'. Career management can then be understood not so much as going for promotion as exploring the possibilities for invigoration within a context over which one has, or chooses to have, little other influence. Career development can mean looking for stimulus – in this case in teaching – in a job that is probably a dead end, with little chance of moving ahead (because of one's age, gender, qualification, history, care commitments, geographical affiliation, specialism etc.) In the 'onward and upward' view of career, career management would be a joke in that situation, but the alternative reading of career as purposeful search for meaning and satisfaction makes career management a matter of concern to all.

Key points

1 Teaching careers are seen, first and foremost, as quests for satisfaction and psychic rewards. Careers may be about manoeuvring for power and money, but that is not their prime meaning in this chapter.
2 Reflection is central to both senses of career management.
3 So is self-presentation. It increasingly involves making claims to teaching achievement through teaching portfolios.
4 A care for career may increase satisfaction but career management guarantees neither tenure nor promotion.

Informed practices

Career opportunities for people fascinated by teaching

This section combines suggestions for lateral career development – growing while staying at the same level of the hierarchy – with indications of the possibilities for promotion that might be created by such evidence of a care for teaching.

Although new academics are likely to be advised to get publications and research grants in order to get ahead, it is no longer disreputable to be interested in teaching. Most higher education institutions say that teaching quality is important in promotion decisions, which may mean that some threshold of competence has to be passed for promotion, although with the threshold passed promotion will then be made on the basis of research. Alverno College is one of the few to identify the teaching achievements commensurate with assistant, associate and full professorships. Where teaching really does count for promotion, expectations are likely to centre on six areas.

1 *Teaching reputation.* What do students and colleagues think? This has been covered at length in Chapter 11.
2 *All-round teaching skill.* There are outstanding classroom performers who will not be promoted for teaching excellence because their virtuosity allows them to get away with a didactic approach to teaching that is less credible in the information age. There are many situations in which performance skill matters (and others, such as on-line teaching, when it doesn't) but promotion committees are also interested in the teacher's whole approach to promoting student learning, including course design (Chapter 10), the management of learning opportunities (Chapter 8) and engaging in assessment conversations (Chapter 9).
3 *Range of teaching activity.* A claim to teaching strength is more persuasive if it is based on experience of teaching large first year classes as well as specialist final year classes.
4 *Innovation.* Innovation, especially in the form of efficient electronic solutions to learning problems, impresses promotion panels. However, a story of continuing quality improvement by a series of small-scale changes that first extended the range of teaching and learning activities, then provided better guidance on study skills and academic practice, next added new assessment criteria and techniques and finally aligned the course with a new programme specification could be more persuasive than the introduction of yet another web-based information transmission module.
5 *Curriculum leadership.* The people most likely to get promoted because of their teaching quality are those who tell others about their work, act as mentors for new teachers and are willing to advise established teachers. They also contribute beyond their own department, perhaps by working with educational development professionals and joining working groups on institutional teaching, learning, assessment and curriculum policies and practices. Curriculum leadership in professional and subject associations is expected by some promotion committees and valued by most.
6 *Scholarly activity.* In most professions it is reckoned that a good practitioner is a reflective practitioner. Reflection that looks scholarly, in the sense that it leads to publication in practitioner journals, is generally taken as good evidence of teaching quality. This is not the same as

saying that papers on teaching count as highly as mainstream research articles in an area but it is saying that they are a good way of establishing a seriousness about teaching issues. A promotion to full professor mainly on the grounds of teaching will almost always depend on a series of teaching-centred publications.

Opportunities for establishing a credible profile in these six areas differ quite markedly from department to department, country to country. Apart from the suggestions in Part 2, some of the things people commonly do to keep growing as teachers are:

1 Reading, particularly books in which writers have space to set out fresh ideas in satisfying ways. The simple resolution to spend time with one such book on teaching a year is more than enough to keep a teaching career alive.

2 Reading groups. There is much more to be gained if reading can be done in a group. If members are prepared to read, identify one or two things to try out, report back, try something else, read some more . . . then there is enormous potential for excitement and satisfaction in what has become an action learning group or teaching circle.

3 Working with staff/educational/instructional development professionals. They are gatekeepers to the courses that are the only legitimate forms of staff development in some people's minds and, as such, they can make a great difference to promotion proposals. In most institutions they offer a great deal more by: bringing together groups of people interested in the same teaching theme; providing modest funding for teaching development or workshop attendance; advising on problems and – sometimes – working with academic staff trying to resolve them; acting as guides to the literature or to other people working in the same field; alerting colleagues to new issues and, ideally, to good ways of responding to them.

4 National networks. *Active* membership of an organization concerned with teaching improvement: for example, those mentioned in Chapter 3; professional bodies and subject associations with interests in teaching matters; and the Learning and Teaching Support Network in the UK. I find these networks particularly helpful because it is comforting to know that colleagues in other universities have the same problems or worse and networks provide easy access to good, practical thinking about teaching improvement issues.

5 Taking administrative responsibility. Departments, faculties and colleges need academic staff who will sit on validating committees, take on quality assurance tasks and have oversight of degree programmes. Dull and wearisome though these jobs can be, they can have a lot of creative potential. For example, suppose each department were required to set out its programme goals in terms of the knowledge and understanding,

practical skills, key skills, intellectual skills and learning culture to be promoted; suppose, too, that it then had to show how each course contributed to the attainment of those programme goals. A programme leader could make a great difference to the quality of teaching in a department by the ways in which she, or he, helped colleagues to respond to this mandate. Considerable satisfaction and career enhancement could follow and success at this level might lead to an interest in working with other departments.

6 Practitioner research. By 'research' I mean systematic enquiry, using such means as are fit for the purpose and audience. Often practitioner research is small-scale work which is distinguished from tinkering by an awareness of what others have said and done in an area and by a concern to collect evidence systematically. It may not be sophisticated as research, and it is unlikely that strong claims could be made about the generalizability of the findings, but stories of careful investigations that are well connected to the knowledge in a community of enquiry have a great deal of value. The enquirer (or group of enquirers) learns and, all being well, gets satisfaction in the process, while accounts of the work have value for others who judge for themselves how it may be generalized to their settings and concerns. These ideas are considerably developed in Knight (2002d).

Whether 'career' is understood as progression upwards or as having opportunities for satisfaction, these two lists have shown some of the ways in which academic staff might create a career in teaching. The next section is about career planning to help to realize that potential.

Career planning and action

If there was ever a time when achievement, pure and simple, led to advancement, it is not now. Sennett (1998) argues that portfolio careers, which mean that people are forever having to present themselves favourably to new employers to get the next job, have led to a corrosion of character through a new emphasis on self-presentation – on image over substance – so that self-presentation matters at least as much as 'objective' achievement. With increased competition, organizations are increasingly trying to differentiate themselves by quality of service, which means employees are expected to do their job with a smile and to surpass client expectations. Hochschild (1983) draws attention to the emotional labour involved in many jobs, particularly those providing services to others, and Hargreaves (1998) has extended the idea to schoolteaching, observing that teachers have to manage and manipulate their own emotions as part of their work, often at a cost to themselves. Research for the UK's Industrial Society (reported in the *Observer*, 12 February 2001) found employers preferring those with 'open' body language, emotion management skills, poise in social settings, nice appearance and good body shape. Popular advice on getting promotion, as in an article in *The Guardian* of 17 February 2001, instructs us 'never to turn down the chance to network', 'don't hide your light under a bushel' and 'don't be yourself'. If such analyses hold good for the academic world – and there is no reason to think otherwise in this most casualized of professions – two conclusions are:

1 That a portfolio of documented achievements is not enough: you need to look the part and, according to many women academics (Chilly Editorial Collective, 1995), to have the right networks.
2 That there are limits to what can be achieved by rational career planning; not only are opportunities unpredictable, but promotion and appointment committees can still be capricious. (I recently heard that research is not worthy of merit pay because it is taken for granted that all academic staff are excellent researchers – a twist on the more common cant that all staff are assumed to be good teachers, and hence good teaching needs no special reward.)

The suggestions that follow concentrate on the teaching elements of faculty work and come from a literature that assumes that careers can be planned and managed. Anyone wanting to get ahead has to make that assumption but career analysis, planning and management do not guarantee career success. It might be better to invest in good clothes, gym membership and being visible at conferences and cross-institutional meetings.

Career planning involves scanning past, present and future.

Past
The backwards gaze has some similarity to portfolio making, which is covered later in this chapter. The aim is to become clearer about what has been associated with achievement and what might be associated with underdeveloped areas. Behind both is an attempt to appreciate better how we work and why – for example, do we have routines or beliefs that thwart improvement resolutions? Notice the view of growth here, which is that it is a natural process that is often blocked: therefore development is less about energizing growth than about weakening impediments to it (Moshman, 1999). The backward gaze, then, has at least three purposes: to identify achievements; to identify areas of failure or stagnation; and to explore what goes with success and what limits achievement.

The first two purposes need little comment. It helps to have a checklist as a reminder of what teaching involves, so that course development improvements, one-to-one teaching and pastoral work do not get overlooked. The section on teaching portfolios identifies some areas to look at. It also helps to involve friends or appreciative colleagues because analyses get amplified, clarified and qualified through conversations that prompt reflection to go outside its customary range and which may encourage diffident teachers to be more upbeat about their achievements. In good departments and teams, staff appraisals do this rather than get snagged on monitoring compliance with accountability routines and recording precise scores on inappropriate performance indicators.

Reflection is usually seen as a way to make best guesses about why what has happened has happened. Appreciative reflection tells me that my best teaching occurs when:

- I am dealing with fresh material about which I am enthusiastic.
- I have large groups.
- I have room for manoeuvre – I am not constricted by having to get them good exam grades.
- I can easily improvise between presentation, small group work, seatwork, role play, activities etc.
- Somehow the learners have been interested: sometimes I think I make interest happen, other times I think it is something they bring.
- I have time to think about what I have done, what I am going to do, to get together the wherewithal to do it and to do it.
- I am at ease in myself.
- I get signals from the learners that they are with me.
- We laugh.

My worst teaching points to my weaknesses. When I look at what I have not done well I try to remain appreciative in the sense of appreciating why things were askew. My reflective story is that I teach poorly when:

- I am not patient enough.
- I am bored.
- I know too much and am concerned that learners should know it too.
- Learners aren't skilled learners (I still can't express this clearly because I am quite comfortable working with 5-year-olds and probably have enjoyed working with 10–14-year-olds more than any other groups).
- I don't *understand* what I'm teaching, in the sense that I don't have a feel for why it matters and what it means.
- I am stressed (trying to busk my teaching because I am writing too much, marking too much, frazzled by meetings, pulled awry by life outside work).
- I have lost their attention – I am corpsing – and can't get them back.
- I am working with OHP slides (or worse, with Powerpoint) rather than creating on the board.

Three things strike me about my reflections. First, I could not have got these insights from a portfolio, although portfolios have their place. Reflections have to come from recalling, imagining, feeling and comparing. Second, none of this suggests that I could teach better if only I went on a course. Third, reflection has created a story about who I am that happens to have teaching as its focus. On this analysis, becoming a better teacher has a lot to do with working on me, less on teaching.

Beguiling though reflection may be, it has limits as a basis for career planning. The problem is not simply that some people find it hard to reflect. They can be helped by: writing stories or vignettes (Winter, 1999); making or choosing pictures that speak of their teaching experiences, both good and bad; drawing lines to represent their teaching careers and talking about them (Orland, 2000); concept mapping; and any other devices that creatively prompt thinking and, preferably, provide a focus for conversations with others. A career management questionnaire can help to identify priorities for general development (Pedler *et al.*, 1994), and Knight *et al.* (2000) provide a chart to help thinking about priorities for teaching development. Nor is the problem that we tend to fall into a rut when it comes to explaining why we do what we do and end up just reflecting back to ourselves the image of the world with which we started. Others can nudge us out of this rutted thinking and remind us that there are alternative ways of seeing ourselves in the world. The problem is that reflection is not all-powerful (Donnelly, 1999). It may appear that we can know ourselves by reflection but, even with the help of others, there is that which is recognized but beyond the grasp of cognition (mood, for example) and that which is not recognized and so, by definition, unknown (the subconscious). Dreyfus (1991: 70) quotes John Dewey saying 'It is a commonplace that the more suavely efficient a habit the more unconsciously it operates. Only a hitch in its workings occasions emotion and provokes thought.' Furthermore, in so far as reflection puts the emphasis on 'me', it runs counter to the theme that teaching quality is a social and an individual achievement. The price of emphasizing the individual over the social is excessive guilt about failure and false consciousness about achievement.

Appreciative reflection on self and on past teaching is, then, a necessary part of career planning. It is best done with help (people and techniques), with an openness to fresh ways of making sense of the pasts (and of the nows) and on the understanding that just as teaching and living twine together, so too teaching quality is a social and individual achievement.

Present

What is seen through reflection on the past should be appraised by comparing it with a list, such as the one on p. 202 above, of things promotion committees look for and then by considering what is desirable in terms of what you would like to be doing in five years' time and what you think you can achieve in the context in which you work. Ask the question, 'What can I learn in this post that I want to learn and that will help me to get my next job?' This involves scanning the work environment to identify opportunities to innovate, lead and publish, and spot people who can help.

These affordances may be within the institution, to be had by bidding for regional or national funds or by making a strategic sideways career move. Scanning also needs to be strategic. Professional obsolescence is ever-looming (Dubin, 1990), so advancement through teaching means positioning oneself in the forefront of developments, which will often amount to knowing what to do about government initiatives to, for example, improve student employability. Likewise, it is important to be able to claim competence in pedagogical developments such as problem-based learning and web-based teaching. Lastly, it would also be helpful to scan for opportunities to tell people about your promotion-worthy trajectory, which will mean networking, possibly taking on extra administrative duties (serving on a validation board or teaching committee) and probably some strategic positioning.

Future

When imagining where you would like to be in five years' time imagine a whole life, not just a career-as-promotion. It involves starting with the person and working back to what that implies in terms of being a teacher in higher education. If we take seriously the idea that career is about trying to get the best chance of having self-fulfilment, it has to be recognized that for some teachers this will mean disengaging themselves from teaching, perhaps because they want to get satisfaction by being more active as researchers or by attending to the non-work things that are becoming more important in their lives. They may find strategic disengagement from teaching a good move, particularly when it is limited so that learners barely notice it, if at all. For example, a summer spent on thorough preparation of undergraduate teaching may be sufficient for strong classroom performance for the next five years, allowing more time for research, family or hobbies. This preparation will begin to wear out as new research is published, new teaching expectations continue to creep in and repetition brings staleness, but it need not be assumed that wear will have serious effects on teaching quality in the short term.

Where the five-year vision includes better teaching, then there is an ambiguous need to clarify one's goals. On the one hand, goal theories of motivation (see Chapter 4) hold that goals should be specific (so that we know when we have achieved them and can feel pleased by the achievement), feasible (so we have a good chance of feeling pleased by achievement) and worth the effort that success will take (so that we will not be disgruntled at spending ages on some footling activity, such as writing government-compliant course documentation). On the other hand, it has been suggested that these are the counsels of false precision and the best that can be done is to have a fuzzy notion of teaching better, some specific and achievable changes to make (improving the quality of handouts), some specific actions to take (going on a course to learn how to use

Powerpoint) and ideas about the sorts of things that teaching improvement might lead to over the next five years.

Somewhere between tight and fuzzy goals lies the strategy of making a
major investment in teaching, by being active in POD, SEDA, STLHE, ILT
or HERDSA, for example, without having a firm notion of where it might
lead. Given this uncertainty about the extrinsic outcomes – promotion or
new responsibilities – it follows that any substantial investment in teaching
improvement is best if it is intrinsically driven. Extrinsic motivation is
vulnerable to disappointment if rewards do not materialize or if effort
appears to be disproportionate to the rewards of success. Intrinsic motivation is widely thought to be superior (Chapter 4). What, then, are the
likely sources of intrinsic motivation for individuals to try to surpass the
departmental norm for teaching development work? Standard answers
talk of interest and enjoyment but they say little about how enjoyment and
interest get to be associated with teaching. Perhaps it just happens, but
that is not helpful enough if we want insights to help us to strengthen our
intrinsic motivation. A more promising analysis may come from recalling
the view of development as the removal of obstacles to natural growth.
*Assume that we prefer to teach well and have a disposition to try to improve, as long
as the costs are not too high.* Our career development then centres on reducing barriers to growth, looking for ways of reducing the time backstage
work takes, of encysting irritants and of putting the most in to those things
that give us pleasure. Many of the ideas in Table 12.1 apply.

Teaching portfolios, profiles and dossiers

A teaching portfolio, also known as a dossier or profile, is widely used to
document teaching quality. Baume (2001) sees a portfolio as a growing,
changing creation, a well indexed collection of resources, a database that
links claims to achievement with a store of evidence. I find it best to
organize a portfolio into four sections that are revised in the light of
regular reviews of achievement and intentions for development.

Claims to achievement

This section will be written in continuous prose, highlighting the points
that you think present you to best advantage. I find 2000 words to be a
good length for it. This section will usually begin with a short statement of
your prime principles as far as teaching goes – a statement of teaching
philosophy, of aims and aspirations. Ideally, it denotes an enquiring,
reflective cast of mind and all that follows will show how you try to come
up to the ideals you profess. Overall, this first section should develop into
an accessible, crisp summary of the highlights to be amplified later in the
portfolio. What counts as 'crisp' varies from audience to audience – a
promotion committee in your own institution may expect to read some

---

Box 13.1   Information commonly expected in section 2 of a teaching portfolio

- What you have taught, to whom and when. (Don't forget postgraduate work.)
- Teaching methods/techniques used, including electronic ones and one-to-one work with research students.
- Assessment methods used, including giving feedback. (Refer to plentiful, detailed, formative conversations with research students.)
- Your part in course design.
- Contributions within the department/team to curriculum, teaching, learning and assessment developments. (Improved supervision practices or training sessions for postgraduates, especially on professional degrees, should be mentioned.)
- Contributions at institutional or national levels to curriculum, teaching, learning and assessment developments.
- Teaching qualifications, membership of societies concerned with teaching (in general or in a subject area), relevant course and conference attendance, teaching-related publications, including student texts.

---

two or three thousand words that set out your claims to good teaching. On the other hand, when you are applying for a job you may condense this first section to provide two or three paragraphs in a letter of application, mentioning that a fuller statement and evidence are available should an interviewing panel wish to consider them. A virtual portfolio at http://amby.com.kimeldorf/sampler/intro.html has a first, introductory section of a dozen sentences in four paragraphs (e.g. 'over the years I have survived by becoming a quick-study. Put me on any new assignment and I'll quickly get up to speed'). Ten supporting sections follow, each clearly headed by a claim.

Range statements
Claims are taken more or less seriously depending on the extent of the practices on which they are built, which means that the second section should give some account of the range of your teaching duties over, say, the past five years – what they are, what they involve and what you do. Of course, if it is helpful to refer to work in earlier times, do so. Box 13.1 lists information that is frequently expected. Although I have the strong impression that people who read teaching portfolios are really expecting to get information about whole-class teaching with undergraduates, I tell them about my one-to-one supervision of postgraduates, my work on taught postgraduate classes and any 'clinical' work, such as supervising students' classroom practice. These are teaching duties. So are contributions to teaching design and policy, such as being a member of a team reviewing

some practices at departmental or institutional level, chairing a teaching committee and participating in curriculum innovation.

The index or database

The third section is really nothing more than an index that lists the strengths to which you wish to lay claim, the range of practices in which they are grounded, references to the evidence that fleshes out the claim and some indication of why the evidence should be read as substantiating the claim. It is best understood as a database that matches up claims and evidence. In many cases almost all of the portfolio, including evidence of achievement, can be stored electronically, in which case the index will contain hypertext links from claims to pieces of evidence substantiating them. A database, such as Lotus Notes (or even a qualitative data analysis program such as Atlas-ti or NU*DIST), will hold documents and allow you to search among them to identify material relevant to changing self-presentation purposes. When this file is edited to create a version of the portfolio for a particular audience and purpose, it may be worth printing section 3 in full as an efficient way of summarizing your claims and showing the depth of evidence to support them. Figure 13.1 shows the bare bones of this section.

The archive

The last and bulkiest section is a sack, or a more sophisticated filing system, containing the evidence you want to use in support of your claims. Box 13.2 lists some of the sources of evidence that are commonly used in portfolios, but an overriding principle should be that anything that can be used as evidence for a claim can be evidence for a claim. Many people who keep portfolios get into the habit of dumping anything likely to be of use in a box or computer folder and sorting this accumulation when they come to review their teaching practices and priorities. Collection becomes habitual, while reflecting, editing, claiming and substantiating are likely to come together at key points in the year. (For me that is usually August when we have had done the annual programme reviews and I rewrite my course handbooks for the classes beginning in October.) It probably goes without saying that only a selection of this evidence gets presented to others and that the selection will vary according to purpose, audience and time. The index in section 3 provides a way of keeping track of the evidence and the claims related to each item. When you are presenting the evidence to others, each piece needs to be clearly indexed against section 3, perhaps with coloured Post-its, and labelled to show how exactly you think it supports your claim to achievement.

This has implied that portfolios are a vital part of the rituals of appointment and promotion. The corollary could be drawn that only those on

Illustrative claims to teaching strength	Range: can the claim be sustained in a variety of settings and levels? Which ones?	(a) Reference number identifying the items of evidence (or parts) substantiating the claim. (b) Explanation of how each piece or part backs up the claim – it is often not clear why something should be read as evidence for a claim
1 A student- and learning-centred approach to teaching		
2 A commitment to continuing and incremental development in all aspects of teaching		
3 Performance skill in undergraduate teaching, especially with large classes		
4 A concern to help undergraduates to work with one another, becoming more autonomous in the process		
5 Innovative course design		
6 Distinctiveness in the use of authentic assessment methods		
7 A concern to develop a good range of skills and qualities in addition to subject understanding		
8 Engagement in teaching and learning development in the national community of teaching practice		

Figure 13.1   A template for section 3 of a teaching portfolio

short-term contracts or with a career, in the sense of a quest for tenure or promotion, need take them seriously. The rest could relax. I think there is a lot of sense in this, as long as relaxing does not mean ceasing to care about teaching and its improvement. Creating and keeping portfolios takes a lot of time and I am not convinced that thinking well about teaching needs all the paraphernalia of a portfolio. People working in good departments or teams where teaching is regularly appraised, discussed and revised have reflection and commitment designed into daily practice. Previous chapters have made it clear that I value this embedded commitment

---

Box 13.2   Evidence commonly indexed in section 4 of a teaching portfolio

- Evidence that you are working or have worked in departments committed to teaching quality. It is infectious.
- Lecture notes, OHTs, references to course websites and printouts of some material on them, videos or other records of teaching performance, handouts, course handbooks or syllabi.
- Samples of student work, assessment criteria and your written feedback.
- Student evaluation comments or summaries of evaluation forms *plus* notes of action taken in the light of student evaluations. Include 'thank you' notes and other appreciative acts, reviews in alternative prospectuses/calendars published by student bodies etc.
- Any evaluative comments from colleagues, such as peer review reports, classroom observation comments, messages from colleagues with whom you have worked.
- Other evidence of teaching effectiveness. In many places this means a summary of student course grades. More sophisticated institutions have alternatives to these 'raw score' data, while some are sceptical about the value of course-level outcome scores and prefer to rely on the other sources of evidence listed here.
- Evidence of change to teaching practices over time – for example, a course handbook from five years ago compared to the current version.
- Evidence of engagement with teaching matters: for example, service on institutional validation and teaching committees; a record of participation in local or national teaching improvement events, networks, initiatives etc.

---

to being a teacher far more highly than any events. In these ideal circumstances, reflection happens and metacognition grows. In these circumstances it is hard to see that the opportunity cost of keeping a portfolio is justified. Of course, that depends upon what it means to keep a portfolio. If it means keeping a dump file and referring to it at key times, then the opportunity cost is low and the advantages are considerable. However, like so many things to do with teaching improvement, it can become bloated, with administrators or staff developers seeming to vie with one another to identify new things to be documented, supported with evidence and analysed in depth. Visit http://celt.ntu.ac.uk/se/portfolio24.html to see screens of prompts to guide teaching portfolio construction around nine major headings (summary of teaching responsibilities; approach to teaching; curriculum design, content and organization; teaching, learning and assessment; student progression and achievement; student support and guidance; learning resources; quality management and enhancement; continuing professional development). Each heading and each prompt is defensible but, for me, enthusiasm has outstripped efficiency. I do not believe that finding evidence to back up my response to each prompt would do much to improve my teaching. I understand that if I had such evidence I could produce a splendid portfolio for promotion purposes, although, rather like PCs that seem to become obsolete the moment they are purchased, expectations keep growing and even more will be needed to make an equally strong case in two years' time. Besides, working to lists like those in Boxes 12.1 and 12.2 feels soulless. I like the felt-ness of the electronic portfolio at http://amby.com.kimeldorf/sampler/intro.html, with section headings like 'Facing any challenge' and 'Dramatizing instruction', with its attention to 'applied creativity'.

Yet 'felt' portfolios, which are about what matters in the personal experience of being a teacher, are risky because committees have been taught to expect blockbusters with nine sections and there is a difficulty with my view that portfolio-keeping is primarily something for job-seekers to do: career intentions change and a teaching portfolio can be needed quite unexpectedly. The next section contains suggestions that are sensitive to such ambiguities.

Action points

Those concerned with departmental cultures, with the sort of place a department is, can help teaching career development by weakening some of the barriers to teaching improvement by, for example, encouraging people to get student evaluations of teaching that appreciate strengths as well as identifying areas for development. It is also helpful to challenge entity self-theories – beliefs that lukewarm teaching is no one's fault because you either have the teaching gift or you don't. It is better to give a high profile to incremental theories and say that the resolution of teaching problems often calls for sustained, well considered effort. There are many ways of providing low-cost, high-gain opportunities for teaching improvement. For example, The Boyer Commission (Kenny, 1998) recommend that research universities value good teaching more and reward it better and encourage faculty to get a better match between the curriculum and the topics concerning researchers, and argue that undergraduate teaching methods can be more enquiry-based, with students emulating the enquiry methods of the research community. Departmental teaching seminars addressing pressing pedagogical or curriculum topics also bring teaching improvement, and hence career development opportunities, into normal discourse, as do performance appraisals that always identify opportunities to tinker and ways of presenting routine teaching achievements to best advantage.

Further reading

There is no shortage of guides to career management, although academic career management is not well served. *A Manager's Guide to Self-development* (Pedler *et al.*, 1994) understands the research literature on management and contains a good series of self-assessment and career/life planning activities. Although I am influenced by the work on portfolios done in Canada by Alan Wright (O'Neil and Wright, 1996), Peter Seldin's (1997) is better known. His suggestions are securely based in wide experience and accessible, although readers in other parts of the world will occasionally need to replace North American terms with local ones.

14

Being a teacher in higher education

Pressure to publish; quality assurance procedures; marketization; grants-manship; greater student diversity; casualization; larger classes; codification and formalization; resource constrictions; proliferating backstage work; intensification – these are some of the structural forces that demand more from teachers, while leaving them fewer spaces in which to create their own satisfactions.

This grim list misleads. The experience of being a teacher varies according to:

- Who you are – your age, gender, aspirations, family care responsibilities, self-theories.
- Where you are – the state, institution and department in which you work and how tightly coupled you are to the policies set by others.
- Your status – part- or full-time, senior or junior, full academic contract or teaching only.
- Your academic discipline, although disciplines are more fragmented and locally constructed than is sometimes assumed (Knight and Trowler, 2000).

This non-determinist analysis can be enriched by summarizing Argyle's (1999) review of the literature on happiness. He wrote:

- 'A busy social life is correlated with happiness, as are regular exercise and an active sex life' (p. 41).
- Job satisfaction is a major cause of overall satisfaction and vice versa: '[it] is caused by the essential nature of the work – autonomy, use of skills, etc. – and by social interactions, formal and informal, with co-workers' (p. 40).
- 'People can get used to almost anything – from winning the lottery to becoming paraplegic; after a while their happiness returns to somewhere near where it was before' (p. 41).
- 'Cognitive styles, such as optimism and not blaming yourself when things go wrong, also correlate with happiness: this opens the door to

psychotherapy for happiness, by persuading people to look at things differently' (p. 40).

- 'It looks as if happiness is to a large extent in the mind, i.e. it depends how we perceive things' (p. 41).

Environments can be depressing and if we are vexed by the structural conditions of our work, it is increasingly hard to be happy teachers. Yet Argyle's analysis of happiness suggests that it is something that people make for themselves. And while structural conditions can be bleak, public discourses have warmed to teaching. Where an interest in teaching once seemed to show a lack of seriousness about an academic career, there is now no shortage of people saying that teaching is important. Some people even get rewarded for teaching. Acting on the assumption that being a good or fulfilled teacher is an achievement in a deteriorating environment, this book (or heft, to use an obsolete synonym) has said a lot about teaching well. Some of the more distinctive points are:

1 The assumption that we are in the business of stimulating complex learning: learning for understanding subject matter; learning to develop subject-specific and generic skills; learning that favours efficacy beliefs and fruitful self-theories; and learning that promotes metacognition.
2 Good teaching is an individual and social achievement, an emergent property of a person networking with others and connecting with systems and communities.
3 Programme teams (activity systems) and departments (communities of practice) create affordances while also limiting what it is easy or possible to do.
4 Task setting and giving feedback are crucial teaching tasks.
5 So too is the design of affordances for complex learning.
6 Learning happens: complex learning often happens slowly. Teachers, teams and departments should design programmes that capitalize on these insights.
7 Good teaching goes with knowing students: they should know about the programme, learning culture and goals, and teachers should know them.
8 Teaching well involves the whole person. Van Manen (1995: 45–6) writes of 'epistemologies of practice [that] . . . locate practical knowledge not primarily in the intellect or the head but in the existential situation in which the person finds himself or herself. In other words, the practical active knowledge that animates teaching is something that belongs phenomenologically more closely to the whole embodied being of the person as well as to the social and physical world in which this person lives.'
9 Intrinsic motivation for teaching, with its emphasis on creating opportunities for self-fulfilment in work, is preferred to motivational strategies

that rely on extrinsic forces. This runs counter to attempts to improve teaching by means of sceptical surveillance.

10 An extension of that thinking leads to the idea that, whatever else they do, good evaluations and good careers help people to feel the psychic rewards of teaching.

11 Teachers' self-theories and attributional tendencies contribute considerably to the ways in which they experience being a teacher. There is evidence that we can choose to change them.

12 Professional learning might best be understood as something that happens through working in systems and communities. This view probably explains what I am told is 'rather an anti-staff development tone in a couple of places in this book'. My reservations about what I see as the most common forms of staff development come from their poor fit with my analysis of professional learning and my belief that effective educational development operations should be based upon modern, extensive theories of professional and other workplace learning.

13 It is not enough to give teachers a set of techniques: scripts (or memes), courses and programmes matter (more).

One way of summarizing these points is by exploring other meanings of 'heft'. Good teaching is hefty in the sense that it has weight – as educational developers are wont to say, it is, at its best, a scholarly activity. The list shows some of what is weighty about being a good teacher. But the list breaks with mainstream thinking about how to get this weight of expertise by saying that teaching is hefted in the sense that expertise is something we come into possession of by being in activity systems and communities of teaching practice. Herdwick sheep, the tough, wiry-fleeced sheep that survive on the mountains of the English Lake District, are hefted: flocks have survival memes which have passed from ewe and ram to lamb. Farmers fear that 2001's mass slaughter of Lakeland sheep will destroy the heft and that unhefted Herdwicks put on the mountains to replace those culled in the foot and mouth epidemic will not manage. Good teaching is hefty and hefted but I don't think it ought to be hefted in the sense of weighed. Connectionist metaphors, talk of complexity and contingency, and the problems of making valid judgements of teaching quality (Chapters 7 and 10) combine to suggest that the quintessence of teaching eludes commodification and measurement, although connoisseurship can disclose its subtle shapes (Eisner, 1985).

And here I see a major problem for those keen to stimulate better teaching. In many states those with power – policy-makers and politicians – have an inordinate fondness for the technical-rationalist discourse of Taylorist work science, Fordist practices and hard managerialist technologies of surveillance. In *Being a Teacher* I have hefted – picked up and carried – an alternative discourse that says that hard managerialism is not fit for the complex purpose of helping teachers to engage students with good complex learning. This leads me to argue that being committed to teaching also carries with it the need to be a teacher of policy wonks and their sort. I see a need to show that the quality enhancements that can stimulate complex teaching for complex learning are not to be had from quality assurance or quality control systems. (Quality improvement, of which connoisseurship is a part, is a different matter.)

I finish with words from Jo Tait, who inspired the process of inventing this book:

> In his preface, Peter describes how I originally planned a book about 'inspiring higher education' – a book full of inspirational ideas and practices that might incorporate (give body to) the sense of breathing in fresh life and a spirit of expansion.
>
> The proposal for the 'inspiring' book was drafted almost immediately after co-editing *The Management of Independent Learning* (Tait and Knight, 1996). David Boud, one of the contributors, had become the hero of my undergraduate learning because of his insistence on the value of experience in learning (see, for example, Boud and Griffin, 1987). Editing this book – part of one of my post-graduation jobs – gave me a chance to meet this champion of learning and, once I'd recovered from the fact that he didn't ride a white horse and tilt at dragons, we talked briefly about where my part-time jobs might lead. His advice, 'Follow your heart', helped me imagine that I might write a book that persuaded individuals and institutions to embody more connected, holistic learning principles, driven and rewarded by inspiration. As Peter explains, after writing the proposal a series of short-term and part-time jobs in higher education – each taking up more than its allotted percentage of my life – got in the way of actually writing the book. And more than once I have doubted the wisdom of that heart-centred advice as, in the personal and global pursuit of learning, I found myself pouring my enthusiasm into poorly paid work with no security or career prospects. Although I can now tell a good – not necessarily inspiring – story about how following my heart has got me where I am today – just beginning a 'proper' job as a lecturer.
>
> As I approach the end of my reading of *Being a Teacher*, and wonder about the next chapter of my working life, I reflect on my various lives in different communities of academic practice – or in one vast community. The connectionist webs and networks of learning in Chapter 1 of the book might also be a map of the routes that my 'heart' has followed or declined. The lines of the web may be drawn between my ever-changing identity and friends and colleagues (as peers, research participants and bosses), or they might emerge from fictional

and 'real' heroes and heroines in my story. Sometimes the connections are easy paths and, at other times, dilemmas and choices – times of confusion where the web gets tangled.

Perhaps a friend has thrown me a line – a common one has been 'Don't be so hard on yourself!' I might hear and ignore it, not believing that anything other than the harshest criticism will keep me on track. Or, on another occasion, I might take notice and incorporate some kindnesses to myself into my daily routine. At other times, a group of colleagues – a reading group looking at subject matter I don't fully understand – offers me threads that I have to decide whether or not to incorporate into my web of learning. And, in the informal conversations that run between the analytical clever-talk, there are supports for continuing the struggle to make sense of the text and to absorb some of the ideas into my practices, if I choose to become that sort of person. Sometimes the stimulus to reflect has come from a boss or an authority-figure – perhaps to urge me to 'Just focus on what we're supposed to be doing here and get the job done.' How do I decide whether this is useful advice or managerialist power-games? Perhaps that line connects with what I read in this book about the need for academic survival skills – it is just a job, after all.

As I claimed in my original 'inspiration' idea, I am constantly breathing in new ideas – inspirations and affordances for dissonance, improvement, discomfort and learning. But what I was, in my naive way, at risk of forgetting is the other part of breathing, the need to exhale, too. We exhale waste products and retain life-giving oxygen. In *Being a Teacher* we are invited to breathe through some very rich material and to retain what gives us life – what allows us to grow and to continue to learn. We are also helped to select out – to exhale, as it were – ideas and responsibilities that really don't support us. For example, we need to reject any idea that we alone are responsible for our continuing improvement and the associated belief that if we fall short of expectations, it is a personal failing. This, then, does feel like a book on inspiring higher education, partly because of the freshness of some of the things it recommends but also because of the things it invites us to reject.

References

Abrami, P. C., d'Appollonia, S. and Rosenfield, S. (1997) The dimensionality of student ratings of instruction: what we know and what we do not, in R. Perry and J. C. Smart (eds) *Effective Teaching in Higher Education: Research and Practice*, pp. 321–67. New York: Agathon Press.

Adey, P. and Shayer, M. (1994) *Really Raising Standards*. London: Routledge.

Ali, L. and Graham, B. (2000) *Moving on in Your Career: A Guide for Academic Researchers and Postgraduates*. London: Continuum.

Allee, V. (1997) *The Knowledge Evolution*. Boston, MA: Butterworth-Heinemann.

Altbach, P. G. and Lewis, L. S. (1996) The academic profession in international perspective, in P. G. Altbach (ed.) *The International Academic Profession*. Princeton, NJ: The Carnegie Foundation for the Advancement of Teaching.

American Institute of Stress (2001) *Stress – America's #1 Health Problem*. www.stress.org, accessed 23 January 2001.

Anderson, V. and Skinner, D. (1999) Organizational learning in practice: how do small businesses learn to operate internationally?, *Human Resource Development International*, 2(3): 235–58.

André, R. and Frost, P. J. (eds) (1997) *Researchers Hooked on Teaching*. Thousand Oaks, CA: Sage.

Angelo, T. and Cross, P. (1993) *Classroom Assessment Techniques*, 2nd edn. San Francisco: Jossey-Bass.

Argyle, M. (1999) In quest of happiness, *Oxford Today*, 11(3): 40–1.

Askew, S. and Lodge, C. (2000) Gifts, ping-pong and loops – linking feedback and learning, in S. Askew (ed.) *Feedback for Learning*, pp. 1–17. London: Routledge/Falmer.

Astin, A. W. (1997) *Four Years that Matter: The College Experience Twenty Years On*. San Francisco: Jossey-Bass.

Atkins, M. (1999) Over-ready and self basting: taking stock of employability skills, *Teaching in Higher Education*, 4(2): 267–80.

Atkinson, T. and Claxton, G. (eds) (2000) *The Intuitive Practitioner. On the Value of Not Always Knowing what One Is Doing*. Buckingham: Open University Press.

Bailey, J. G. (1999) Academics' motivation and self efficacy for teaching and research, *Higher Education Research and Development*, 18(3): 343–59.

Ball, S. J. (1994) *Education Reform: A Critical and Post-Structural Approach*. Buckingham: Open University Press.

Balloch, S., Pahl, J. and McLean, J. (1998) Working in the social services: job satisfaction, stress and violence, *British Journal of Social Work*, 28(3): 329–56.

Balloch, S., McLean, J. and Fisher, M. (1999) *Social Services: Working under Pressure*. Bristol: The Policy Press.

Bandura, A. (1997) *Self-efficacy: The Exercise of Control*, 2nd edn. New York: Freeman.

Banta, T., Lund, J. P., Black, K. E. *et al.* (eds) (1996) *Assessment in Practice*. San Francisco: Jossey-Bass.

Barnett, R. (2000) *Realizing the University in an age of supercomplexity*. Buckingham: Society for Research into Higher Education and Open University Press.

Barr, R. B. and Tagg, J. (1995) From teaching to learning – a new paradigm for undergraduate education, *Change*, November/December, 13–25.

Bascia, N. and Hargreaves, A. (2000) Teaching and leading on the sharp edge of change, in N. Bascia and A. Hargreaves (eds) *The Sharp Edge of Educational Change: Teaching, Leading and the Realities of Reform*, pp. 3–26. London: Routledge/Falmer.

Baume, D. (2001) Enrich a teaching portfolio, *Times Higher Education Supplement*, 16 March, 21.

Becher, T. (1999) *Professional Practices: Commitment and Capability in a Changing Environment*. New Brunswick, NJ: Transaction Publishers.

Beckett, F. (2001) The truth exposed, *AUT Look*, 217: 8–10.

Bennett, N., Desforges, C. W., Cockburn, A. and Wilkinson, B. (1984) *The Quality of Pupil Learning Experiences*. London: Lawrence Erlbaum Associates.

Bess, J. L. (ed.) (1997) *Teaching Well and Liking It*. Baltimore: Johns Hopkins University Press.

Bett, Sir Michael (1999) *Independent Review of Higher Education Pay and Conditions*. London: The Stationery Office.

Biggs, J. (1999a) *Teaching for Quality Learning at University*. Buckingham: Society for Research in Higher Education and Open University Press.

Biggs, J. (1999b) What the student does: teaching for enhanced learning, *Higher Education Research and Development*, 18(1): 57–75.

Black, P. (1998) Learning, league tables and national assessment, *Oxford Review of Education*, 24(1): 57–68.

Black, P. (2001) Dreams, strategies and systems: portraits of assessment past, present and future, *Assessment in Education*, 8(1): 65–85.

Black, P. and Wiliam, D. (1998) Assessment and classroom learning, *Assessment in Education*, 5(1): 7–74.

Blackburn, R. T. and Lawrence, J. H. (1995) *Faculty at Work*. Baltimore: Johns Hopkins University Press.

Blackler, F. (1993) Knowledge and the theory of organizations: organizations as activity systems and the reframing of management, *Journal of Management Studies*, 30(6): 863–84.

Blackwell, A. and Williamson, E. (1999) Modularisation and staff satisfaction. Paper presented to the European Association of Institutional Research Forum, Lund, Sweden, August.

Blackwell, R., Channell, J. and Williams, J. (2001) Teaching circles: a way forward for part-time teachers in higher education?, *The International Journal for Academic Development*, 6(1): 40–53.

Bland, C. J. and Schmitz, C. C. (1990) An overview of research on faculty and institutional vitality, in J. Schuster, D. Wheeler and associates (eds) *Enhancing Faculty Careers*, pp. 41–61. San Francisco: Jossey-Bass.

Bloom, B. S. (1956) *Taxonomy of Educational Objectives. Handbook 1: Cognitive Domain*. London: Longman.

Boden, M. A. (1991) Horses of a different color?, in W. Ramsey, S. Stich and D. Rumelhart (eds) *Philosophy and Connectionist Theory*, pp. 3–19. Hillsdale, NJ: Lawrence Erlbaum Associates.

Boice, R. (1992) *The New Faculty Member: Supporting and Fostering Professional Development*. San Francisco: Jossey-Bass.

Bolles, R. N. (1997) *What Color Is Your Parachute?* Berkeley, CA: Ten Speed Press.

Bolton, G. (2001) *Reflective Practice: Writing and Professional Development*. London: Paul Chapman Publishing.

Bottery, M. (1998) *Professionals and Policy: Management Strategy in a Competitive World*. London: Cassell.

Boud, D. and Griffin, V. (eds) (1987) *Appreciating Adults Learning*. London: Kogan Page.

Bourner, T., O'Hare, S. and Barlow, J. (2000) Only connect; facilitating reflective learning with statements of relevance, *Innovations in Education and Training International*, 37(1): 68–75.

Boyatis, R. E. and associates (1995) *Innovation in Professional Education*. San Francisco: Jossey-Bass.

Boyer, E. L. (1990) *Scholarship Reconsidered: Priorities of the Professoriate*. Princeton, NJ: Carnegie Foundation for the Advancement of Learning.

Boyle, M. and Woods, P. (1996) The composite head: coping with changes in the primary headteacher role, *British Educational Research Journal*, 22(5): 549–68.

Boyle, P. and Boice, R. (1998) Systematic mentoring for new faculty teachers and graduate teaching assistants, *Innovative Higher Education*, 22(3): 157–79.

Brennan, R. (1992) *The Alexander Technique Workbook*. Shaftesbury: Element Books.

Briner, R. (1997) Improving stress assessment, *Journal of Psychosomatic Research*, 43(1): 61–71.

Broadfoot, P. (2000) Assessment and intuition, in T. Atkinson and G. Claxton (eds) *The Intuitive Practitioner. On the Value of Not Always Knowing what One Is Doing*, pp. 199–219. Buckingham: Open University Press.

Brockbank, A. and McGill, I. (1998) *Facilitating Reflective Learning in Higher Education*. Buckingham: Open University Press.

Brookfield, S. (1999) *Becoming a Critically Reflective Teacher*. San Francisco: Jossey-Bass.

Brown, G., Bull, J. and Pendlebury, M. (1997) *Assessing Student Learning in Higher Education*. London: Routledge.

Brown, J. S. and Duguid, P. (2000) *The Social Life of Information*. Boston, MA: Harvard Business School Press.

Brown, S. and Knight, P. (1994) *Assessing Learners in Higher Education*. London: Kogan Page.

Bryson, C. (2001) The rising tide of casualisation, *AUT Look*, 217: 5–7.

Buzan, T. (1995) *Use Your Head*. London: BBC Books.

Callon, M. (1999) Actor–network theory – the market test, in J. Law and J. Hassard (eds) *Actor Network Theory and After*, pp. 181–95. Oxford: Blackwell.

Campbell, R. J. and Neill, S. R. St J. (1994) *Primary Teachers at Work*. London: Routledge.

Caplan, P. J. (1994) *Lifting a Ton of Feathers: A Woman's Guide to Surviving in the Academic World*. Toronto, ON: University of Toronto Press.

Carrington, W. and Carey, S. (1992) *Explaining the Alexander Technique*. London: The Sheildrake Press.

Chilly Editorial Collective (1995) *Breaking Anonymity: The Chilly Climate for Women Faculty*. Waterloo, ON: Wilfrid Laurier University Press.

Chitnis, A. and Williams, G. (1999). *Casualisation and Quality: A Study of the Issues for Quality in Teaching and Research Raised by Employment of Part Time and Fixed Term Staff in UK Higher Education*. London: NAFTHE.

Chivers, G. and Cheetham, G. (2001) Professional development and lifelong learning, in L. West, N. Miller, D. O'Reilly and R. Allan (eds) *Travellers' Tales: From Adult Literacy to Lifelong Learning . . . and Beyond*, pp. 70–2. Nottingham: SCUTREA.

Claxton, G. (1998) *Hare Brain, Tortoise Mind*. London: Fourth Estate.

Cohen, J. and Stewart, I. (1995) *The Collapse of Chaos*. London: Penguin.

Cooper, C. L. and Cartwright, S. (1997) An intervention strategy for workplace stress, *Journal of Psychosomatic Research*, 43(1): 7–16.

Cowan, J. (1998) *On Becoming an Innovative University Teacher*. Buckingham: Open University Press.

Cox, M. D. (1997) Long-term patterns in a mentoring program for junior faculty: recommendations for practice, *To Improve the Academy*, 16: 225–68.

Csikszentmihalyi, M. (1997) *Living Well: The Psychology of Everyday Life*. Little Rock, AR: Phoenix Press.

Currie, J. (1996) The effects of globalization on 1990s academics in greedy institutions, *Melbourne Studies in Education*, 37(2): 101–28.

CVCP (1992) *Resourceful Induction: A Manual of Materials for Higher Education*. London: Committee of Vice Chancellors and College Principals.

Davenport, T. H. and Prusak, L. (1998) *Working Knowledge*. Cambridge, MA: Harvard University Press.

Deci, E., Kasser, T. and Ryan, R. (1997) Self-determined teaching: opportunities and obstacles, in J. Bess (ed.) *Teaching Well and Liking It*, pp. 57–71. San Francisco: Jossey-Bass.

De Corte, E. (1996) Learning theory and instructional science: introduction, in P. Reimenn and H. Spada (eds) *Learning in Humans and Machines: Towards an Interdisciplinary Learning Science*, pp. 97–108. London: Pergamon.

Dennett, D. C. (1991) Mother nature versus the walking encyclopedia, in W. Ramsey, S. Stich and D. Rumelhart (eds) *Philosophy and Connectionist Theory*, pp. 21–30. Hillsdale, NJ: Lawrence Erlbaum Associates.

Donnelly, J. F. (1999) Schooling Heidegger: on being in teaching, *Teaching and Teacher Education*, 15: 933–49.

Doyle, C. and Hind, P. (1998) Occupational stress, burnout and job status in female academics, *Gender, Work and Organization*, 5(2): 67–82.

Doyle, W. (1983) Academic work, *Review of Educational Research*, 53(2): 159–99.

Dreyfus, H. (1991) *Being-in-the-world: A Commentary on Heidegger's Being and Time*. Cambridge, MA: MIT Press.

Dreyfus, H. and Dreyfus, S. (1986) *Mind Over Machine*. Oxford: Blackwell.

Dubin, S. S. (1990) Maintaining competence through updating, in S. L. Willis and S. S. Dubin (eds) *Maintaining Professional Competence*, pp. 125–43. San Francisco: Jossey-Bass.

Dweck, C. (1999) *Self-theories: Their Role in Motivation, Personality and Development.* Philadelphia: Psychology Press.

Edworthy, A. (2000) *Managing Stress.* Buckingham: Open University Press.

Eisner, E. (1985) *The Educational Imagination*, 2nd edn. New York: Macmillan.

Eisner, E. (2000) Those who ignore the past . . . , *Journal of Curriculum Studies*, 32(2): 343–57.

Elton, L. (1996) Strategies to enhance student motivation: a conceptual analysis, *Studies in Higher Education*, 21(1): 57–68.

Engeström, Y. (1999) Innovative learning in work teams, in Y. Engeström, R. Miettinem and R.-L. Punamäki (eds) *Perspectives on Activity Theory*, pp. 377–404. Cambridge: Cambridge University Press.

Engeström, Y. (2001) Expansive learning at work: towards an activity theoretical reconceptualization, *Journal of Education and Work*, 14(1): 133–56.

Entwistle, N. (1996) Recent research on student learning, in J. Tait and P. Knight (eds) *The Management of Independent Learning*, pp. 97–112. London: Kogan Page.

Entwistle, N. (2000) Promoting deep learning through teaching and assessment: conceptual frameworks and educational contexts. Paper presented to the TLRP Conference, Leicester, November.

Entwistle, N. and Ramsden, P. (1983) *Understanding Student Learning.* London: Croom Helm.

Eraut, M. (1995) Schön shock: a case for reframing reflection-in-action?, *Teachers and Teaching: Theory and Practice*, 1(1): 9–22.

Eraut, M. (2000) Non-formal learning and tacit knowledge in professional work, *British Journal of Educational Psychology*, 70: 113–36.

Evans, L. (1998) *Teacher Morale, Job Satisfaction and Motivation.* London: Paul Chapman.

Everett, J. E. and Entrekin, L. (1994) Changing attitudes of Australian academics, *Higher Education*, 27(2): 203–27.

Exworthy, M. and Halford, S. (1999) *Professionals and the New Managerialism in the Public Sector.* Buckingham: Open University Press.

Farrell, J. P. (2000) Why is educational reform so difficult?, *Curriculum Inquiry*, 30(1): 83–103.

Fay, B. (1975) *Social Theory and Political Practice.* London: Allen & Unwin.

Filer, A. and Pollard, A. (2000) *The Social World of Pupil Assessment.* London: Continuum.

Fineman, S. (1996) Emotion and organizing, in S. Clegg, C. Hardy and W. R. Nord (eds) *Handbook of Organizational Studies*, pp. 543–64. London: Sage Publications.

Fisher, S. (1994) *Stress in Academic Life.* Buckingham: Open University Press.

Fourie, M. and Alt, H. (2000) Challenges to sustaining and enhancing quality of teaching/learning at South African universities, *Quality in Higher Education*, 6(2): 115–24.

Fry, H., Ketteridge, S. and Marshall, S. (eds) (1999) *A Handbook for Teaching and Learning in Higher Education.* London: Kogan Page.

Fullan, M. (1991) *The Meaning of Educational Change*. London: Cassell.

Fullan, M. (1993) *Change Forces*. Brighton: Falmer.

Fullan, M. (1999) *Change Forces: The Sequel*. London: Falmer.

Gaff, J. G. and Ratcliff, J. L. (eds) (1996) *Handbook of the Undergraduate Curriculum*. San Francisco: Jossey-Bass.

Gage, N. (1978) *The Scientific Basis of the Art of Teaching*. New York: Teachers' College Press.

Galton, M. and Williamson, J. (1992) *Group-work in the Primary Classroom*. London: Routledge.

Gappa, J. M. and Leslie, D. W. (1993) *The Invisible Faculty*. San Francisco: Jossey-Bass.

Gee, J. P. and Lankshear, C. (1997) Language, literacy and the new work order, in C. Lankshear (ed.) *Changing Literacies*, pp. 83–101. Buckingham: Open University Press.

Gibbs, G. (1992) *Teaching More Students I. Problems and Course Design Strategies*. Oxford: Oxford Centre for Staff Development.

Gibbs, G. (1995) Changing lecturers' conceptions of teaching and learning through action research, in A. Brew (ed.) *Directions in Staff Development*, pp. 21–35. Buckingham: Society for Research into Higher Education and Open University Press.

Gibbs, G. (1999a) Using assessment strategically to change the way students learn, in S. Brown and A. Glasner (eds) *Assessment Matters in Higher Education*, pp. 41–54. Buckingham: Open University Press.

Gibbs, G. (1999b) *Teaching in Higher Education: Theory and Evidence. Designing Courses*. Milton Keynes: The Open University.

Gibson, G. W. (1992) *Good Start: A Guidebook for New Faculty in Liberal Arts Colleges*. Bolton, MA: Anker Publishing.

Gibson, J. J. (1986) *The Ecological Approach to Visual Perception*. Hillsdale, NJ: Lawrence Erlbaum Associates.

Glassick, C. E., Huber, M. T. and Maeroff, G. I. (1997) *Scholarship Assessed: Evaluation of the Professoriate*. San Francisco: Jossey-Bass.

Glynn, C. and Holbeche, L. (2000) *The Management Agenda 2000*. Horsham: Roffey Park Management Institute.

Goleman, D. (1998) *Working with Emotional Intelligence*. New York: Bantam Books.

Grasha, A. F. (1996) *Teaching with Style*. Pittsburgh, PA: Alliance Publishers.

Griffiths, J., Steptoe, A. and Cropley, M. (1999) An investigation of coping strategies associated with job stress in teachers, *British Journal of Educational Psychology*, 69(4): 517–32.

Grunert, J. (1997) *The Course Syllabus*. Bolton, MA: Anker Publishing.

Guile, D. and Young, M. (1998) Apprenticeship as a conceptual basis for a social theory of learning, *Journal of Vocational Education and Training*, 50(2): 173–92.

Hacker, D., Dunlosky, J. and Graesser, A. (eds) (1998) *Metacognition in Education Theory and Practice*. Mahwah, NJ: Lawrence Erlbaum Associates.

Halford, S. and Leonard, P. (1999) New identities? Professionalism, managerialism and the construction of self, in M. Exworthy and S. Halford (eds) *Professionals and the New Managerialism in the Public Sector*, pp. 101–21. Buckingham: Open University Press.

Hargreaves, A. (1994) *Changing Teachers, Changing Times.* London: Cassell.

Hargreaves, A. (1998) The emotional practice of teaching, *Teaching and Teacher Education*, 14(8): 835–54.

Hargreaves, D. (1983) *The Challenge of the Comprehensive.* London: Routledge and Kegan Paul.

Harvey, L. and Knight, P. T. (1996) *Transforming Higher Education.* Buckingham: Society for Research in Higher Education and Open University Press.

Harvey, L., Moon, S. and Geall, V., with Bower, R. (1997) *Graduates' Work: Organisation Change and Students' Attributes.* Birmingham, Centre for Research into Quality and Association of Graduate Recruiters.

Hay, L. (1999) *You Can Heal Your Life.* New York: Hay House.

HEFCE (2000) *Review of Research.* Bristol: Higher Education Funding Council for England.

Helsby, G. (1999) *Changing Teachers' Work: The 'Reform' of Secondary Schooling.* Buckingham: Open University Press.

Henkel, M. (2000) *Academic Identities and Policy Change in Higher Education.* London: Jessica Kingsley.

Herskowitz, M. (1997) *Emotional Armoring.* Hamburg: Lit Verlag.

Hesselbein, F., Goldsmith, M. and Beckhard, R. (eds) (1996) *The Leader of the Future.* San Francisco: Jossey-Bass.

Heywood, J. (2000) *Assessment in Higher Education.* London: Jessica Kingsley.

Hochschild, A. R. (1983) *The Managed Heart: The Commercialization of Human Feeling.* Berkeley, CA: University of California Press.

Hogarth, T., Hasluck, C. and Pierre, G. (2000) *Work-life Balance 2000: Baseline Study of Work–Life Balance Practices in Great Britain.* London: DfEE.

Hounsell, D., McCulloch, M. and Scott, M. (eds) (1996) *The ASSHE Inventory.* Edinburgh: University of Edinburgh and Napier University.

Hoyles, C. (1990) Neglected voices: pupils' mathematics and the national curriculum, in P. Dowling and R. Noss (eds) *Mathematics versus the National Curriculum.* Basingstoke: Falmer.

Huberman, M. (1993) *The Lives of Teachers.* London: Cassell.

Husbands, C. T. and Davies, A. (2000) The teaching roles, institutional locations, and terms and conditions of employment of part-time teachers in UK higher education, *Journal of Further and Higher Education*, 24(3): 337–62.

Jenkins, A. (1998) *Curriculum Design in Geography.* Cheltenham: Geography Diciple Network.

Jones, E. A. (1996) National and state policies affecting learning expectations, in E. A. Jones (ed.) *Preparing Competent College Graduates: Setting New and Higher Expectations in Student Learning*, pp. 7–17. San Francisco: Jossey-Bass.

Karpiak, I. E. (1997) University professors in mid-life, *To Improve the Academy*, 16: 21–40.

Karpiak, I. (2000) The 'second call': faculty renewal and recommitment at midlife, *Quality in Higher Education*, 6(2): 125–34.

Kember, D. (2000) *Action Learning and Action Research.* London: Kogan Page.

Kenny, S. S. (1998) *The Boyer Commission on Education. Reinventing Undergraduate Education: A Blueprint for America's Research Universities.* New York: State University of New York at Stony Brook.

Knight, P. T. (1993) Overview, in P. T. Knight (ed.) *The Audit and Assessment of Teaching Quality*, pp. 5–25. Birmingham: Standing Conference on Educational Development.

Knight, P. T. (1998) Professional obsolescence and continuing professional development in higher education, *Innovation in Education and Training International*, 35(3): 241–8.

Knight, P. T. (2000) The value of a programme-wide approach to assessment, *Assessment and Evaluation in Higher Education*, 25(3): 236–51.

Knight, P. T. (2001) Complexity and curriculum: a process approach to curriculum-making, *Teaching in Higher Education*, 6(3): 369–82.

Knight, P. T. (2002a) Summative assessment in higher education: practices in disarray, *Studies in Higher Education*, 27(2).

Knight, P. T. (2002b) Learning from schools, *Higher Education*, 43(3).

Knight, P. T. (2002c) A systemic approach to professional development: learning as practice, *Teaching and Teacher Education*, 18(3).

Knight, P. T. (2002d) *Small-scale Research*. London: Sage Publications.

Knight, P. T., Aitken, N. and Rogerson, R. (2000) *Forever Better: Fine-tuning Your Teaching Practises*. Oakland, OK: New Forums Press.

Knight, P. T. and Trowler, P. R. (1999) It takes a village to raise a child, *Mentoring and Tutoring*, 7(1): 23–34.

Knight, P. T. and Trowler, P. R. (2000) Department-level cultures and the improvement of learning and teaching, *Studies in Higher Education*, 25(1): 69–83.

Knight, P. T. and Trowler, P. R. (2001) *Departmental Leadership in Higher Education*. Buckingham: Open University Press.

Kolb, D. (1984) *Experiential Learning: Experience in the Service of Learning and Development*. Englewood Cliffs, NJ: Prentice Hall.

Kreber, C. (ed.) (2001) Revisiting scholarship: identifying and implementing the scholarship of teaching, *New Directions in Teaching and Learning 86*. San Francisco: Jossey-Bass.

Lapham, A. (1999) Reflections on the groupware experience, *Active Learning*, 10: 14–20.

Latham, G., Daghighi, S. and Locke, E. A. (1997) Implications of goal setting for faculty motivation, in J. Bess (ed.) *Teaching Well and Liking It*, pp. 125–42. San Francisco: Jossey-Bass.

Laurillard, D. (1993) *Rethinking University Teaching*. London: Routledge.

Laurillard, D., Stratfold, M., Luckin, R., Plowman, L. and Taylor, J. (2000) Affordances for learning in a non-linear narrative medium, *Journal of Interactive Media in Education*, 2: 1–17.

Law, J. (1999) After ANT: complexity, naming and typology, in J. Law and J. Hassard (eds) *Actor Network Theory and After*, pp. 1–14. Oxford: Blackwell.

Lazarus, R. (1991) *Emotion and Adaptation*. New York: Oxford University Press.

Lea, M. (2001) Computer conferencing and assessment, *Studies in Higher Education*, 26(2): 165–83.

Leadbeater, C. (2000) *Living on Thin Air*. London: Penguin.

Leithwood, K., Jantzi, D. and Steinbach, R. (1999) *Changing Leadership for Changing Times*. Buckingham: Open University Press.

Lejk, M. and Wyvill, M. (2001) Peer assessment of contributions to a group project, *Assessment and Evaluation in Higher Education*, 26(1): 61–72.

Leslie, D. W. (ed.) (1998) The growing use of part-time faculty, *New Directions for Higher Education 44*. San Francisco: Jossey-Bass.

Levine, A. and Cureton, J. (1998) Collegiate life: an obituary. *Change*, May/June, 14–17.

Li, L. K. Y. (2001) Some refinements on peer assessments of group project, *Assessment and Evaluation in Higher Education*, 26(1): 5–18.

Loacker, G. (ed.) (2000) *Self Assessment at Alverno College*. Milwaukee: Alverno College.

Lucas, A. (1994) *Strengthening Departmental Leadership*. San Francisco: Jossey-Bass.

Ludema, J. D., Cooperrider, D. L. and Barrett, F. J. (2001) Appreciative inquiry: the power of the unconditional positive question, in P. Reason and H. Bradbury (eds) *Handbook of Action Research*, pp. 189–99. London: Sage Publications.

Luhmann, N. (1995) *Social Systems* (trans. J. Bednarz). Stanford, CA: Stanford University Press.

Luntley, M. (1999) *Performance Pay and Professionals*. Ringwood: Philosophy of Education Society of Great Britain.

McCulloch, G., Helsby, G. and Knight, P. T. (2000) *The Politics of Teacher Professionalism*. London: Cassell.

MacDonald, B. and Walker, R. (1976) *Changing the Curriculum*. London: Open Books.

McInnis, C. (2000) Changing academic work roles: the everyday realities challenging quality in teaching, *Quality in Higher Education*, 6(2): 143–52.

McKeachie, W. (1994) *Teaching Tips*, 9th edn. Lexington, MA: D. C. Heath.

McKeachie, W. J. (1997) Good teaching makes a difference – and we know what it is, in R. Perry and J. C. Smart (eds) *Effective Teaching in Higher Education: Research and Practice*, pp. 396–408. New York: Agathon Press.

McLeod, S. and Jennings, J. (1990) Fit for the future, in M. Pedler, J. Burgoyne, T. Boydell and G. Welshman (eds) *Self Development in Organizations*, pp. 67–83. London: McGraw-Hill.

Magin, D. (2001) A novel technique for comparing the reliability of multiple peer assessments with that of single teacher assessments of group process work, *Assessment and Evaluation in Higher Education*, 26(2): 139–54.

Malina, D. and Maslin Prothero, S. (eds) (1998) *Surviving the Academy: Feminist Perspectives*. London: Falmer.

Marmot, M. (1999) Introduction, in M. Marmot and R. Wilkinson (eds) *Social Determinants of Health*, pp. 1–16. Oxford: Oxford University Press.

Marmot, M., Siegrist, J., Theorell, T. and Feeney, A. (1999) Health and the psychosocial environment at work, in M. Marmot and R. Wilkinson (eds) *Social Determinants of Health*, pp. 105–31. Oxford: Oxford University Press.

Martin, E. (1999) *Changing Academic Work: Developing the Learning University*. Buckingham: Society for Research in Higher Education and Open University Press.

Menges, R. *et al.* (1999) *Faculty in New Jobs*. San Francisco: Jossey-Bass.

Mentkowski, M. and associates (2000) *Learning that Lasts*. San Francisco: Jossey-Bass.

Morley, L. and Walsh, V. (eds) (1996) *Breaking Boundaries: Women in Higher Education*. London: Falmer.

Moshman, D. (1999) *Adolescent Psychological Development*. Mahwah, NJ: Lawrence Erlbaum Associates.

Murphy, L. R. (1988) Workplace interventions for stress reduction and prevention, in C. L. Cooper and R. Payne (eds) *Causes, Coping and Consequences of Stress at Work*, pp. 301–39. Chichester: John Wiley.

Murray, H. and Renaud, R. D. (1995) Disciplinary differences in classroom teaching behaviors, in N. Hativa and M. Marincovich (eds) *Disciplinary Differences in Teaching and Learning*, pp. 31–40. San Francisco: Jossey-Bass.

Murray, H. G. (1997) Effective teaching behaviours in the college classroom, in R. Perry and J. C. Smart (eds) *Effective Teaching in Higher Education: Research and Practice*, pp. 171–204. New York: Agathon Press.

Newton, J. (2000) Feeding the beast or improving quality?, *Quality in Higher Education*, 6(2): 153–63.

Nias, J. (1996) Thinking about teaching: the emotions in teaching, *Cambridge Journal of Education*, 26(3): 293–306.

Nilson, L. B. (1998) *Teaching at its Best*. Bolton, MA: Anker Publishing.

Nonaka, I. and Takauchi, H. (1995) *The Knowledge-creating Company*. New York: Oxford.

Ohlsson, S. (1996) Learning to do and learning to understand, in P. Reimenn and H. Spada (eds) *Learning in Humans and Machines: Towards an Interdisciplinary Learning Science*, pp. 37–62. London: Pergamon.

O'Neil, M. C. and Wright, A. W. (1996) *Recording Teaching Accomplishment: A Dalhousie Guide to the Teaching Dossier*, 5th edn. Halifax: Dalhousie University.

Orland, L. (2000) What's in a line? Exploration of a research reflection tool, *Teachers and Teaching*, 6(2): 197–213.

Palloff, R. M. and Pratt, K. (1999) *Building Learning Communities in Cyberspace*. San Francisco: Jossey-Bass.

Palmer, P. J. (1998) *The Courage to Teach*. San Francisco: Jossey-Bass.

Parker, S. (1997) *Reflective Thinking in the Postmodern World*. Buckingham: Open University Press.

Pascarella, E. T. and Terenzini, P. T. (1991) *How College Affects Students*. San Francisco: Jossey-Bass.

Patton, M. Q. (1997) *Utilization-focused Evaluation*, 3rd edn. Thousand Oaks, CA: Sage Publications.

Pedler, M., Burgoyne, J. and Boydell, T. (1994) *A Manager's Guide to Self Development*, 3rd edn. London: McGraw-Hill.

Pellegrino, J., Baxter, G. and Glaser, R. (1999) Addressing the 'two disciplines' problem: linking theories of cognition and learning with assessment and instructional practice, *Review of Research in Education*, 24: 307–53.

Perrenoud, P. (1998) From formative evaluation to a controlled regulation of learning processes, *Assessment in Education*, 5(1): 85–102.

Perret-Clérmont, A.-N. (1985) *Social Interaction and Cognitive Development in Children*. London: Academic Press.

Perry, R. (1997) Perceived control in college students: implications for instruction, in R. Perry and J. Smart (eds) *Effective Teaching in Higher Education*. New York: Agathon Press.

Perry, R., Menec, V. H. and Struthers, C. W. (1999) Feeling in control, in R. Menges and associates (eds) *Faculty in New Jobs*, pp. 186–215. San Francisco: Jossey-Bass.

Perry, R. P., Menec, V. H., Struthers, C. W. *et al.* (1996) *Faculty in Transition: The Adjustment of New Hires to Postsecondary Institutions.* Winnipeg, MB: Centre for Higher Education Research and Development.

Peterson, C., Maier, S. and Seligman, M. (1993) *Learned Helplessness: A Theory for an Age of Personal Control.* New York: Oxford University Press.

Prosser, M. and Trigwell, K. (1998) Teaching in Higher Education, in B. Dart and G. Bolton-Lewis (eds) *Teaching and Learning in Higher Education*, pp. 250–68. Melbourne: Australian Council for Educational Research.

Prosser, M. and Trigwell, K. (1999) *Understanding Learning and Teaching.* Buckingham: Society for Research in Higher Education and Open University Press.

Putnam, L. L. and Mumby, D. K. (1993) Organizations, emotion and the myth of rationality, in S. Fineman (ed.) *Emotions in Organizations*, pp. 36–57. London: Sage.

Qualter, D. (2000) Creating faculty community, *National Teaching and Learning Forum*, 9(4), n.p.

Rahim, M. A. and Psenicka, C. (1996) A structural equations model of stress, locus of control, social support, psychiatric symptoms and propensity to leave a job, *Journal of Social Psychology*, 136(1): 69–84.

Ramsden, P. (1992) *Learning to Teach in Higher Education.* London: Routledge.

Ramsden, P. (1998a) *Learning to Lead in Higher Education.* London: Routledge.

Ramsden, P. (1998b) Managing the effective university, *Higher Education Research and Development*, 17(3): 347–70.

Reynolds, F. (1997) Studying psychology at degree level: would problem-based learning enhance students' experiences?, *Studies in Higher Education*, 22(3): 263–74.

Rice, E., Sorcinelli, M. D. and Austin, A. E. (2000) *Heeding New Voices. Academic Careers for a New Generation.* Washington, DC: American Association for Higher Education.

Rosenholtz, S. (1991) *Teachers' Workplace.* New York: Macmillan.

Rowland, S. (2000) *The Enquiring University Teacher.* Buckingham: Society for Research into Higher Education and Open University Press.

Rust, C. (1998) The impact of educational development workshops on teachers' practice, *International Journal for Academic Development*, 3(1): 71–80.

Ryan, R. M. and La Guardia, J. G. (1999) Achievement motivation within a pressurized society, in T. C. Urdan (ed.) *The Role of Context: Advances in Achievement and Motivation*, pp. 45–85. Stamford, CT: JAI Press.

Salmon, G. (2000) *E-moderation. The Key to Teaching and Learning Online.* London: Kogan Page.

Schön, D. A. (1983) *The Reflective Practitioner.* New York: Basic Books.

Schuster, J. (1990) The need for fresh approaches to faculty renewal, in J. Schuster and D. Wheeler (eds) *Enhancing Faculty Careers: Strategies for Development and Renewal*, pp. 3–19. San Francisco: Jossey-Bass.

Seldin, P. (1997) *The Teaching Portfolio*, 2nd edn. Bolton, MA: Anker Publishing.

Seligman, M. (1998) *Learned Optimism.* New York: Pocket Books.

Senge, P. (1994) *The Fifth Discipline Fieldbook.* New York: Doubleday.

Senge, P., Kleiner, A., Roberts, C. *et al.* (1999) *The Dance of Change.* London: Nicholas Brearley.

Sennett, R. (1998) *The Corrosion of Character.* New York: Norton.

Shulman, M. (1987) Knowledge and teaching foundations of the new reform, *Harvard Education Review*, 57(1): 1–22.

Slavin, R. (1996) *Education for All*. Lisse, Netherlands: Swets & Zeitlinger.

Soliman, I. and Soliman, H. (1997) Academic workload and quality, *Assessment and Evaluation in Higher Education*, 22(2): 135–58.

Sorcinelli, M. (2000) Department chairs and deans, *The Department Chair*, 10(3): 15–18.

Spender, J.-C. (1998) The dynamics of individual and organizational knowledge, in C. Eden and J.-C. Spender (eds) *Managerial and Organizational Cognition*, pp. 13–39. London: Sage.

Sternberg, R. J. (1997) *Successful Intelligence*. New York: Plume.

Stenhouse, L. (1975) *An Introduction to Curriculum Research and Development*. London: Heinemann.

Stigler, J. W. and Hiebert, J. (1999) *The Teaching Gap*. New York: The Free Press.

Strauss, C. and Quinn, N. (1997) *A Cognitive Theory of Cultural Meaning*. Cambridge: Cambridge University Press.

Tait, J. (2002) From competence to excellence: a systems view of staff development for part-time tutors, *Open Learning*, 17(1).

Tait, J. and Knight, P. (eds) (1996) *The Management of Independent Learning*. London: Kogan Page.

Thorley, L. and Gregory, R. (1994) *Using Group-based Learning in Higher Education*. London: Kogan Page.

Thorsen, E. J. (1996) Stress in academe: what bothers professors?, *Higher Education*, 31(4): 471–89.

Tierney, W. and Bensimon, E. M. (1996) *Promotion and Tenure: Community and Socialization in Academe*. Albany: State University of New York Press.

Tompkins, J. (1992) The way we live now, *Change*, 24(6): 12–19.

Toohey, S. (1999) *Designing Courses for Higher Education*. Buckingham: Open University Press.

Torrance, H. and Pryor, J. (1998) *Investigating Formative Assessment: Teaching, Learning and Assessment in the Classroom*. Buckingham: Open University Press.

Trigwell, K. (2001) Judging university teaching, *International Journal for Academic Development*, 6(1): 65–73.

Troman, G. and Woods, P. (2001) *Primary Teachers' Stress*. London: Routledge/Falmer.

Trowler, P. (1998) *Academics Responding to Change: New Higher Education Frameworks and Academic Cultures*. Buckingham: Society for Research into Higher Education and Open University Press.

Trowler, P. R. and Knight, P. T. (2000) Coming to know in higher education: theorising faculty entry to new work contexts, *Higher Education Research and Development*, 19(1): 27–42.

Trowler, P. and Knight, P. T. (2002) Social practice policy innovations: exploring the implementation gap, in P. Trowler (ed.) *Higher Education Policy and Institutional Change: Intentions and Outcomes in Turbulent Environments*, pp. 142–63. Buckingham: Society for Research into Higher Education and Open University Press.

Upcraft, M. L. (1996) Teaching and today's college students, in R. J. Menges and M. Weimer (eds) *Teaching on Solid Ground*, pp. 21–41. San Francisco: Jossey-Bass.

van Geert, P. (1994) *Dynamic Systems of Development: Change between Complexity and Chaos*. Hemel Hempstead: Harvester Wheatsheaf.

van Manen, M. (1995) On the epistemology of reflective practice, *Teachers and Teaching*, 1(1): 33–50.

Vitale, M. (2001) Being in the classroom: there's nothing like the real thing, *South China Morning Post*, Education Section, 31 March, 9.

Walker, C. J. and Quinn, J. W. (1996) Fostering instructional vitality and motivation, in R. J. Menges and M. Weimer (eds) *Teaching on Solid Ground*, pp. 315–36. San Francisco: Jossey-Bass.

Walvoord, B. E. and Anderson, V. J. (1998) *Effective Grading: A Tool for Learning and Assessment*. San Francisco: Jossey-Bass.

Webb, J. (1999) Work and the new public service class?, *Sociology*, 33(4): 747–66.

Weimer, M. and Lenze, L. F. (1991) Instructional interventions: a review of the literature on efforts to improve instruction, in J. C. Smart (ed.) *Higher Education: A Handbook of Theory and Practice, Volume 3*. New York: Agathon.

Wenger, E. (2000) Communities of practice and social learning systems, *Organization*, 7(2): 225–46.

Wertsch, J. V. (1998) *Mind as Action*. Oxford: Oxford University Press.

Winter, R. (1999) *Professional Experience and the Investigative Imagination*. London: Routledge/Falmer.

Wisner, A. (1995) Situated cognition and action, *Ergonomics*, 38(8): 1542–57.

Wolf, A. (1997) *Assessment in Higher Education and the Role of 'Graduateness'*. London: HEQC.

Wright, W. A. and O'Neil, C. (1995) Teaching improvement practices: international perspectives, in W. A. Wright and associates (eds) *Teaching Improvement Practices*, pp. 1–57. Bolton, MA: Anker Publishing.

Wright, W. A. and associates (1995) *Teaching Improvement Practices*. Bolton, MA: Anker Publishing.

Yorke, M. (1999) The skills of graduates: a small enterprise perspective, in D. O'Reilly, L. Cunningham and S. Lester (eds) *Developing the Capable Practitioner*, pp. 174–83. London: Kogan Page.

Index

The Society for Research into Higher Education

The Society for Research into Higher Education (SRHE) exists to stimulate and coordinate research into all aspects of higher education. It aims to improve the quality of higher education through the encouragement of debate and publication on issues of policy, on the organization and management of higher education institutions, and on the curriculum, teaching and learning methods.

The Society is entirely independent and receives no subsidies, although individual events often receive sponsorship from business or industry. The Society is financed through corporate and individual subscriptions and has members from many parts of the world.

Under the imprint *SRHE & Open University Press*, the Society is a specialist publisher of research, having over 80 titles in print. In addition to *SRHE News*, the Society's newsletter, the Society publishes three journals: *Studies in Higher Education* (three issues a year), *Higher Education Quarterly* and *Research into Higher Education Abstracts* (three issues a year).

The Society runs frequent conferences, consulations, seminars and other events. The annual conference in December is organized at and with a higher education institution. There are a growing number of networks which focus on particular areas of interest, including:

Access	Learning Environment
Consultants	Legal Education
Curriculum Development	Managing Innovation
Eastern European	New Technology for Learning
Educational Development Research	Postgraduate Issues
FE/HE	Quantitative Studies
Funding	Student Development
Graduate Employment	Vocation at Qualification

Benefits to members

Individual

- The opportunity to participate in the Society's networks
- Reduced rates for the annual conferences
- Free copies of *Research into Higher Education Abstracts*

- Reduced rates for *Studies in Higher Education*
- Reduced rates for *Higher Education Quarterly*
- Free copy of *Register of Members' Research Interests* – includes valuable reference material on research being pursued by the Society's members
- Free copy of occasional in-house publications, e.g. *The Thirtieth Anniversary Seminars Presented by the Vice-Presidents*
- Free copies of *SRHE News* which informs members of the Society's activities and provides a calendar of events, with additional material provided in regular mailings
- A 35 per cent discount on all SRHE/Open University Press books
- Access to HESA statistics for student members
- The opportunity for you to apply for the annual research grants
- Inclusion of your research in the *Register of Members' Research Interests*

Corporate

- Reduced rates for the annual conferences
- The opportunity for members of the Institution to attend SRHE's network events at reduced rates
- Free copies of *Research into Higher Education Abstracts*
- Free copies of *Studies in Higher Education*
- Free copies of *Register of Members' Research Interests* – includes valuable reference material on research being pursued by the Society's members
- Free copy of occasional in-house publications
- Free copies of *SRHE News*
- A 35 per cent discount on all SRHE/Open University Press books
- Access to HESA statistics for research for students of the Institution
- The opportunity for members of the Institution to submit applications for the Society's research grants
- The opportunity to work with the Society and co-host conferences
- The opportunity to include in the *Register of Members' Research Interests* your Institution's research into aspects of higher education

Membership details: SRHE, 3 Devonshire Street, London
W1N 2BA, UK Tel: 020 7637 2766. Fax: 020 7637 2781.
email: srhe@mailbox.ulcc.ac.uk
world wide web: http://www.srhe.ac.uk./srhe/
Catalogue: SRHE & Open University Press, Celtic Court,
22 Ballmoor, Buckingham MK18 1XW. Tel: 01280 823388.
Fax: 01280 823233. email: enquiries@openup.co.uk